Terms and conditions

IMPORTANT – PERMITTED USE AND WARNINGS – READ CAREFULLY BEFORE USING

Recommended system requirements:

- Windows: XP (Service Pack 3), Vista (Service Pack 2), Windows 7 or Windows 8 with 2.33GHz processor
- Mac: OS 10.6 to 10.8 with Intel Core™ Duo processor
- 1GB RAM (recommended)
- 1024 x 768 Screen resolution
- CD-ROM drive (24x speed recommended)
- 16-bit sound card
- Adobe Reader (version 9 recommended for Mac users)
- Broadband internet connections (for installation and updates)

For all technical support queries, please phone Scholastic Customer Services on 0845 6039091.

Book End, Range Road, Witney, Oxfordshire, OX29 0YD
www.scholastic.co.uk

© 2014, Scholastic Ltd

456789 67890123

British Library Cataloguing-in-Publication Data
A catalogue record for this book is available from the
British Library.

ISBN 978-1407-12765-1
Printed by Bell & Bain Ltd, Glasgow

Author
Gillian Ravenscroft

Consultant
Juliet Gladston

Series Editor
Peter Riley

Editorial team
Rachel Morgan, Pollyanna Poulter, Melissa Somers
and Louise Titley

Cover Design
Andrea Lewis

Design Team
Sarah Garbett, Shelley Best and Andrea Lewis

CD-ROM development
Hannah Barnett, Phil Crothers, MWA Technologies
Private Ltd

Typesetting
Tracey Camden

Illustrations
Jackie Stafford

Contents

Introduction

About the series

The *100 Science Lessons* series is designed to meet the requirements of the 2014 Curriculum, Science Programmes of Study. There are six books in the series, Years 1–6, and each book contains lesson plans, resources and ideas matched to the new curriculum. It can be a complex task to ensure that a progressive and appropriate curriculum is followed in all year groups; this series has been carefully structured to ensure that a progressive and appropriate curriculum is followed throughout.

About the new curriculum

The curriculum documentation for Science provides a single-year programme of study for each year in Key Stage 1 and 2. However schools are only required to teach the relevant programmes of study by the end of the key stage and can approach their curriculum planning with greater flexibility than ever before in the following ways. Within each key stage they can introduce content earlier or later than set out in the programme of study and they can introduce key stage content during an earlier key stage if appropriate. Whatever plan is used the school curriculum for science must be set out on a year-by-year basis and made available online.

Knowledge and conceptual understanding

The national curriculum for science aims to ensure that all children develop scientific knowledge and conceptual understanding through the specific disciplines of Biology (Plants, Animals including humans, Seasonal changes, Living things and their habitats, Evolution and inheritance), Chemistry (Everyday materials, Uses of everyday materials, Rocks, States of matter, Properties and changes of materials) and Physics (Seasonal changes, Light, Forces and magnets, Sound, Electricity, Earth and space). It is vitally important that the children develop a secure understanding of each key block of knowledge and its concepts in order to progress to the next stage. As they do so they should also be familiar with and use technical terminology accurately and precisely and build up an extended specialist vocabulary. Equally they should also apply their mathematical knowledge to their understanding of science including collecting, presenting and analysing data.

The nature, processes and methods of science

The requirements needed for the understanding of the nature, processes and methods of science are set out at the beginning of Key Stage 1, Lower Key Stage 2 and Upper Key Stage 2 in a section called Working scientifically. This section of the curriculum replaces the Science enquiry section of the previous science curriculum. It is important that Working scientifically is not taught as a separate strand and guidance is given in the non-statutory notes to help embed it in the scientific content of each area of the programme of study. In the working scientifically section the children are introduced to a range of types of scientific enquiry. These include observing over time, classifying and grouping, identifying, comparative and fair testing (making controlled investigations), pattern seeking and researching using secondary sources. The questions used to stimulate the enquiry should be answered by the children through collecting, presenting and analysing data and drawing conclusions from their findings.

■SCHOLASTIC

About the book

This book is divided into six chapters; each chapter contains a half-term's work and is based around one of the content areas in the programme of study. Each chapter follows the same structure:

Chapter introduction

At the start of each chapter there is an introduction with the following features. This includes:

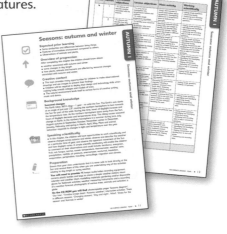

- **Expected prior learning:** What the children are expected to know before starting the work in the chapter.
- **Overview of progression:** A brief explanation of how the children progress through the chapter.
- **Creative context:** How the chapter could link to other curriculum areas.
- **Background knowledge:** A section explaining scientific terms and suchlike to enhance your subject knowledge, where required.
- **Speaking scientifically:** A section highlighting some of the key words featured in the chapter for building up the children's scientific vocabulary. This is also a feature of every lesson (see below).
- **Preparation:** Any resources required for the teaching of the chapter, including things that need to be sourced or prepared and the content that can be located on the CD-ROM. As part of the preparation of all practical work you should consult your school's policies on practical work and select activities for which you are confident to take responsibility. The ASE *Be Safe Forth Edition* gives very useful guidance on health and safety issues in primary science.
- **Chapter at a glance:** This is a table that summarises the content of each lesson, including: the curriculum objectives, lesson objectives, the main activity or activities and the working scientifically statutory requirements that are featured in each lesson.

Lessons

Each chapter contains six weeks' of lessons, each week contains three lessons. At the start of each half term there is an introductory lesson revisiting relevant content from work in previous years then introducing the new area of study. There is also a checkpoint section to check on the children's knowledge before proceeding to the next lesson.

All lessons including the introductory lesson have lesson plans that include the relevant combination of headings from below.

- **Lesson objectives:** A list of objectives for the lesson.
- **Resources:** What you require to teach the lesson.
- **Speaking scientifically:** A list of words to use in the lesson. The children should learn to spell them, understand their meanings and use them when talking about their activities, particularly when working scientifically.
- **Introduction:** A short and engaging activity to begin the lesson.
  - **Whole-class work:** Working together as a class.
  - **Group/Paired/Independent work:** Children working independently of the teacher in pairs, groups or alone.
  - **Differentiation:** Ideas for how to support children who are struggling with a concept or how to extend those children who understand a concept without taking them onto new work.
  - **Science in the wider world:** The information in this section may develop some of the content and concepts in the lesson and show how they relate to the wider world in their implications for humanity (such as health care) or impact on the environment (such as initiating conservation strategies).
  - **Review:** A chance to review the children's learning and ensure the outcomes of the lesson have been achieved.

Assess and review

At the end of each chapter are activities for assessing and reviewing the children's understanding. These can be conducted during the course of the chapter's work, saved until the end of the chapter or done at a later date.

All assessment and review activities follow the same format:

- **Curriculum objectives:** These are the areas of focus for the assess and review activity. There may be one focus or more than one depending on the activity.
- **Resources:** What you require to conduct the activities.
- **Working scientifically:** Each activity features one or more of the Working scientifically objectives for assessment.
- **Revise:** A series of short activities or one longer activity to revise and consolidate the children's learning and ensure they understand the concept(s).
- **Assess:** An assessment activity to provide a chance for the children to demonstrate their understanding and for you to check this.
- **Further practice:** Ideas for further practice on the focus, whether children are insecure in their learning or you want to provide extra practice or challenge.

Photocopiable pages

At the end of each chapter are some photocopiable pages that will have been referred to in the lesson plans.

These sheets are for the children to use; there is generally a title, an instruction, an activity and an 'I can' statement at the bottom. These sheets are also provided on the CD-ROM alongside additional pages as referenced in the lessons (see page 7 About the CD-ROM). The children should be encouraged to complete the 'I can' statements by colouring in the traffic lights to say how they think they have done (red – not very well, amber – ok, green – very well).

■ SCHOLASTIC

About the CD-ROM

The CD-ROM contains:

- Printable versions of the photocopiable sheets from the book and additional photocopiable sheets as referenced in the lesson plans.
- Interactive activities for children to complete or to use on the whiteboard.
- Media resources to display.
- Printable versions of the lesson plans.
- Digital versions of the lesson plans with the relevant resources linked to them.

Getting started

- Put the CD-ROM into your CD-ROM drive.
  - For Windows users, the install wizard should autorun, if it fails to do so then navigate to your CD-ROM drive. Then follow the installation process.
  - For Mac users, copy the disk image file to your hard drive. After it has finished copying double-click it to mount the disk image. Navigate to the mounted disk image and run the installer. After installation the disk image can be unmounted and the DMG can be deleted from the hard drive.
- To complete the installation of the program you need to open the program and click 'Update' in the pop-up. Please note – this CD-ROM is web-enabled and the content will be downloaded from the internet to your hard-drive to populate the CD-ROM with the relevant resources. This only needs to be done on first use, after this you will be able to use the CD-ROM without an internet connection. If at any point any content is updated you will receive another pop-up upon start up with an internet connection.

Navigating the CD-ROM

There are two options to navigate the CD-ROM either as a Child or as a Teacher.

Child

- Click on the 'Child' button on the first menu screen.
- In the second menu click on the relevant class (please note only the books installed on the machine or network will be accessible. You can also rename year groups to match your school's naming conventions via the Teacher > Settings > Rename books area).
- A list of interactive activities will be displayed, children need to locate the correct one and click 'Go' to launch it.
- There is the opportunity to print or save a PDF of the activity at the end.

Teacher

- Click on the 'Teacher' button on the first menu screen and you will be taken to a screen showing which of the *100 English* books you have purchased. From here, you can also access information about getting started and the credits.
- To enter the product click 'Next' in the bottom right.
- You then need to enter a password (the password is: login).
- On first use:
  - Enter as a Guest by clicking on the 'Guest' button.
  - If desired, create a profile for yourself by adding your name to the list of users. Profiles allow you to save favourites and to specify which year group(s) you wish to be able to view.
  - Go to 'Settings' to create a profile for yourself – click 'Add user' and enter your name. Then choose the year groups you wish to have access to (you can return to this screen to change this at any time). Click on 'Login' at the top of the screen to re-enter the disk under your new profile.
- On subsequent uses you can choose your name from the drop-down list. The 'Guest' option will always be available if you, or a colleague, wish to use this.
- You can search the CD-ROM using the tools or save favourites.

For more information about how to use the CD-ROM, please refer to the help file which can be found in the teacher area of the CD-ROM. It is a red button with a question mark on it on the right-hand side of the screen just underneath the 'Settings' tab.

Curriculum grid

The tables below show the weekly curriculum coverage for each chapter.

Curriculum objectives	Autumn 1						Autumn 2					
	W1	W2	W3	W4	W5	W6	W1	W2	W3	W4	W5	W6
Plants												
To identify and name a variety of common wild and garden plants, including deciduous and evergreen trees												
To identify and describe the basic structure of a variety of common flowering plants, including trees												
Animals, including humans												
To identify and name a variety of common animals including fish, amphibians, reptiles, birds and mammals									✓	✓	✓	✓
To identify and name a variety of common animals that are carnivores, herbivores and omnivores									✓			
To describe and compare the structure of a variety of common animals (fish, amphibians, reptiles, birds and mammals, including pets)									✓	✓	✓	✓
To identify, name, draw and label the basic parts of the human body and say which part of the body is associated with each sense							✓	✓				
Everyday materials												
To distinguish between an object and the material from which it is made												
To identify and name a variety of everyday materials, including wood, plastic, glass, metal, water, and rock												
To describe the simple physical properties of a variety of everyday materials												
To compare and group together a variety of everyday materials on the basis of their simple physical properties												
Seasonal changes												
To observe changes across the four seasons	✓			✓	✓	✓						
To observe and describe weather associated with the seasons and how day length varies		✓	✓	✓	✓							

Curriculum objectives	Spring 1						Spring 2					
	W1	W2	W3	W4	W5	W6	W1	W2	W3	W4	W5	W6
Plants												
To identify and name a variety of common wild and garden plants, including deciduous and evergreen trees							✓				✓	✓
To identify and describe the basic structure of a variety of common flowering plants, including trees								✓	✓	✓		✓
Animals, including humans												
To identify and name a variety of common animals including fish, amphibians, reptiles, birds and mammals												
To identify and name a variety of common animals that are carnivores, herbivores and omnivores												
To describe and compare the structure of a variety of common animals (fish, amphibians, reptiles, birds and mammals, including pets)												
To identify, name, draw and label the basic parts of the human body and say which part of the body is associated with each sense												
Everyday materials												
To distinguish between an object and the material from which it is made	✓											
To identify and name a variety of everyday materials, including wood, plastic, glass, metal, water, and rock		✓										
To describe the simple physical properties of a variety of everyday materials			✓	✓	✓	✓						
To compare and group together a variety of everyday materials on the basis of their simple physical properties				✓	✓	✓						
Seasonal changes												
To observe changes across the four seasons	✓			✓	✓	✓						
To observe and describe weather associated with the seasons and how day length varies	✓	✓	✓	✓	✓							

Curriculum objectives	Summer 1						Summer 2					
	W1	W2	W3	W4	W5	W6	W1	W2	W3	W4	W5	W6
Plants												
To identify and name a variety of common wild and garden plants, including deciduous and evergreen trees												
To identify and describe the basic structure of a variety of common flowering plants, including trees												
Animals, including humans												
To identify and name a variety of common animals including fish, amphibians, reptiles, birds and mammals												
To identify and name a variety of common animals that are carnivores, herbivores and omnivores												
To describe and compare the structure of a variety of common animals (fish, amphibians, reptiles, birds and mammals, including pets)												
To identify, name, draw and label the basic parts of the human body and say which part of the body is associated with each sense												
Everyday materials												
To distinguish between an object and the material from which it is made							✓					
To identify and name a variety of everyday materials, including wood, plastic, glass, metal, water, and rock							✓	✓				
To describe the simple physical properties of a variety of everyday materials									✓	✓	✓	✓
To compare and group together a variety of everyday materials on the basis of their simple physical properties										✓	✓	✓
Seasonal changes												
To observe changes across the four seasons	✓	✓		✓	✓							
To observe and describe weather associated with the seasons and how day length varies		✓	✓	✓	✓							

Seasons: autumn and winter

Expected prior learning
● Some similarities and differences between living things.
● Features of immediate environment compared to others.
● Observations of animals and plants.

Overview of progression
After completing this chapter the children should know about:

● weather associated with autumn and winter
● some changes in day length
● how plants, animals and humans are affected by seasonal changes associated with autumn and winter.

Creative context
● This topic provides many opportunities for children to make observational drawings and use images to present their findings.
● Children will be required to deploy their design and technology skills when making holly-wreath collages and models of trees.
● The natural environment lends itself to various forms of creative writing, music and dance.

Background knowledge

Seasonal changes
The Earth takes 365¼ days – 1 year – to orbit the Sun. The Earth's axis slants at an angle of just over 23°, causing the northern hemisphere to lean towards the Sun for part of this orbit. During this time, hours of daylight increase and the temperature rises. As the northern hemisphere leans away from the Sun, hours of daylight decrease and temperatures drop. This tilting causes seasonal change on Earth. In the northern hemisphere it is summer during June, July, August; autumn in September, October, November; winter in December, January, February; and spring in March, April, May. Plant and animal behaviour responds to changes in light and temperature over the year.

Speaking scientifically
● In this chapter, the children will have opportunities to work scientifically and observe changes across autumn and winter, observe and describe the weather at a particular time of year, and observe the apparent movement of the Sun and how daylight varies. A simple scientific vocabulary will enable the children to comment on their observations and could include: deciduous, evergreen, fruit, nut, fungus, sunrise, sunset, temperature, thermometer, weather vane, precipitation, rainfall, air pressure, anemometer, nocturnal, insulation, evaporation, perspiration, moulting, camouflage, migration and climate.

Preparation
Ensure that your class understands that it is never safe to look directly at the Sun and remind them of this when you are undertaking any of the activities relating to day length or sunny weather.

You will need to provide: PE hoops; audio/video recording equipment, camera; plastic bottles and bags to create a simple weather station; visual calendar and weather chart; modelling materials; gardening and/or disposable gloves for fieldwork activities; weather measuring instruments and a recording of a weather forecast; photographs of various trees, animals and activities; a globe

On the CD-ROM you will find: photocopiable pages 'Seasons diagram', 'Our tree', 'Timeline image sheet', 'Autumn weather'; interactive activities 'Trees in different seasons', 'Changing seasons', 'Day and night', 'Wind', 'Dress for the season' and 'Animals in winter'

Chapter at a glance

Week	Lesson	Curriculum objectives	Lesson objectives	Main activity	Working scientifically
1	1	• To observe changes across the four seasons (autumn/winter).	• To review knowledge of the seasons. • To recognise changes to the natural environment that happen in autumn. • To identify and record evidence of autumn. • To identify some common tree species.	Making a list of their ideas and questions about autumn and winter. Looking for signs of autumn in a local park: photograph/draw/collect examples of changing trees.	• Asking simple questions. • Identifying and classifying. • Observing closely. • Gathering and recording data to help in answering questions.
	2	• To observe changes across the four seasons.	• To observe changes across the seasons. • To name the seasons and their order. • To link the months of the year to the relevant season. • To identify characteristics of each season.	Dividing a PE hoop into four sections. Hanging labels with months in order. Adding photos of children to birthday month.	• Asking simple questions. • Identifying and classifying. • Observing closely. • *Making comparisons and deciding how to sort and group.*
	3	• To observe changes across the four seasons.	• To observe changes across the seasons. • To name the seasons and their order. • To link the months of the year to the relevant season. • To identify characteristics of each season.	Making a simple visual calendar to show differences/ similarities between each season. Recording with photos/drawings.	• Asking simple questions. • Identifying and classifying. • Observing closely. • *Making comparisons and deciding how to sort and group.*
2	1	• To observe and describe how day length varies.	• To observe shadows. • To measure and record shadows over the course of a day. • To describe how shadows change in shape and size over the course of a day.	Investigating changes in shadow length over a day: drawing around children's shadows. Using string to measure from head to toe of shadows. Recording with photos.	• Asking simple questions. • Observing closely. • Gathering and recording data to help in answering questions.
	2	• To observe and describe how day length varies.	• To create a timeline of a day, from sunrise to sunset. • To relate the apparent position of the Sun to the time of day. • To relate shadow size to time of day.	Making a simple timeline showing when they do certain activities – linking with telling the time and the shadow measurements made in previous lesson.	• Asking simple questions. • Observing closely. • Making comparisons.
	3	• To observe and describe how day length varies.	• To observe differences between day and night. • To compare light and dark in summer and autumn evenings. • To identify some differences between summer and autumn.	Using video/images to observe differences between the seasons. Using photos and drawings to identify examples such as long summer evenings/long autumn nights.	• Asking simple questions. • Observing closely. • Making comparisons.
3	1	• To observe and describe weather associated with the seasons.	• To identify different types of weather. • To match the different weather types to weather symbols. • To create weather reports using weather symbols.	Looking at weather charts, symbols and forecasts. Making their weather forecasts.	• Asking simple questions. • Identifying and classifying. • Observing closely. • *Making comparisons and deciding how to sort and group.* • Gathering and recording data to help in answering questions.
	2	• To observe and describe weather associated with the seasons.	• To consider how to measure rainfall. • To consider how to site a rain gauge. • To record rainfall regularly. • To be able to read back measurements from a rainfall record.	What happened when Dr Foster went to Gloucester? What made the puddle so deep? Siting a simple rain gauge. Predicting amounts of rainfall and taking measurements.	• Asking simple questions. • Observing closely. • Gathering and recording data to help in answering questions.
	3	• To observe and describe weather associated with the seasons.	• To observe signs of wind. • To identify differing wind strengths. • To create a wind measurer using appropriate materials. • To identify wind direction.	Looking at images of washing on a line, smoking chimneys, and so on and discussing what causes the movement. Using plastic strips to identify direction and strength of wind.	• Asking simple questions. • Identifying and classifying. • Observing closely. • Gathering and recording data to help in answering questions.

Chapter at a glance

Week	Lesson	Curriculum objectives	Lesson objectives	Main activity	Working scientifically
4	1	• To observe and describe weather associated with the seasons.	• To carry out an investigation into temperatures indoors and outdoors. • To make simple temperature recordings.	Using a thermometer to record observations about temperature. Investigating differences in temperature: leave ice balloons out overnight.	• Asking simple questions. • Observing closely. • Gathering and recording data to help in answering questions.
	2	• To observe and describe how day length varies.	• To identify some nocturnal animals. • To consider why some animals are nocturnal.	Discussing nocturnal animals. Using video and images to identify and describe other nocturnal animals. Talking about day length in different parts of the world.	• Asking simple questions. • Identifying and classifying. • Observing closely. • Gathering and recording data to help in answering questions.
	3	• To observe changes across the four seasons (summer/ autumn).	• To recall the names of some deciduous trees. • To observe the leaves of some deciduous trees and sort them. • To identify trees by closely observing their leaves.	Displaying images of autumnal leaves and discussing what is happening to the trees. Looking at a collection of fallen leaves and sorting into groups by colour, size and shape.	• Asking simple questions. • Identifying and classifying. • Observing closely. • *Making comparisons and deciding how to sort and group.* • Gathering and recording data to help in answering questions.
5	1	• To observe and describe weather associated with the seasons.	• To compare weather in different seasons. • To explain why specific clothing is suited to different seasons.	Listening to the story of a competition between the Sun and the Wind. Acting out the story. Choosing suitable clothes.	• Asking simple questions. • Identifying and classifying. • Observing closely. • Making comparisons. • Gathering and recording data to help in answering questions.
	2	• To observe changes across the four seasons.	• To consider how animals cope with cold winter weather. • To establish the purpose of some animals' winter coats.	Comparing arctic foxes and mountain hares in summer and winter. Matching task to describe how they cope with cold weather.	• Asking simple questions. • Observing closely.
	3	• To observe changes across the four seasons.	• To investigate the concept of bird/animal migration. • To correctly order images of a swallow's annual migration.	Discussing bird and animal migration. Reading a swallow's 'postcard' from South Africa. Ordering images to tell the story of swallow migration.	• Asking simple questions. • Making comparisons.
6	1	• To observe changes across the four seasons (autumn/ winter).	• To observe and predict seasonal changes in the park. • To record their observations. • To compare their observations with those from their previous park visit.	Looking at pictures from the previous visit to the park and asking children to predict how it will have changed. Revisiting the park.	• Asking simple questions. • Identifying and classifying. • Observing closely. • Making comparisons. • Gathering and recording data.
	2	• To observe changes across the four seasons (autumn/ winter).	• To observe one tree in detail. • To record their observations. • To identify the tree.	Observing one particular tree in detail.	• Asking simple questions. • Identifying and classifying. • Observing closely. • Gathering and recording data to help in answering questions.
	3	• To observe changes across the four seasons.	• To identify the characteristics of an evergreen tree. • To sort trees according to whether they are evergreen or deciduous. • To name some evergreen trees. • To name some deciduous trees.	Looking at images of plants associated with winter festivals. Discussing how traditions evolved. Comparing evergreen and deciduous plants. Making holly-wreath collages.	• Asking simple questions. • Identifying and classifying. • Observing closely. • *Making comparisons and deciding how to sort and group.* • Gathering and recording data.
Assess and review					

Objectives
- To review knowledge of the seasons.
- To recognise changes to the natural environment that happen in autumn.
- To identify and record evidence of autumn.
- To identify some common tree species.

Resources
Audio recording of summer sounds; cameras; paper; clipboards and pencils; disposable or gardening gloves; collecting bags; laminated photocopiable page 36 'Tree identification chart'; photocopiable page 37 'Autumn in the park'

Speaking scientifically
deciduous, evergreen, temperature, fruit, nut, berry, sycamore and ash keys, fungus

Lesson 1: The hunt for autumn

Previous knowledge
During the Early Years Foundation Stage, children will have had opportunities to develop their understanding of the world and find out about differences and similarities between some living things. They will have been encouraged to talk about features of their own environment and how others might vary; and make some observations about plants and animals.

Introduction
Play the children some summer sounds – birds singing, waves lapping on a beach, an ice-cream van's tune, and so on – and ask the children to say what time of year these sounds remind them of. Show the class a photograph of yourself on holiday during the summer break. Typical scenes to help the children begin thinking about the seasons include a visit to the seaside, camping or a family barbeque. Describe what the weather was like when the photograph was taken and include details such as the length of time you were able to spend outside before it got dark. Invite the children to talk about their own summer holidays and encourage them to add any details they can remember about the weather and day length.

Check that the children can name and order the seasons and that they are aware that autumn has started and that winter will follow on afterwards. Ask them what will change now autumn has started and make a list of their ideas and any questions they may have.

Whole-class work
Prior to this lesson, prepare for an off-site educational visit, in line with school policy, by carrying out a thorough risk assessment and obtaining permission from parents and carers. Consider details such as transport, food, clothing, medical requirements and an appropriate level of adult support. (Be aware of allergies. In particular, chestnuts can trigger an allergic reaction in some children. Check whether anyone in your class could be at risk and take appropriate action, tailoring the activities as appropriate.)

1. Tell the children that you are going on a 'hunt for autumn' in a park. Show them some photographs of where they will be looking and ask what they might expect to see there. Explain that they will be taking photographs and making drawings of what they find and establish some ground rules for staying safe. Children should use gloves to collect fallen leaves, twigs, conkers and so on; on no account should they taste any nuts, berries or fungi; and they should tell an adult if they come across any rubbish, dog mess or similar.

2. Begin your visit to the park by looking at the trees. Encourage the children to notice any changes in the colour of the leaves and whether any have started to fall onto the ground. Take photographs of general scenes and anything particular from children's initial observations.

Group work
3. Divide the class into small adult-led groups and direct them to different locations in the park. Tell the children to look carefully at the trees and plants in their area and collect any evidence of autumnal changes – such as fallen leaves and nuts – using gloves and their special collection bags. Ask them to record their findings in a number of ways, for example by making drawings and taking photographs and bark rubbings of trees that they notice are changing. Encourage them to observe tree and leaf shapes closely, comparing them against laminated versions of photocopiable page 36 'Tree identification chart', which lists some common species of tree.

4. At various points during the visit, bring the whole class back together and talk about what they have found. Compare each group's observations about autumn and send the children out to a new location to repeat their investigations.

Checkpoint
● What are the months of the year?
● What are the names of the seasons?
● Which season has just ended?
● Which season is just beginning?
● What happens in autumn?
● How do trees change?
● What will change between now and winter?

5. Make an autumnal path for the class to follow by laying out a trail of natural materials among the trees. Include some twists and turns and doubling back and challenge the children to collect treasure-hunt clues, such as a twig with an acorn attached to it, some sycamore keys or a yellow, five-fingered leaf from a horse chestnut tree.

6. At the end of the visit, collect the whole class together again and review all their findings. Collate their drawings, photographs and other autumnal evidence for a classroom display.

7. Back in class, remind children of their visit to the park and invite them to recall what they saw. Challenge them to start noticing and reporting their observations as they travel to and from school or are out and about at weekends.

Independent work
8. Provide children with photocopiable page 37 'Autumn in the park', showing an autumnal scene, and ask them to fill it in using appropriate colours they have observed.

Introducing the new area of study
Teach the class some songs about autumn such as 'Autumn Days when the Grass is Jewelled' or sing about autumn leaves to the tune of 'London Bridge is Falling Down' and talk about the lyrics. Display a simple weather chart and tell the children that they will be finding out how the weather changes over the next few weeks. Show them pictures of animals such as swallows and arctic foxes and explain that they will also be finding out about changes these creatures go through during autumn in preparation for the cold, dark winter months.

> **Differentiation**
> ● Support children during the photocopiable sheet activity by giving them labels with first-letter clues to glue onto their autumnal scene.
> ● Challenge children to label their autumnal scene and write sentences about their visit to the park.

Science in the wider world
Deciduous trees are those which shed all their leaves in autumn. This is the beginning of a period of dormancy during which these trees can conserve energy and water. The most common deciduous trees in the UK include ash, horse chestnut, lime, oak and sycamore. Evergreen trees often have dark, needle-like leaves or tough waxy surfaces, which do not lose as much moisture as broad-leaved varieties. Evergreens tend to lose leaves on a gradual basis, retaining enough to photosynthesise during the winter months, providing there is enough moisture. In autumn, many flowering plants will have produced nuts and berries that contain the seeds from which new plants grow. These need to be dispersed away from the parent plant and may be carried by the wind, as in the case of sycamore and ash keys; or taken by animals as in the case of acorns and blackberries.

Review
Children could be assessed on the observations they have made about signs of autumnal change and any evidence they have collected in the form of drawings or photographs of fallen leaves, nuts and berries. They could also be assessed on their completion of the autumnal photocopiable sheet and inclusion of relevant details such as colour, labels and sentences about their observations.

Objectives
● To observe changes across the seasons.
● To name the seasons and their order.
● To link the months of the year to the relevant season.
● To identify characteristics of each season.

Resources
A large PE hoop; a large yellow ball; a small practice ball; a piece of wire or paperclip; crepe paper in four seasonal colours; string or ribbon; four pictures of a tree in each season; labels for months of the year; photocopiable page 'Seasons diagram' from the CD-ROM; a small photograph of each child attached to a length of string with their birthday month written on the back; interactive activity 'Trees in different seasons' on the CD-ROM

Speaking scientifically
spring, summer, autumn, winter, season, lighter, darker, shorter, longer, day length

Lesson 2: The seasons mobile

Introduction
Look at the photographs and drawings the children made during their visit to the park. Talk about the signs of autumn they observed. Ask what the park might look like in other seasons. Display images of trees in each season or use the interactive activity 'Trees in different seasons' on the CD-ROM.

Whole-class work
1. Seat the children in rows and show them the small practice ball. Explain that this represents the Earth and that the children are going to help it make its yearly journey by passing it round and calling out the months in order. Hand one child the ball and ask them to start with January. After December, the next child should start again with January. Repeat until all the children are familiar with the order.

2. Next, seat the children in a circle and put the large yellow ball in the middle of the circle. Explain that this is the Sun and that it takes our planet, the Earth, a year to go around it once. Place the large PE hoop – divided into four sections covered in seasonally appropriate crepe paper (white for winter, green for spring, yellow for summer and red for autumn) – on the floor so that the Sun is inside. Use string or ribbon to divide the circle of children into four sections. Lay crepe paper around the edge of the children's circle to indicate which season they are sitting in. Give each group a picture of a tree in the particular season.

3. Tell the children that they are helping the Earth on its journey again, but this time the months are divided into seasons. Ask which months go where. Hand the ball to the winter quarter. Tell them to call out the winter months December, January and February as a group and then pass the ball on to spring.

4. Continue until all the children are familiar with the order of the seasons and the months in each. Turn the hoop so that the groups call out different months.

Independent work
5. Show the class the photocopiable page 'Seasons diagram' from the CD-ROM and ask them to label and colour the trees appropriately.

Whole-class work
6. While the children complete their independent task, suspend the yellow ball using wire or a paper clip as a hook. Hang the PE hoop horizontally, with the ball in the centre. Attach labels for each month of the year.

7. Hand out the children's photographs and ask those with winter birthdays to stand up. Check that their birthdays are in December, January or February. Attach their photographs to the winter quarter of the hoop. Repeat for the other three seasons.

Differentiation
● Support children with labels for each season to glue onto their diagram.
● Challenge children to write the name of the season by each tree on their photocopiable sheet and describe how the trees change over the year.

Science in the wider world
Seasonal change is most noticeable in the Earth's temperate zones. At the equator, day length and temperatures remain constant throughout the year (although rainfall can vary significantly). The poles experience continuous darkness in the winter and continuous daylight in summer.

Review
Children could be assessed on listing months of the year and linking them to the seasons; also on colouring and labelling the 'Seasons diagram'.

Objectives
- To observe changes across the seasons.
- To name the seasons and their order.
- To link the months of the year to the relevant season.
- To identify characteristics of each season.

Resources
Seasons mobile from previous lesson; completed examples from previous lesson of photocopiable page 'Seasons diagram' from the CD-ROM; photographs of children taking part in seasonally appropriate activities; photographs of plants and animals that change colour in different seasons; a commercially produced calendar; blank sheets of paper equally divided into four boxes; a list of seasons and months of the year; images reflecting changes in the seasons; old seasonal greetings cards; interactive activity 'Changing seasons' on the CD-ROM

Speaking scientifically
spring, summer, autumn, winter, season, calendar, temperature, daylight

Lesson 3: Comparing seasons

Introduction
Show the class the completed seasons mobile from the previous lesson, with each child's photograph hanging by their birthday month. Play a guessing game to check that the children can recall which season their birthday month is in. Ask everyone to stand up and give instructions such as, *Sit down if your birthday is in summer*, or *I am thinking of a child with a birthday in early spring – can you guess who?* and so on. Choose some children to check that their classmates are following instructions according to when their birthday is by comparing with the photographs attached to the hoop.

Whole-class work
1. Remind the children about the diagram they completed in the previous lesson showing trees in different seasons. Look at some of these and talk about how the trees are different in each picture. Ask the children to suggest other changes that happen around us over the seasons. Make a list of their ideas. This could include what they wear or do at various times of the year, certain festivals, how animals change, flowers grow, and so on.

2. Display photographs of different activities that reflect changes in the seasons and match these with the children's suggestions.

3. Show the children a commercially produced calendar and talk about how it works. Demonstrate how it lists all the months of the year in order and has space to write in important events.

Paired work
4. Give pairs of children a sheet of paper that has been divided into four equal boxes. They will also need a list of seasons and months of the year, as well as a series of images reflecting changes in the seasons.

5. Ask the children to begin by labelling each box with a season. They should then identify and glue the appropriate month labels into each box. Tell them to leave room by these for some illustrations.

6. Next, ask the children to choose some images to represent each season. They should make comparisons and decide how to sort and group them and then add them to their boxes. Old seasonal greetings cards could also be cut out and glued into the correct season or by the appropriate month.

7. Ask the children to complete their calendars by colouring them in.

Differentiation
- Support children by providing sheets with the months already attached and asking them to choose and add the correct season label.
- Challenge children by providing them with a month of the year wordbank and asking them to write in each month on their calendar, or by asking them to complete the interactive activity 'Changing seasons' on the CD-ROM.

Science in the wider world
The Earth takes 365¼ days to orbit the Sun, but for most years calendars are based on the 365 full days of the year. Every four years, however, the quarters are added together to make an extra day. This is a leap year and the day that is added on is 29 February.

Review
Children could be assessed on the completion of their visual calendar: check that they have matched the seasons and months of the year correctly and illustrated their work with images appropriate to each season.

Objectives
- To observe shadows.
- To measure and record shadows over the course of a day.
- To describe how shadows change in shape and size over the course of a day.

Resources
Different coloured chalks; a camera; lengths of string

Speaking scientifically
sun, shadow, sunlight, direction, length

Lesson 1: Sun and shadows

Introduction

Show the children some images of unusual shadows and ask them to guess what objects might have cast them. Talk about how shadows are made by blocking out light with something. Use the projector and whiteboard in your classroom to make some shadow shapes using your hands. Challenge the children to make birds, rabbits, and so on. Ask them to suggest how shadows are made when they are outdoors and to think about whether these are always the same. Encourage the children to describe times when they may have noticed a very long shadow – in early morning or late afternoon – or when their shadow has seemed shorter than them. Remind them that the Sun can be dangerous and it is very important that they never look directly at it.

Whole-class work

1. Choose a sunny day with a settled forecast before embarking on this activity! Take the class into the playground early in the morning and tell them to run around and watch what happens to their shadows. Stop them after a few minutes and talk about their observations, ensuring that they notice their shadows are always 'attached' to their feet and move with them.

2. Next, ask the children to stand on a spot and turn slowly around, checking as they do so to see if their shadow turns with them. Continue with this activity until every child is able to notice that their shadow might change shape as they turn their bodies, but always stays on the same part of the playground.

3. Find an area in the playground that is unobstructed by buildings or large trees and mark out a line with chalk. Explain that the children are going to put their toes on this line and stand still while their partner draws around the shape of their shadow on the ground with chalk. They will then swap over so that everyone has a shadow recorded on the ground. Ensure that there is enough space for every child's shadow and that they all write their names at the base of their shadow outlines.

4. Make a note of the time and the colour of chalk used. Take photographs of the children and their shadows. Lay a piece of string from head to toe of some of the shadows and cut it to show their lengths. Label these with name and time.

5. After an hour or so, return to the shadow outlines and line the children up with their shadow shapes again. Are their shadows the same shape and size as before? Ask them to take it in turns to draw around the new shadow outlines in a different colour. Talk about any changes the children notice.

6. Repeat the chalking, photographing and measuring activities over the course of the school day.

7. Use the lengths of string to make a simple bar chart as a record and display this alongside the photographs. Encourage the children to describe how the size and direction of their shadows changed over the course of the day.

Science in the wider world

The Sun appears to move across the sky, although actually it is the movement of the Earth that makes it appear to rise and fall in the course of a day. Shadows are longest when the Sun is low in the sky and shortest in the middle of the day when it reaches its highest point.

Review

Children could be assessed on their observations of changes in shadow size and direction.

Objectives
● To create a timeline of a day, from sunrise to sunset.
● To relate the apparent position of the Sun to the time of day.
● To relate shadow size to time of day.

Resources
Photographs and bar chart from previous lesson; large and small clock faces; a long sheet of card for a timeline; yellow paper discs; images of sunrise and sunset; pictures of significant events in the school day; small sheets of paper; paints; long sheets of paper for timelines; interactive activity 'Day and night' on the CD-ROM

Speaking scientifically
sunrise, dawn, dusk, sunset, dusk, midday, noon, higher, lower, east, west

Lesson 2: What time is it?

Introduction
Remind the class of their work on shadows by displaying the photographs and bar chart from the previous lesson. Ask the children to recall what they did and what they noticed about shadows over the course of the school day. Display a large clock face showing what time it was when each of the measurements was taken (approximate to the nearest hour or half hour, as appropriate). Create smaller clock faces set to these times and add them to the bar chart, asking questions such as, *At what time did we have the shortest shadows?* to practise relating these times to the measurements on the bar chart.

Whole-class work
1. Show the class a long strip of card with a line ruled horizontally across it and a small clock face set to 12 attached in the middle. Explain that this is a 'timeline' and that they are going to add some events from their day to it. Place a yellow disc above the clock face to represent the midday Sun.

2. Remind the children about how the shadows were longer when the Sun was lower in the sky. Ask if they know what happens to the Sun at the beginning and end of each day.

3. Display images of sunrise and sunset. Invite the children to recall occasions when they have witnessed either. Establish that the Sun 'rises' at the beginning of the day (dawn) and attach a sunrise image at the left-hand end of the timeline. Label it 'sunrise'. Repeat for sunset (dusk) at the right-hand end. Extend by explaining that the Sun rises in the east and sets in the west.

4. Work with the children to transfer pictures of significant daily events, such as assembly, playtime and lunchtime, onto the timeline.

5. Ask the children to suggest events that happen before and after school, such as waking up, breakfast, travelling, teatime and bedtime.

Paired work
6. Provide pairs of children with small sheets of plain paper and paints. Ask one of them to create a sunrise picture, and the other a sunset picture.

7. While their paintings are drying, ask each pair to work on a timeline with midday marked on it. Provide them with small pictures of significant daily events. Ask them to work out where these should go and attach them.

8. When their paintings are dry, ask the children to place these at either end of their timeline with the labels 'sunrise' and 'sunset'.

Differentiation
● Support children by limiting the events you ask them to place on their timeline.
● Challenge children to add more events to their timeline and to make clock faces to show when these happen. You can also challenge them to complete the interactive activity 'Day and night' on the CD-ROM.

Science in the wider world
Day and night are caused by the Earth rotating on its axis. As it turns, the half of the Earth facing the Sun experiences day, while the other half is in darkness. It is this rotation that creates sunrise and sunset and makes the Sun appear to move across the sky.

Review
Children could be assessed on how accurately they are able to order daily events and show a link with the apparent movement of the Sun.

Objectives
• To observe and identify differences between day and night.
• To compare light and dark in summer and autumn evenings.
• To identify some differences between summer and autumn.

Resources
Video/images of autumnal festivals such as Diwali, Halloween and bonfire night; plain paper divided into two equal sections

Speaking scientifically
sunrise, dawn, sunset, dusk, higher, lower, sunlight, shortest, longest

Lesson 3: Day or night?

Introduction

Talk about the timelines the children made in the previous lesson. Point out the sunrise and sunset pictures they painted to go at the beginning and end of their day. Remind them about what these terms mean and ask the children to describe what it is like after sunset and before sunrise. Establish that the period in between is night-time. Talk about some of the activities they might do at night and make a list of these – at this stage, the children may suggest that all they do when it is dark is go to bed!

Whole-class work

1. Ask the children to think about any after-school activities they may do during the week, or other occasions when they are later returning home than usual. Talk about what their return journey is like and encourage them to recall details such as whether street and car lights are on and whether they have to switch lights on when they get home. If so, why? What has happened? Establish that the lights are on because the Sun has set before bedtime.

2. Show video footage or display images of autumnal festivals such as Diwali, Halloween and bonfire night. Encourage the children to make observations about how dark it is outside on these occasions, though there are still lots of people about.

3. Remind the class about the first lesson in this topic, when they began their work on seasons by thinking about what they did during the summer holidays. Ask them to remember some of their summer evening activities, such as barbeques, camping trips or simply playing out before bedtime. Establish that there was enough daylight to do these activities then. Question whether it would still be possible to do these activities in the autumn.

Independent work

4. Provide the children with paper divided into two equal sections. Ask them to draw a picture of a summer evening activity in one box. Remind them that they should include the Sun in their picture, although it would be low in the sky or even setting. In the other box, ask them to draw an autumnal festival with a bonfire and fireworks. This time, the night sky should be dark.

> **Differentiation**
> • Support children by asking them to make one drawing of a night-time activity such as a firework display.
> • Challenge children to add labels showing the difference between summer and autumn and to write sentences about their experiences.

Science in the wider world

The summer solstice occurs at the point in the Earth's orbit where it leans most towards the Sun. After it, the northern hemisphere begins to tilt away from it again. The length of daylight starts to decrease and the days will continue to shorten until the winter solstice, around 21 December.

Review

Children could be assessed on the detail they can add to their night-time pictures and the observations they make about variations between these.

Objectives
- To identify different types of weather.
- To match the different weather types to weather symbols.
- To create weather reports using weather symbols.

Resources
Simple weather symbols; a recorded televised weather forecast; weather chart backgrounds or images of the school grounds; a video recorder; examples or images of weather measuring instruments

Speaking scientifically
temperature, thermometer, weather vane, rainfall, rain gauge

Lesson 1: Weather monitoring

Introduction
Teach the class some songs or rhymes about the weather, such as 'Rain, Rain Go Away', 'The North Wind Doth Blow' or 'I'm a Little Snowman'. Ask the children to come up with a list of different types of weather and to describe their recent experiences of it, such as wet playtimes, walking into a strong wind or feeling warm in the sunshine. Tell them to look out of the classroom windows and describe what the weather is like. Talk about how weather affects humans, plants and animals and why it is helpful to know what it is doing and what it might do next.

Whole-class work
1. Display a range of simple weather symbols, including symbols for clouds, sunshine, rain, a thermometer, a weather vane and a personified cloud blowing, to represent the wind. Ask the children to suggest what each one means. Match up as many as possible to the list you made at the start of the lesson and fill in any gaps. Check the children understand that temperature is a measure of how warm or cold it is and that a weather vane moves to show which direction the wind is blowing from.

2. Show the children a recording of a televised weather forecast. Challenge them to list the types of weather mentioned in the forecast and describe the symbols that they saw. Talk about any differences between these symbols and the ones in the classroom and decide which ones are easier to use.

3. Select some symbols and tell the children that you are going to give a weather report. Include the temperature, wind direction and whether it is rainy or sunny in your summary, and attach the symbols to a weather chart or a picture of the school playground as you explain each one.

Paired work
4. Provide pairs of children with a selection of weather symbols and a background to attach them to. Ask them to make up their own reports by describing their chosen weather and selecting appropriate symbols. Encourage the children to practise with their partner and then invite them to perform their forecast to the class. Some of the forecasts could be recorded on video.

Whole-class work
5. Explain that, in order to make an accurate weather report, forecasters need to use some special measuring equipment to record conditions. Display a thermometer, rain gauge and weather vane and ask the children to suggest what they are and how they work. Tell the children that, over the next few lessons, they will be using similar equipment to make and record their own weather observations. Ask them what they think the weather will be like at this time of year and in what ways it might differ from other seasons.

Science in the wider world
Modern weather forecasting is based on the science of meteorology and involves a range of sophisticated equipment and satellite imaging to measure atmospheric conditions and observe the development of weather systems and patterns. Accurate weather predictions are of vital importance to farmers, as well as those involved in shipping and aviation.

Review
Children could be assessed on their choice of weather symbols and how accurately they are able to use these to make a weather report.

● To consider how to measure rainfall.
● To consider how to site a rain gauge.
● To record rainfall regularly.
● To be able to read back measurements from a rainfall record.

Resources
A rain gauge – either commercially produced or made from a plastic drinks bottle; a measuring cylinder; a class rainfall chart; photocopiable rainfall charts

Speaking scientifically
precipitation, rainfall, rain gauge

Lesson 2: Measuring rainfall

Introduction
Sing the rhyme 'Dr Foster Went to Gloucester' with your class. Ask the children to recap the doctor's story and suggest why the puddle went up to his middle. Talk about how the rainwater must have collected in a hollow to make a deep puddle. Encourage the children to think about ways in which they could measure how much rain falls over a period of time.

Whole-class work
1. Discuss the fact that we have different amounts of rain on different days and that it can be important to know how much rain has fallen. Perhaps if Dr Foster had known how heavily it had been raining in Gloucester, he might have postponed his journey!

2. Show the class a commercially produced rain gauge, or one that has been made by cutting, inverting and reinserting the top third of a clear plastic drinks bottle. Talk about how it might work and then use a watering can to demonstrate how it collects the rain as it falls.

3. Tell the children to practise pouring the water from the rain gauge into a measuring cylinder and reading the measurement from the scale on the side. Encourage them to think about why they should be careful not to spill any water, as well as why the gauge might be empty when they go to check it.

4. Take your class out into the school grounds to find a suitable place to site the rain gauge. Encourage the children to think about what would happen if they put the gauge next to a wall or under a tree. Once you have agreed on the best position, ensure that the gauge is firmly fixed into the ground so that it cannot fall over or blow away.

5. Back in the classroom, decide how often you are going to take rainfall measurements and for how many weeks. Demonstrate how to record the information on a class table. This needs to be a large sheet of paper divided into columns for days of the week and the amount of rain collected. Display the table prominently. Model recording rainfall for the first day and talk about how the numbers could be added together at the end of each week to find out the total amount of rain that has fallen. Guide the children to recognise that there might be more water in the gauge on a Monday because no one will have emptied it on a Saturday or Sunday!

Independent work
6. Provide individual photocopiable sheets for the children to keep their own rainfall records on and ask them to begin to fill these in by listing the days of the week.

> **Differentiation**
> ● Support children by providing labels with days of the week to be attached to their rainfall charts.
> ● Challenge children to write the days of the week on independently and add dates, if appropriate.

Science in the wider world
2012 was one of the wettest years in the UK on record. There is some academic research on climate (such as at the University of Reading) to suggest that periods of very heavy rain are becoming more common – increasing the likelihood of flooding.

Review
Children could be assessed on how accurately they can take rainfall measurements and record these on their charts. Note those who can read information from their charts at the end of the collection period.

Objectives
● To observe signs of wind.
● To identify differing wind strengths.
● To create a wind measurer using appropriate materials.
● To identify wind direction.

Resources
A story about a windy day; images of the effects of a windy day; interactive activity 'Wind' on the CD-ROM; strips cut from three or four different weights of plastic sheeting (carrier bags, freezer bags, and so on); large curtain rings or lengths of cane; a camera

Speaking scientifically
wind, wind sock, Beaufort scale: calm, light air, light breeze, gentle breeze, moderate breeze, fresh breeze, strong breeze, near gale, gale, strong gale, storm, violent storm, hurricane

Lesson 3: When the wind blows

Introduction
Read the class a story about a windy day, such as *The Wind Blew* by Pat Hutchins, and make a list of how the strength of the wind can affect us. Talk about being outside on a windy day and how washing moves on a line, smoke rises from chimneys and the size and noise of waves at the seaside. Display images of these examples and invite the children to describe their own experiences.

Whole-class work
1. Ask the children to look out of the classroom window to see if there are any signs of the wind. Draw their attention to swaying trees or leaves being blown across the playground. Explain that there is a measure called the 'Beaufort scale' that can help us describe how strong the wind is. Use the interactive activity 'Wind' on the CD-ROM to identify differing wind strengths further.

2. Practise describing wind strength by looking at a variety of images, including a flag extended on a flagpole, an umbrella blowing inside out, a tree bending over and tiles blown off a roof.

3. Remind the children of the weather vane they saw in lesson 1 and talk about how it works. Establish that it is a way of finding out which direction the wind is blowing from. Explain that the children are going to make their own instruments for finding the wind direction to try out in the playground.

4. Show the class the strips of plastic sheeting and ask them to compare the thickness of these. Talk about which one might move with only a little wind and whether the thicker one might need a stronger wind to move. Explain that the children will use one strip of each thickness for their wind measurer.

Paired work
5. Provide pairs of children with some strips of plastic and tell them to tie three different types to their curtain ring or length of cane. Support children as necessary to tie knots – or have adults on hand with wall staplers to quickly attach the plastic.

6. Once all the wind measurers have been prepared, take the class into the playground. Find a suitable open area for the children to stand in and observe what happens to their streamers. Tell them to point to the direction the wind is blowing from and check that they all agree. Look at which pieces of plastic are blowing, and discuss how strong the wind is. Take photographs to make a visual record of their observations. Repeat this activity regularly over the next week or two weeks, alongside your class rainfall measurements.

Independent work
7. Back in class, tell the children to draw a picture of themselves in the playground with their wind measurers. Display these drawings and photographs and update with further measurements, alongside their records of rainfall.

Science in the wider world
In the UK, periods of late-summer weather at the beginning of September are often replaced with much more unsettled conditions at the end of the month. Traditionally, seafarers have equated the autumnal equinox with stormy winds. While statistics may not support the idea that gales occur more frequently at the equinoxes, records do show an increase in the occurrence of high winds around the British coastline at this time of year.

Review
Children could be assessed on whether they are able to say which direction the wind is blowing from and understand that, the heavier the streamer, the more wind is required to move it.

Objectives
• To carry out an investigation into temperatures indoors and outdoors.
• To make simple temperature recordings.

Resources
Enlarged photocopiable page 38 'Weather chart'; a large thermometer; ice balloons (fill balloons with coloured water, freeze and then carefully peel away the rubber); empty fish tanks or large trays; a camera; string; sheets of plain paper divided into two equal sections

Speaking scientifically
thermometer, temperature, Celsius

Lesson 1: Temperature differences

Introduction

Play some of the weather forecast videos the children made in week 3, lesson 1. Remind them of the symbols they used and the measurements these represented. Look at the data collected so far for rainfall and wind direction and strength, and talk about what other weather measurements the class could make. Display a large thermometer and talk about what it measures and how it works. Use one with a comparative scale for 'cold', 'colder', 'warm' and 'warmer', or a standard one adapted with similar labels.

Whole-class work

1. Talk about what is meant by 'warm' and 'cold' weather and how we can check. Place a thermometer outside with the rain gauge and – after a few minutes – take your first reading.

2. Back in class, add the temperature reading to an enlarged version of photocopiable page 38 'Weather chart', then complete the other weather observations for the day. Explain that you will carry on measuring the temperature and recording it alongside the other weather observations.

3. Ask the children if they think the temperature will vary each day. Talk about warm and cold days. Encourage them to suggest appropriate clothing. Display some of the pictures the children made in week 2, lesson 3 on light and dark evenings. Ask if they would need to dress differently for the night-time activities. Establish that generally it is colder at night-time because there is no heat from the Sun.

4. Explain that the children are going to investigate what happens to temperatures during the night. Display two ice balloons. Place these in separate fish tanks or on large plastic trays. Label them 'indoor' and 'outdoor'. Photograph the ice balloons and ask some of the children to measure around the fattest part of each one with a length of string. Keep the photographs and pieces of string for later.

5. Leave one balloon outside and the other in the classroom overnight. Repeat the photographs and measurements the following day. Ask the children to compare the balloons and say which one has melted the most, and why.

Independent work

6. Provide children with a sheet of paper divided into two sections. Ask them to draw the indoor and outdoor balloons.

Differentiation
• Support children by providing labels and photographs for the ice balloons to glue onto their sheets.
• Challenge children by asking them to compare the lengths of string and write sentences about their observations.

Science in the wider world

By the end of September and into October, the UK weather generally becomes more unsettled, with a greater likelihood of rain and strong winds. Temperatures start to fall, particularly at night.

Review

Children could be assessed on whether they are able to say that the outdoor ice balloon melted less because it was colder outside overnight.

■ SCHOLASTIC

Objectives
- To identify some nocturnal animals.
- To consider why some animals are nocturnal.

Resources
The Owl Who Was Afraid of the Dark by Jill Tomlinson; video clip or images of nocturnal animals in the UK; enlarged photocopiable page 39 'Nocturnal animals'; television clip of polar animals in winter

Speaking scientifically
nocturnal, diurnal, Arctic, Antarctic

Lesson 2: Nocturnal

Introduction
Remind the children of their previous work on light and dark evenings and encourage them to make further observations about changes they have noticed recently in day length. Read your class an extract from *The Owl Who Was Afraid of the Dark* by Jill Tomlinson. The story is about a baby barn owl who is struggling to come to terms with the fact that owls are nocturnal. In each chapter, he meets a character who describes a positive night-time experience, such as a campfire or firework display. He also meets an artist who draws nocturnal animals. Talk about what 'being nocturnal' means and ask if the children know any other examples of nocturnal animals.

Whole-class work
1. Choose a suitable clip from a wildlife programme or children's television series on nature to show your class some video footage of nocturnal animals in the UK.

2. Make a class list of the animals mentioned in the video. This might include mice, hedgehogs, bats, moles, owls or badgers. Talk about what the animals do at night-time and why they might be active in the dark, rather than the daylight. Encourage the children to consider factors such as finding food that is also nocturnal (for example, moths).

3. Display an enlarged version of photocopiable page 39 'Nocturnal animals' and ask the children to identify the animals depicted on it. Talk about what the children could write about for each animal and make a list of their ideas. These could include activities such as catching food, building nests and feeding their young.

Independent work
4. Tell the children to complete the photocopiable sheet. Once they have had time to do this, share their work and ideas with the rest of the class.

Whole-class work
5. Remind children that nights in the UK are currently getting longer, and this will continue until the shortest day of the year in December. Explain that, soon, they will be switching lights on when they get home from school. However, after that the hours of daylight will start to get longer. Explain that in some parts of the world the nights get so long that by the end of the autumn there is no daylight at all. This happens at the north and south poles in winter. Talk about what it would be like to live near one of the poles – for humans and animals – and, if possible, show further video footage of polar bears emerging from their winter burrow with cubs, or emperor penguins huddling in the dark.

Differentiation
- Support children in the completion of their photocopiable sheet with short statements describing what each animal does.
- Challenge children to write more detailed descriptions of the habits of nocturnal animals.

Science in the wider world
Above the Arctic Circle in the northern hemisphere and below the Antarctic Circle in the southern hemisphere, the Sun does not set in summer, or rise in winter. Hence these regions experience either midnight sun or complete darkness for several months of the year – the further north or south you go the longer these extremes will last.

Review
Children could be assessed on whether they are able to list nocturnal animals and on their completion of the photocopiable sheet.

Objectives
● To recall the names of some deciduous trees.
● To observe the leaves of some deciduous trees and sort them.
● To identify trees by closely observing their leaves.

Resources
Photographs taken during park visit in week 1, lesson 1; pictures of deciduous trees; laminated photocopiable page 36 'Tree identification chart' as used in week 1, lesson 1; a selection of clean autumn leaves; children's disposable or gardening gloves; large sheets of paper; trays or PE hoops for sorting activities; photocopiable page 40 'Leaf sorting'

Speaking scientifically
deciduous, evergreen, ash, horse chestnut, lime, oak, sycamore

Lesson 3: Falling leaves

Introduction

Remind the children about their visit to the park in week 1, lesson 1. Look at some of the photographs taken during this visit and encourage the children to describe what the trees looked like. Talk about leaves changing colour and explain that some trees begin to shed their leaves as the weather turns cooler in autumn. Sing about autumn leaves to the tune of 'London Bridge is Falling Down'. Challenge the children to recall any names of deciduous trees (trees that lose their leaves), prompting as necessary, and make a class list. This might include ash, horse chestnut, lime, oak and sycamore.

Whole-class work

1. Display some pictures of deciduous trees. Point out and name one tree. Ask the children to describe its leaves. Repeat, to identify one tree at a time.

2. Distribute laminated photocopiable page 36 'Tree identification charts'. Tell the children that they are going to use it to play a game. Describe a tree and ask the class to identify it by looking at their card. Play a few times so that the children begin to associate the names and features of trees. Choose children to describe a tree for the rest of the class to guess.

3. Show the class the pile of autumn leaves you have brought in. Tell them that they are going to sort these leaves into different groups.

Group work

4. Provide each group with a pile of leaves and trays, large sheets of paper or PE hoops to sort into. Ensure that the children wear gloves before touching the leaves. Each child will also need photocopiable page 40 'Leaf sorting'. Ask them to begin sorting their leaves by putting different colours into groups. Talk about the least and most common colours and ask them to record this on the photocopiable sheet.

5. Ask the children to make groups of large and small leaves, count how many are in each group, and add this to the photocopiable sheet.

6. For the final sorting activity, the children will group according to leaf shape. Remind them of the pictures of leaves on their identification chart and tell them to separate those with individual leaflets from those with one broad surface, and those with a smooth edge from those that are crinkly or jagged.

7. Challenge the children to use their identification charts to name a tree by carefully observing its leaf shape. Ask them to glue a leaf to the photocopiable sheet and write the name of the tree it comes from below it.

Differentiation
● Support children with the leaf-sorting activity by limiting the number of leaves they need to count.
● Challenge children to identify other trees from their leaves.

Science in the wider world

Some regions – such as New England in the USA – are famous for the colours produced by their large forests of deciduous trees during autumn. Spectacular shades of red, yellow and orange foliage are produced as the trees begin to shut down for the winter.

Review

Children could be assessed on whether they can sort leaves according to their characteristics and whether they can name any deciduous trees.

Objectives
● To compare weather in different seasons.
● To explain why specific clothing is suited to different seasons.

Resources
A variety of children's clothing, such as t-shirts, sandals, coats, hats, scarves; a camera or video recorder; photocopiable page 41 'Dress for the season'; interactive activity 'Dress for the season' on the CD-ROM

Speaking scientifically
temperature, insulation, heat loss, evaporation, perspiration

Lesson 1: Dressing for the season

Introduction
Display some articles of children's clothing appropriate for different seasons and ask the class to say when they might wear them. Talk about the type of clothing children are currently wearing to travel to and from school and go outside at playtimes. Establish that they may now need coats and enclosed shoes rather than sandals, along with long-sleeved fleecy tops, full-length trousers, and so on. Ask them to explain why they can no longer wear t-shirts, shorts and other summer clothing and link their observations with falling autumnal temperatures and the weather records they have been keeping.

Whole-class work
1. Tell the children Aesop's fable of 'The Sun and the Wind'. Begin by explaining that, once upon a time, the Sun and the Wind were having a quarrel. All day long, they argued about who was the stronger. The Wind claimed it was obviously him because he could send leaves rolling along the road, make trees fall over and knock tiles off roofs. The Sun on the other hand said that there was great strength in his gentleness.

At last, they decided to hold a contest to prove who was stronger. The Sun spotted a traveller on the road and said to the Wind: 'Whoever can make that traveller lose his coat is the stronger.' The Wind readily agreed and began to blow as hard as he could. But as the cold wind blew, the man just buttoned up his coat and turned up his collar, and no matter how hard the Wind blew, he couldn't blow the coat off the traveller.

At last, the Wind gave up and agreed that it was the Sun's turn. So the Sun began to shine on the traveller and warm him up again. Soon the man had undone the buttons on his coat, and after a while he took it off completely. The Sun had won!

2. Talk about the season when the Sun is likely to be warmest and what time of the year cold winds are most likely to blow.

Independent work
3. Ask the children to complete photocopiable page 41 'Dress for the season' by choosing appropriate clothing for a child in autumn. Tell them to begin by selecting appropriate clothing and then attaching it to one of the models. Once they have dressed one model for autumn, ask them to think about how this would differ from summer, and to dress the other model for that season. Some children could complete the interactive activity 'Dress for the season' on the CD-ROM.

Group work
4. Tell the children to act out the story of 'The Sun and the Wind' in their groups and take photographs or use a video recorder to capture their efforts.

Science in the wider world
In cooler weather, fibres that trap air, such as wool or fleecy fabrics, help to insulate the body and reduce heat loss. In warm weather the body keeps cool by evaporating moisture through perspiration. Light, loose clothing enables this to happen more efficiently and comfortably.

Review
Children could be assessed on their choice of clothing for different seasons.

Objectives
● To consider how animals cope with cold winter weather.
● To establish the purpose of some animals' winter coats.

Resources
Completed photocopiable page 41 'Dress for the season' from previous lesson; images of emperor penguins; photocopiable page 42 'Animals in winter'; interactive activity 'Animals in winter' on the CD-ROM

Speaking scientifically
temperature, insulation, heat loss, moulting, camouflage

Lesson 2: Animals dressing for winter

Introduction

Recap on the work the children carried out in the previous lesson on dressing for the season. Look at some of their completed photocopiable sheets and talk about the clothes they chose to keep their model warm during autumn. Talk about how other animals keep warm or cool and ask children if they have a pet at home that moults as the weather warms up. Talk about what this means and why it happens; establish that in order to moult a coat in spring, the animal must have grown a thicker one for the winter months. Display some images of animals, including mountain hares and arctic foxes before their coats have turned white.

Whole-class work

1. Look at the images of summer-coated mountain hares and arctic foxes from 'Animals in winter' on the CD-ROM. Tell the children that the animals only look like this for certain parts of the year. Show further images of these animals in their white winter coats and encourage the children to compare them and identify how the animals have changed. Ask them to suggest which images they think were taken in the summer and which were in the winter and to explain their ideas. Establish that both the hares and the foxes live in very cold places where there is a lot of snow in winter, so their coats not only need to keep them warm, but also need to make them harder to spot against the snowy landscape. Show the children an image of emperor penguins. Remind them, if appropriate, that they were introduced to this animal in an earlier lesson: it lives in Antarctica – the coldest place on Earth, where it is continuously dark in the winter months.

2. List the animals that you have covered and display an enlarged version of photocopiable page 42 'Animals in winter'. Check that the children are able to identify each animal as you point to it. Show them the speech bubbles and ask them to imagine that the animals are talking to us about how they cope in winter. Read the statements out and challenge the children to suggest which animal might be speaking.

3. Complete the interactive activity 'Animals in winter' on the CD-ROM with the class.

Independent work

4. Provide children with the photocopiable sheet. Ask them to draw a line to match each speech bubble to the correct animal.

> **Differentiation**
> ● Support children by providing labels that can be cut and glued onto each animal and shortening the information in the speech bubbles.
> ● Challenge children by asking them to add more information to the speech bubbles.

Science in the wider world

Mammals and birds are warm-blooded animals and need to maintain a constant body temperature, whatever the surrounding conditions. Having bodies that are covered in fur or feathers helps guard against heat loss in cold weather.

Review

Children could be assessed on whether they are able to match the animals to their speech bubbles correctly.

Objectives
● To investigate the concept of bird/animal migration.
● To correctly order images of a swallow's annual migration.

Resources
Images of planes and passengers; a 'postcard' from South Africa – a large piece of card with images of South Africa on one side and a message on the other, as provided in text of lesson; a globe; image of swallows gathering on telegraph wires or similar; image of swallows in flight; photocopiable page 43 'Swallow's story'

Speaking scientifically
migration, climate, northern hemisphere, southern hemisphere

Lesson 3: Heading south for winter

Introduction
Display an image of a passenger plane. Encourage the children to suggest where it might be going. Show another image, of passengers at an airport, and talk about where they might be on their way to or from. Ask the children to describe any occasions when they have travelled on a plane. Talk about their experiences. Make a list of any destinations they mention. Explain that many humans like to go on holiday to somewhere warm and sunny when the weather is cold at home and that some animals do this as well – only they don't get on planes!

Whole-class work
1. Show the class the 'postcard' and tell them it is from a country called South Africa. Point out where South Africa is on the globe. It is a very long way from Britain; if the children were to fly there on a jet plane, the journey would take about 11 hours. Equate this to the children's school day: getting on a plane as school starts and not getting off again until bedtime. Display the image side of the postcard and ask the children what they think South Africa looks like and what sort of weather they have there. Make a list of their ideas.

2. Read the message on the postcard; it is from a young swallow, describing his migration from the UK to South Africa:

● Dear children, I am having a lovely time here in South Africa. It has been a very long flight and my wings feel very tired, but we have seen lots of interesting places along the way and the weather here is sunny and warm – just how we swallows like it!

3. Display an image of swallows gathering on telegraph wires or similar. Explain that, while these birds nest and hatch in Britain and spend their summers here, it is too cold for them to stay during the winter. Each September, as autumn begins, they get ready to fly off to South Africa, on the other side of the world. While it is winter in the top, northern half of the world, it is summer in the bottom, southern half so South Africa will be warm and sunny for the birds.

4. Show your class an image of a large flock of swallows in flight. Tell the children that the journey to South Africa takes the birds several weeks. They fly during the day and rest at night, always at the same places each year. They eat flying insects, so feed as they fly. They travel around 200 miles a day.

5. Look at the postcard image again and explain that the swallows will stay in South Africa for a few months and make the return journey to Britain in the spring. Tell the children that moving from one part of the world to another and back again is called 'migration' and that many animals have very long migrations.

Independent work
6. Ask the children to look at photocopiable page 43 'Swallow's story' and to put the pictures into the correct order to tell the story of the birds' migration.

Differentiation
● Support children by asking them to cut and glue fewer pictures into story order.
● Challenge children to write words or sentences to describe each stage of the migration story.

Science in the wider world
Many animals make remarkable migration journeys each year: bar-headed geese fly over the Himalayas, while monarch butterflies fly around 2,500 miles between Canada and Mexico.

Review
Children could be assessed on their completion of the swallow migration story.

Objectives
● To observe and predict seasonal changes in the park.
● To record their observations.
● To compare their latest observations with those from their previous park visit.

Resources
Photographs and photocopies of work from the visit to the park in week 1, lesson 1; cameras; paper, clipboards and pencils; disposable or gardening gloves; collecting bags; laminated photocopiable page 36 'Tree identification chart'

Speaking scientifically
deciduous, evergreen, temperature, fruit, nut, berry, sycamore and ash keys, fungus

Lesson 1: Seasonal change

Introduction
Remind the children of their visit to the park in week 1, lesson 1. Look at photographs and drawings from the trip. Check that they can recall some signs of autumn and ask them to think about what they would see in the park now. Make a list of their ideas and explain that they are going back to see how autumn has moved on.

Whole-class work
As before, prior to this lesson, you will need to prepare for an off-site educational visit by carrying out a thorough risk assessment and obtaining permission from parents and carers. Consider details such as transport, food, clothing, medical requirements (including any allergies) and an appropriate level of adult support. Once again, establish some ground rules for staying safe and remind the children to use gloves to collect natural objects, not eat any nuts, berries or fungi, and tell an adult if they come across rubbish or dog mess.

1. Provide children with clipboards and paper. Begin your visit in the same place as last time. Encourage the children to notice any changes in the colour and number of the leaves on the trees. Take photographs of general scenes. Gather the children to compare their new observations with the work they did previously.

Group work
2. Divide the class into small adult-led groups and direct them to the various locations they investigated last time. Tell the children to carefully observe the trees and plants and collect any further evidence of autumn, using gloves and collection bags. Ask them to make more drawings and take photographs and bark rubbings.

3. Bring the class back together at various points. Compare groups' observations, then send them to new locations.

4. At the end of the visit, review all the findings. Collate drawings, photographs and other evidence of change to update your classroom display with.

Whole-class work
5. Back in class, ask the children to describe how the park has changed. Compare their observations from the visit.

Paired work
6. Ask children to put photographs from both trips into pairs showing the same area, then to glue two onto a recording sheet. They could then add words to describe what they notice.

Differentiation
● Support children by giving them a sentence with missing words to complete, such as 'When we went back to the park the leaves had...'
● Challenge children to write their own sentences to describe how the park has changed.

Science in the wider world
When deciduous trees lose their leaves will vary depending on the weather. A dry summer can mean that trees do not get enough moisture and so begin to shed leaves early. High winds can also bring leaves down quickly.

Review
Children could be assessed on the observations they make about autumnal changes and their comparison work on photographs.

■ SCHOLASTIC

Objectives
- To observe one tree in detail.
- To make recordings of their observations.
- To identify the tree.

Resources
A tree in the locality – preferably in the school grounds – and a photo of it; paper, clipboards and pencils; a length of string or measuring tape; disposable or gardening gloves; collecting bags; a camera; laminated photocopiable page 36 'Tree identification chart' as used in week 1, lesson 1; photocopiable page 'Our tree' from the CD-ROM, large sheet of paper

Speaking scientifically
change, grow, branch, trunk, leaf, flower, fruit, spring, summer, autumn, winter

Lesson 2: Changing trees

Introduction
Tell your class that, in addition to their visits to the park to watch what is happening as the seasons change, they are also going to keep an eye on a tree that is much closer at hand. Display a zoomed-in photograph of the tree you have selected and ask the children if they recognise it. Gradually reveal more background to help them identify it as a tree that is either within, or very nearby, their own school grounds. Talk about what they already know about how trees grow and change and ask them if they think this one is deciduous and will be losing its leaves.

Whole-class work
1. Take the class outside to make some observations about the tree they are going to 'adopt'. Begin by looking at it from a distance and asking the children what they notice before going up to it to observe it more closely.

2. Tell the children to look closely and talk about what they can see. Encourage them to check whether the tree still has leaves and what these look like. Ask them to feel the bark to see if it is rough or smooth. Draw their attention to any variations in colour on the trunk and branches. Talk about why the trunk may be a different colour on one side – perhaps because the wind and rain are coming from that direction. Look around to see if any of the roots are visible and talk about the role they play in anchoring the tree in the ground.

3. Tell the children to measure around the trunk with a length of string or a measuring tape, use gloves to collect any fallen leaves and take photographs and bark rubbings of their tree.

4. Back in class, collate all the children's findings and challenge them to name the tree, if it is one that appears on the laminated photocopiable page 36 'Tree identification chart' they have been using for their park visits. Otherwise, you may just have to tell them.

5. Straighten out the length of string that you used to measure the girth of the tree and compare it with the heights of the children.

Independent work
6. Ask the children to complete the photocopiable page 'Our tree' from the CD-ROM and place it on a larger sheet of paper, to decorate around it with photographs, drawings, bark rubbings and dried leaves.

Differentiation
- Support children by providing a wordbank of appropriate vocabulary for them to cut and paste onto the photocopiable sheet.
- Challenge children to write further sentences about their tree.

Science in the wider world
Trees absorb carbon dioxide, which helps to reduce the greenhouse gases that cause global warming. Trees also provide shade to keep us cool in summer and reduce wind chill by blocking or slowing down moving air.

Review
Children could be assessed on the observations they make about their tree and their recording on the photocopiable sheet.

Objectives
- To identify the characteristics of an evergreen tree.
- To sort trees according to whether they are evergreen or deciduous.
- To name some evergreen trees.
- To name some deciduous trees.

Resources
Images of plants used for decorations including mistletoe, Yule logs and Christmas trees, photographs taken during park visits in week 1, lesson 1 and week 6, lesson 1; images of deciduous and evergreen plants for group sorting activity; large sheets of paper; a wordbank of deciduous and evergreen plants; laminated photocopiable page 36 'Tree identification chart'; green and red paper; circular holly-wreath templates

Speaking scientifically
evergreen, deciduous, holly, mistletoe, spruce, berry

Lesson 3: Plants for festivals

Introduction
Teach your class a verse of the carol 'Deck the Halls' and ask them to suggest what 'boughs of holly' are and what is meant by the 'season to be jolly'. Explain that, at different times of the year, people bring plants into their homes for all sorts of reasons. These could be daffodils in the spring, cut flowers on birthdays or mothers' day and in winter – particularly around Christmas time – various plants are used as indoor decorations. Ask the children if they can suggest other plants, in addition to the holly mentioned in the song, and make a list. It could include mistletoe, Yule logs and Christmas trees.

Whole-class work
1. Display some images of plants that are used as Christmas decorations and ask the children to identify them.

2. Play a game of 'odd one out' to help the children identify plants that are in season at different times of the year. For example, show an image of a holly wreath with varieties of spring flowers, or a decorated Christmas tree in a summer garden. Encourage the children to recognise that these are odd and to explain why.

3. Next, display a deciduous tree that is shedding its leaves, alongside holly, mistletoe and a Christmas tree. Challenge the children to identify the odd one out and encourage them to explain that the plants we associate with Christmas do not drop their leaves in winter.

4. Recap on some of the type of trees the children observed at the park and in the school grounds and explain that the Christmas plants are 'evergreens'. This means that they do not drop all their leaves at once, but gradually lose and replace them throughout the year so that they always look green.

5. Look back at the photographs that were taken during the park visits and challenge the children to point out any evergreen trees.

Group work
6. Provide groups of children with images of both deciduous and evergreen plants and ask them to compare and sort them into two groups and glue them onto a large piece of paper. Challenge them to identify any of their plants using their laminated photocopiable page 36 'Tree identification chart' and the wordbank.

7. Next, give each group a selection of green and red papers and ask them to build a holly wreath on a circular template.

Differentiation
- Support children by limiting the number of trees that require sorting and by providing tree names on labels which can be glued onto their work.
- Challenge children to name a wider variety of deciduous and evergreen plants.

Science in the wider world
Common evergreen trees in the UK include the Scots pine, spruce and yew. Privet and laurel are often used for hedging. Many evergreen plants are very poisonous and children should be warned against picking leaves and berries.

Review
Children could be assessed on their sorting activity and the number of trees they can name. You could also ask them some general questions to round up their topic on autumn/winter, such as: listing the seasons in order, naming the autumn and winter months, describing activities they could do at this time of year and how they can tell which season they are in.

Objectives

- To recap seasonal changes.
- To name some deciduous trees.
- To recap how animals manage seasonal change.
- To create and label a recognisable representation of a deciduous tree in autumn.
- To suggest how this tree will look in winter.

Resources

For each child: coloured modelling clay, a board to work on, simple tools such as lolly sticks, tree labels – trunk, branches, bark, twigs, roots, leaves, berries, nuts, keys – two sheets of cardboard, glitter, cotton wool, glue

Working scientifically

- To use their observations and ideas to suggest answers to questions.

Understanding seasonal changes (1)

Revise

- Use photographs and examples of the children's work from this topic to carry out a recap on the seasonal changes they have been finding out about. Remind the children of their visits to the park and the local tree they have adopted. Challenge them to recall some of the names of deciduous trees they have observed, such as ash, horse chestnut, lime, oak and sycamore. Talk about what has been happening to these trees and make a list of the signs of autumn that they have spotted, including changes to leaves and the production of fruits, nuts, berries, and so on. Also recap on ways in which animals change at this time of year and remind the children about animals that grow thick winter coats or migrate to a warmer part of the world.

Assess

- Provide each child with a selection of coloured modelling clay, a board and some simple tools, such as lolly sticks, to work with. Tell them to begin by making a model of a bare tree (just the trunk and branches) on one of their sheets of cardboard.
- Next, ask them to select some of the tree-part labels and gently attach these to their tree model.
- Tell the children to use their clay to make leaves, berries and nuts to add to their tree model. Advise them to think carefully about where they have seen these recently on real trees, and to try to use colours similar to ones they have seen on real trees.
- Ask them to select and add further labels to their model and to label the sheet with the appropriate season.
- Check that the children have made a recognisable representation of a deciduous tree and have attempted to label the main parts of it. Also check that they have selected suitable colours for the leaves, nuts and berries, and have placed these both on their tree and around the bottom of it.
- When the children have completed their autumn tree model, ask them to draw how their tree will look in the next season on their second sheet of card. Suggest that they could add glitter or cotton wool to represent frost and snow. Ask them to label this piece of work with the appropriate season.
- Review each child's model, drawing and labelling to assess their knowledge and understanding of seasonal change associated with autumn and winter.

Further practice

- Support children by pre-labelling their sheets of card with 'autumn' and 'winter' and limiting the number of tree-part labels you ask them to attach; or ask them to point out features on their models and talk about differences between them.
- Challenge children to demonstrate their knowledge and understanding about seasonal change during autumn and winter further, by asking them to draw an animal that grows a thick coat or migrates to a warmer climate at this time of year. Encourage them to name some animals that do either of these things and to describe how they change using some simple scientific vocabulary. These children could also write sentences about their seasonal tree model and drawing.

Objectives
● To recap on the difference in hours of daylight between summer and autumn.
● To create a timeline of a child's day, including sunrise, midday and sunset.

Resources
Long strips of paper to draw timelines on; photocopiable page 'Timeline image sheet' from the CD-ROM; images and labels for sunrise, sunset, midday; scissors and glue

Working scientifically
● To use their observations and ideas to suggest answers to questions.

Understanding changes in day length

Revise

● Remind the children of their observations on shadows earlier in this topic. Show the photographs you took recording how their shadows changed in size and direction over the course of a school day and the string bar charts the children made. Indicate the longest and shortest strings and link these with the position of the Sun in the sky. Ask the children if they can remember the name for the start of the day when the Sun first appears, and what happens as it begins to get dark. Show the children the timelines they made with sunrise and sunset at each end and talk about the times and activities they added to this. Recap on what you can do on a summer evening when it is still light, compared to going to a firework display, for example, at the same time of the day in early November. Ensure that the children can make comparisons and say that evenings are lighter for longer in summer, but dark for bonfires and fireworks in the autumn.

Assess

● Give each child a long strip of paper with a horizontal line drawn across it and explain that they are going to make another timeline. They will also need a sheet of images to cut out and attach to their timelines.
● Tell them to start by finding the image of a child getting out of bed and to glue that onto the left-hand side of their line. Then ask them to glue the image of a child getting into bed onto the opposite end. Everything else they stick on should go between these two markers.
● Next, ask the children to find an image of someone eating their lunch at school and to fix that onto their timeline. They could then add pictures of a child in lessons, in a playground and attending a firework display.
● Tell the children to think carefully about where to attach images of the sunrise and sunset before attaching these to their timeline, and then to draw a picture of the Sun at the time of the day when it will be high in the sky.
● Finally, ask the children to attach the labels 'sunrise', 'sunset' and 'midday' at the appropriate places along the timeline and to write the name of the season on it.
● Check that children are making reasonable guesses about where to attach images and labels and that they can sequence these – for example, the sunset comes before the firework display.

Further practice

● Support children by limiting the images and labels you ask them to stick on their timeline.
● Challenge children to demonstrate their knowledge and understanding of changes to daylight length further by asking them to add in any times they know to the bottom of their timeline. They could also draw some shadows along the line to show how they think these would change over the course of a day. They could then write some sentences to describe how days are shorter in the autumn and winter than they are in the summer.

Objectives
• To know the types of weather associated with autumn and winter.
• To recap how they measured and recorded various weather conditions.
• To choose the correct weather symbols to represent weather conditions.
• To correctly identify some characteristics of animals in winter.
• To correctly identify the animals on the photocopiable page.

Resources
Thermometer; wind measurers; rain gauge; photocopiable page 'Autumn weather' from the CD-ROM; photocopiable page 42 'Animals in winter'; interactive activity 'Animals in winter' on the CD-ROM

Working scientifically
• To use their observations and ideas to suggest answers to questions.

Understanding seasonal weather

Revise
• Remind the children about the instruments they used to collect their weather data. Show them the rain gauge, wind measurers and thermometer and ask them to explain how each of these works. Display the charts you made to record the weather measurements and talk about what you found out, asking the children to say how much rainfall there was in a particular week and which were the warmest and coldest days during their observation period. Show the children an image of a weather vane and talk about how it works. List some of the wind descriptions they learned about in the interactive activity 'Wind' and make some comparisons between a calm day and a very windy one. Display photographs of the ice balloons and talk about the investigation you used these for. Check that the children can recall what they did with the balloons and what they found out about overnight temperatures. Recap on the story of the Wind and the Sun arguing about who was the most powerful and talk about what sort of clothing the children are wearing now, compared to back in the summer holidays. Display the photographs of the arctic fox and mountain hare from 'Animals in winter' on the CD-ROM and talk about what they do to keep warm during the winter and how this is different from some other animals like swallows. Look at the postcard from the swallow in South Africa again and ask the children to describe how the weather there is different from that in the UK during the winter months.

Assess
• Give each child the photocopiable page 'Autumn weather' from the CD-ROM. Tell them to look carefully at the pictures and the weather symbol and label at the bottom of the page. For each image, they will need to think about how warm it looks, whether it is sunny or raining and how hard the wind might be blowing. They will then need to choose the correct weather symbols to portray what is happening in each picture.
• Give each child photocopiable page 42 'Animals in winter'. Ask them to choose one animal and to describe how it copes with the cold winters.

Further practice
• Support children by giving them weather symbol templates to cut and stick onto an enlarged photocopiable page 'Autumn weather'.
• Challenge children to write sentences to describe the weather they can see in each picture. They could also write about how different animals get ready for winter and illustrate their ideas with drawings.

Tree identification chart

■ Can you find these trees?

Ash

Horse chestnut

Lime

Oak

Sycamore

Beech

I can find different kinds of tree.

How did you do?

Autumn in the park

■ Colour this picture to show that it is autumn in the park. Fill in the labels.

I can use autumn colours.

How did you do?

Weather chart

■ Complete the chart with your weather observations for each day.

Monday			
Temperature			
Tuesday			
Temperature			
Wednesday			
Temperature			
Thursday			
Temperature			
Friday			
Temperature			

PHOTOCOPIABLE

SCHOLASTIC
www.scholastic.co.uk

Nocturnal animals

■ Describe what these animals do at night-time. Use these words to help you:

hunt　　　feed　　　build a home

I can describe nocturnal animals.

How did you do?

Leaf sorting

■ Look carefully at your leaves. Write down what you found out when you sorted them.

Colour of leaves

The most common colour was _____

Size of leaves

The biggest leaf looked like this...   The smallest leaf looked like this...

There were _____ large leaves and _____ small leaves.

Shape of leaves

The most common shape was...

This leaf is from a _____ tree.

I can sort leaves by colour, size and shape.

How did you do?

PHOTOCOPIABLE

Dress for the season

■ Dress one child for winter and another for summer. Cut out the clothes and sort them into two groups.

Animals in winter

■ Match the animal with the right speech bubble.

> I live in the coldest place on earth. In the dark winter months I huddle up with other male penguins who are all keeping eggs warm under their very thick feathers.

> I need a thick coat of fur to keep warm. It is white so that I can sneak up on the animals I hunt without being seen.

> I have a thick white furry coat to stop hungry animals from seeing me easily and catching me.

I can work out which animal is speaking.

How did you do?

Swallow's story

■ Tell the story of the swallow's migration by putting these pictures in the right order.

Animals, including humans

Expected prior learning
- Some similarities and differences between living things.
- Features of immediate environment compared to others.
- Observations about animals and explaining why some things occur.

Overview of progression
After completing this chapter the children should know about:
- the names of the main parts of the human body
- the five senses and the body parts associated with them
- animal families and the structure of a variety of common animals.

Creative context
- This topic provides many opportunities for children to make observational drawings and use images to present their findings.
- Children will be required to deploy design and technology skills to make models of animals.
- Animals lend themselves to various forms of creative writing, music and dance.

Background knowledge

The human body
- The main body parts, including: head, neck, arms, elbows, legs, knees and face.
- The five senses: hearing, sight, smell, taste and touch.
- Humans are mammals.

Animal families
- Mammals: generally have fur or hair, need lungs to breathe, have live young, provide milk for their young.
- Birds: bodies covered with feathers, need lungs to breathe, lay eggs.
- Fish: have scales and fins, breathe through gills, lay eggs.
- Amphibians: moist skin, adults have limbs and need lungs to breathe, lay eggs in water where young develop using gills to breathe.
- Reptiles: dry scaly skin, need lungs to breathe, lay eggs.
- Invertebrates: have no interior skeleton, include insects, lay eggs.
- Animals may be carnivores, herbivores or omnivores.
- Note: although invertebrates aren't included in the curriculum for Year 1, lessons have been included here. They are a useful topic to study it often relates directly to work on vertebrates and they provide a useful comparison.

Speaking scientifically
- In this chapter, the children will have opportunities to work scientifically and identify parts of the human body and associated senses; name common animals and describe their structures. A simple scientific vocabulary will enable the children to comment on their observations and could include: skeleton, backbone, odour, aroma, nasal, volume, decibels, pupil, iris, warm blooded, cold blooded, lung, carnivore, herbivore, omnivore, canine, habitat.

Preparation
You will need to provide: familiar foods for taste testing; blindfolds; covered pots containing familiar smells; musical instruments; audio/video recording equipment; camera; 'feely bags' containing a range of textures; modelling clay. You will also need various photographs (including X-rays) and video clips, as well as forehead thermometers and toy medical kits. It is essential that you check whether any of your children have allergies before you introduce foodstuffs

On the CD-ROM you will find: photocopiable pages 'Animal images', 'Bird facts', 'Bird misfit cards', 'Reptile body parts', 'Beetle drive'; interactive activities 'Body parts', 'Animals around us', 'Minibeast hunt', 'What animal family am I?'

Chapter at a glance

Week	Lesson	Curriculum objectives	Lesson objectives	Main activity	Working scientifically
1	1	• To identify, name, draw and label the basic parts of the human body.	• To elicit children's ideas of how our bodies work. • To know the main human body parts. • To measure a partner's body temperature.	Finding out about what's inside our bodies. Labelling body parts on a diagram. Singing 'Head. shoulders, knees and toes'.	• Asking simple questions. • Identifying and classifying. • Observing closely. • Making comparisons. • Gathering and recording data.
	2	• To say which part of the body is associated with each sense.	• To understand the link between taste and the mouth and tongue. • To identify some familiar foods by taste. • To make an accurate record of taste tests.	Tasting familiar foods while blindfolded (check for allergies).Completing photocopiable sheet of tongue with foods sampled.	• Asking simple questions. • Observing closely. • Making comparisons and deciding how to sort and group.
	3	• To say which part of the body is associated with each sense.	• To know that we smell with our noses. • To identify some familiar smells. • To sort substances by smell.	Smelling substances placed in pots with holes in cover. Identifying each correctly.	• Observing closely. • Making comparisons and deciding how to sort and group. • Gathering and recording data.
2	1	• To say which part of the body is associated with each sense.	• To know that we hear with our ears. • To identify a variety of sounds. • To investigate how sound changes in volume as you move away from it.	Identifying musical instruments/other sounds inside and outside the classroom. Comparing inside/outside; close/distant; natural/artificial sounds.	• Observing closely. • Making comparisons and deciding how to sort and group. • Gathering and recording data.
	2	• To say which part of the body is associated with each sense.	• To know that we see with our eyes. • To observe similarities and differences in each other's eyes. • To investigate and record eye colour.	Playing 'I spy'. Using images of signs. Using mirrors to observe eyes and talking about shape and colour.	• Observing closely. • Making comparisons and deciding how to sort and group. • Gathering and recording data.
	3	• To say which part of the body is associated with each sense.	• To know that skin is sensitive to touch. • To identify and describe objects by touch. • To identify which parts of their bodies are most ticklish (sensitive).	Using feely bags. Identifying a range of textures. Investigating tickly spots: the front/back of hand, inside of arm, back of neck and so on.	• Asking simple questions. • Observing closely. • Making comparisons and deciding how to sort and group.
3	1	• To identify and name a variety of common animals including fish, amphibians, reptiles, birds and mammals.	• To name some common animals. • To sort animals according to their characteristics. • To make predictions about animals in the school grounds.	Using the local environment to look for animals in trees, on flowers, under logs and stones, and so on. Completing photocopiable sheet/interactive activity.	• Asking simple questions. • Observing closely. • Making comparisons. • Gathering and recording data.
	2	• To describe and compare the structure of a variety of common animals.	• To compare animal characteristics. • To group animals by their characteristics. • To discover the characteristics of mammals. • To identify humans as mammals.	Looking at images of animals. Identifying and discussing features of mammals. Selecting additional mammals from images of farm and wild animals.	• Asking simple questions. • Observing closely. • Making comparisons and deciding how to sort and group. • Gathering and recording data.
	3	• To identify and name a variety of common animals that are carnivores, herbivores and omnivores.	• To identify a variety of meat- and plant-eating animals. • To sort animals according to their diet. • To correctly use the terms 'omnivore', 'carnivore', 'herbivore'.	Listening to 'Little Red Riding Hood' story. Comparing images of animals and identifying those with large canine teeth. Relating teeth to diet.	• Observing closely. • Making comparisons and deciding how to sort and group. • Beginning to notice patterns and relationships.

Chapter at a glance

Week	Lesson	Curriculum objectives	Objectives	Main activity	Working scientifically
4	1	• To identify and name a variety of common animals including birds.	• To identify some of the characteristics of birds. • To know and name some common birds and their habitats. • To observe and suggest similarities and differences between birds.	Comparing images of birds. Compiling simple bird factfiles describing a variety of birds, including unusual examples such as peacocks.	• Asking simple questions. • Observing closely. • Making comparisons and deciding how to sort and group.
	2	• To describe and compare the structure of a variety of common animals (birds).	• To think about some characteristics of birds. • To compare the structure of a bird with the structure of a human. • To identify the main body parts of a bird.	Looking at a video of birds in flight. 'Misfits' game – matching bird body parts. Labelling different birds' body parts.	• Asking simple questions. • Observing closely. • Making comparisons and deciding how to sort and group.
	3	• To identify and name a variety of common animals including fish.	• To name some varieties of fish. • To identify some of the characteristics of fish. • To identify similarities and differences between fish and mammals. • To begin to group fish.	Comparing images of common fish with unusual examples and discussing similarities and differences. Grouping fish according to shape, size and colour.	• Asking simple questions. • Observing closely. • Making comparisons and deciding how to sort and group. • Gathering and recording data.
5	1	• Describe and compare the structure of a variety of common animals (fish).	• To know the main external parts of fish.	Discussing the shape of fish and making comparisons between fins and tail shapes. Recording their findings with drawings.	• Asking simple questions. • Observing closely. • Make comparisons. • Gathering and recording data.
	2	• Identify and name a variety of common animals including amphibians.	• To identify the characteristics of an amphibian. • To identify some common amphibians. • To compare some common amphibians.	Reading 'The Frog Prince' and comparing frogs and humans. Comparing images of frogs, toads and newts Playing 'What am I?' game.	• Observing closely. • Make comparisons and deciding how to sort and group. • Gathering and recording data.
	3	• Describe and compare the structure of a variety of common animals (amphibians).	• To recognise that amphibians have skeletons. • To understand the life cycle of a frog. • To correctly order the life cycle of a frog.	Ordering life-cycle images to show how frogs grow and change. Identifying characteristics of frogs. Comparing differences/ similarities between frogs, toads and newts.	• Observing closely. • Make comparisons and deciding how to sort and group. • Gathering and recording data.
6	1	• Identify and name a variety of common animals including reptiles. • Describe and compare the structure of common animals.	• To recap on the characteristics of mammals, birds, fish and amphibians. • To establish the differences between reptiles and amphibians.	Looking at images/video footage of reptiles including snakes, crocodiles and lizards. Comparing how they move and identifying main body parts to form jigsaws.	• Observing closely. • Make comparisons and deciding how to sort and group. • Gathering and recording data.
	2	• Identify and name a variety of common animals.	• To know the names of common minibeasts. • To identify that minibeasts have no backbone. • To begin to group minibeasts into subgroups.	Singing minibeast songs. Matching a list of different minibeasts with the correct illustrations and identifying similarities and differences between them.	• Observing closely. • Make comparisons and deciding how to sort and group.
	3	• To identify and name a variety of common animals that are invertebrates. • Describe and compare the structure of a variety of animals.	• To investigate and record common invertebrates and their habitats. • To identify the characteristics of insects.	Using a virtual environment for a minibeast. Making simple classifications based on structure. Playing 'beetle drive' to identify insect parts.	• Asking simple questions. • Observing closely. • Make comparisons and deciding how to sort and group. • Gathering and recording data.
Assess and review					

Objectives
- To elicit children's ideas of how our bodies work.
- To know the main human body parts.
- To measure a partner's body temperature.

Resources
A school nurse or other appropriate health professional; forehead thermometers; toy stethoscopes and other health-related role-play equipment; X-ray pictures of a variety of human bones including the skull, upper and lower arms and legs, feet, toes, hands, fingers and spine; sheets of plain paper – large enough for children to lie down on; crayons or marker pens; labels for main body parts; photocopiable page 69 'Body parts'; interactive activity 'Body parts' on the CD-ROM

Speaking scientifically
temperature, blood, heart, lungs, bone, skeleton, various body parts

Lesson 1: What do we know about our bodies?

Previous knowledge
Check the children's knowledge and understanding of what is inside their bodies. Talk about what they already know from visits they may have made to doctors and hospitals and elicit whether any of them have ever broken any bones. Ask the children if they know the names of any bones and ways in which humans are similar to or different from other animals. Make a list. Encourage the children to suggest simple questions which they could later ask your guest speaker.

Introduction
Arrange for the school nurse, or other appropriate health professional, to visit your class. Ask if it would be possible for them to bring equipment such as a stethoscope or blood-pressure monitor along with them. Explain that you would like them to demonstrate how these are used, either on willing adults in the classroom, or volunteers among your children. They may also be able to provide visual displays of health promotion material on areas such as dental hygiene and taking exercise for your class to consider. Also have to hand some forehead thermometers for the children to try out on each other, as well as pictures of X-rayed human bones for display. The children will enjoy acting out being nurses or doctors with role-play equipment such as toy stethoscopes.

Whole-class work
1. Ask your visitor to begin by briefly describing their role and talking about general healthcare and healthy lifestyles. They could then explain that taking measurements with a blood-pressure monitor or listening to how fast someone's heart is beating helps nurses and doctors decide what sort of treatment their patient might need.

2. Look at the X-ray pictures of human bones and challenge children to identify them, with the help of appropriate clues from your visitor where required. Invite individual children to ask the questions they thought of earlier and allow the health professional time to answer as many as possible.

Paired work
3. Children take turns to measure each other's temperature using a forehead thermometer, making careful observations. Forehead thermometers work when the strip is gently pressed against the forehead and held in place until the coloured areas stop changing – after 15–30 seconds. Normal body temperature for children is around 37°C.

4. Ask pairs of children to look closely at the X-ray pictures and compare these against the outsides of their own bodies.

5. Provide health professional role-play opportunities for children to use the toy stethoscopes and pretend to listen to each other's hearts or breathing.

Group work
6. Lay out large sheets of strong, plain paper on a flat surface and invite children to volunteer to be models. Ask them to lie still on their backs on top of the paper while other group members carefully draw an outline of their body with crayons or marker pens.

7. Provide each group with a set of body-part labels and tell them to attach as many as possible to the shape they have drawn. These should include: head, neck, arms, elbows, legs and knees. Challenge groups to add on any other parts they know and to draw in a face to show the eyes, ears, mouth and teeth. Children could also complete the interactive activity on the CD-ROM.

Checkpoint
● What parts of the body can we name?
● What is inside the body?
● Why do we have bones?
● How do we look after our bodies?

8. Compare each group's finished work, clearing up any misconceptions and altering or adding labels as appropriate. Make a classroom display of the labelled bodies and ask children to use coloured string to link the X-ray pictures to the correct area of the body.

9. Select one child from each group to be 'Simon' and explain how to play the body-part game 'Simon says'. The rules are simple: when instructions are prefaced by 'Simon says' (as in, 'Simon says touch your toes'), they should be obeyed. After several such directions, however, 'Simon' will slip in an instruction without 'Simon says', and any children who move on that occasion are out! Continue playing until only one child remains 'in'; they can then become the next 'Simon'. This activity could also be organised as a whole-class activity, but if run in smaller groups it provides opportunities for differentiation and enables teachers to observe the level of individual children's understanding.

Independent work

10. Display a large version of the photocopiable page 69 'Body parts' with boxes for labels, but no vocabulary, and talk about what should go in each of the boxes. Demonstrate how to complete the photocopiable sheet by writing in one or two body-part labels.

11. Ask the children to fill in the remaining boxes on their photocopiable sheet, which can be differentiated to suit individual needs.

Introducing the new area of study

Teach your class the words and actions to the song 'Head, Shoulders, Knees and Toes'. The children begin by singing and pointing to each body part in turn but with each verse they omit one part from the lyrics, while continuing to include it in the actions. After a penultimate verse of humming and pointing to all the parts in turn, the children finish by singing and pointing as fast as they can. Talk about how the body parts in the song would vary for a four-legged mammal, a bird or an insect, and encourage the children to make comparisons between these and the human body.

Differentiation
● Support children with the photocopiable sheet by reducing the number of boxes to label, providing initial letter clues, or providing ready-made labels, which can be read to children and given to them to glue in the right boxes.
● Challenge children to include additional body-part labels, such as ankle, shin, thigh, hip, chest, shoulder, wrist and spine.

Science in the wider world

Humans and many other animals have bones inside their bodies. The bones are joined together to make a skeleton. Bones are very strong; they help us stand upright and protect important parts of our bodies, like the heart and brain.

Sometimes bones get cracked or broken in accidents. When this happens, a plaster cast is usually put around the appropriate limb to stop it moving and allow the broken bone to grow back together again. Depending on the type of bone and age of the person, this process may take about six weeks.

Review

Remind your class of the words and actions to the song 'Head, Shoulders, Knees and Toes'. Review how accurately – or quickly – children are able to point to different parts of their bodies. Once they are familiar with the song and can confidently carry out the actions, challenge them to suggest and demonstrate different combinations – 'hips, elbows, neck and toes', for instance, to rhyme with 'hair and teeth and chin and nose'. The children could be assessed on the accuracy of their pointing and the ease with which they can recall names of parts of the body.

Objectives
• To understand the link between taste and the mouth and tongue.
• To identify some familiar foods by taste.
• To make an accurate record of taste tests.

Resources
Always check for allergies before introducing any foodstuffs into the classroom environment. Images or video of food advertisements; clean containers and cutlery; a selection of foods, such as small pieces of orange, lemon, ginger biscuit, carrot, apple, flavoured crisps, to be taste tested; images of the foods to be tested; blindfolds; photocopiable page 70 'Tasty surprise'

Speaking scientifically
sweet, sour, bitter, salty

Lesson 2: Sense of taste

Introduction

Talk with the children about their favourite flavours in foods. Display images or watch video footage of food advertisements to establish how much flavour plays a part in making it attractive to us. Identify examples that are salty, like chips or crisps, or sweet, like ice cream or honey, and ask how the children might describe a flavour such as lemon juice or dark chocolate. If appropriate, introduce the words 'sour' and 'bitter'; children may not be as familiar with these as they are with sweet and salty tastes. Encourage the children to think about the part of their body that they need for tasting foods and clarify that it is within the mouth, it is the tongue that is sensitive to different flavours. Explain that taste is one of five important senses they will be learning about.

Paired work

1. Explain to the children that they are going to do some taste testing. Present pairs of children with a variety of foods that have been placed inside clean containers prior to the lesson and kept out of view. They will also need images of each food to be tested, and to either use a blindfold or just agree to keep their eyes tightly shut while tasting. Ensure that their hands are clean before they embark on this activity.

2. Taking it in turns, one child uses a spoon to feed the other a sample food, which they are unable to see. After each tasting, they select the food image they think represents what they have eaten.

3. When all the samples have been tasted, the children can reveal each food and compare with the selected images. Ask each pair to count how many they identified correctly.

Whole-class work

4. Compare each pair's findings with the rest of the class and talk about flavours that were easier or harder to identify.

5. Point out that we can group foods depending on their taste and use the food images to make a class 'sweet and salty' chart.

Independent work

6. Display a large copy of photocopiable page 70 'Tasty surprise'. Explain to the children how to complete it, by writing the names of some of the foods they tasted around the picture of the tongue.

7. Ask children to complete the photocopiable sheet.

> ### Differentiation
> • Support children by providing smaller images of the foods that have been tested for them to cut and glue onto the photocopiable sheet.
> • Challenge children to further classify flavours by adding examples of sour or bitter foods to the photocopiable sheet.

Science in the wider world

Processed foods, such as baked beans and ready meals, often have significant amounts of sugar and salt added to enhance the flavour. Too much salt or sugar in our food is not healthy.

Review

The children could be assessed on how accurately they were able to identify flavours during their taste tests and the level of accuracy in their recording of sweet and salty tastes – both in the whole-class activity and on the photocopiable sheet.

Objectives
● To know that we smell with our noses.
● To identify some familiar smells.
● To sort substances by smell.

Resources
Always check for allergies before introducing foodstuffs – and other possible triggers such as rubber – into the classroom environment. Substances to 'smell test', such as rubber, lemon juice, vinegar, talcum powder, coffee, fresh sawdust, in small, numbered, opaque pots with very small holes made in the lids (put a few drops of each liquid to be smell tested on cotton wool to prevent liquids spilling; cover powders to be smell tested with a thin layer of cotton or cotton wool to prevent them from being inhaled; the numbers and 'smells' should be the same for each group); two trays for each group

Speaking scientifically
odour, aroma, strong, mild, nasal

Lesson 3: Sense of smell

Introduction

Remind children about their taste investigation in the previous lesson and talk about how easy or hard it was to identify certain tastes. Explain that being able to smell a food as you taste it may make it easier to recognise.

Ask children to point to the part of their face that senses smells and to keep a finger there while you play a circle game. Begin by saying 'I love the smell of fresh bread' – or similar – as you lift your finger away from your nose. Ask the child seated immediately next to you to repeat the statement and add on a favourite smell of their own as they lift their finger away. The game then continues as each child takes it in turn to add an enjoyable smell to this list and ends when no one is still pointing to their nose. For a fun alternative you could play a game suggesting unpleasant smells and pinching noses instead – although you might want to establish some firm ground rules on acceptable suggestions before doing so!

Group work

1. Explain that today you are going to be 'smell testing' some items. Provide small groups with a variety of numbered pots. Tell them not to open them, but to try to identify what might be inside by sniffing through the small holes in the lids.

2. Tell the children to sort their pots by putting all the strong-smelling ones onto one tray and all the faint-smelling ones on another. Ask each group in turn to tell you the number of a pot they put on their strong-smelling tray, and then repeat for the faint-smelling tray. Compare each group's choices and discuss any differences.

3. Next, tell the children to sort their pots according to whether they think a smell is pleasant or not. Talk about why different children may have made different choices; have they selected aromas they are more familiar with to put into the 'pleasant' group? Children may class some unusual smells as unpleasant simply because they don't know what they are.

4. Finally, ask the children to sort their pots so that one tray contains smells they recognise and the other smells they cannot place.

5. Collect in each group's trays and gather the whole class together again. Compare the pots placed on the various trays and then reveal what each smell was.

Differentiation
● Support children who may not have the vocabulary to identify the smells by giving appropriate clues.
● Challenge children to suggest other ways of grouping their smell pots.

Science in the wider world

Our sense of smell does not just provide us with enjoyment it can also help to keep us safe; for example, we might smell whether food has gone bad before we eat it or notice smells such as smoke, burning or a gas leak.

Review

Children could be assessed on how accurately they were able to identify a range of smells, and whether they were able to group the pots successfully in a number of ways and talk about their observations.

Objectives
● To know that we hear with our ears.
● To identify a variety of sounds.
● To investigate how sound changes in volume as you move away from it.

Resources
A selection of percussion instruments; examples of stringed instruments, recorders and whistles; audio recording equipment

Speaking scientifically
volume, loud, quiet, decibels, ear defenders

Lesson 1: Sense of hearing

Introduction
Invite the class to sit quietly with their eyes closed. Play your selection of percussion instruments to them from various points around the classroom. Ask the children to listen carefully to the sounds around them. After a minute, ask the children to describe what they could hear and where they think the sounds were being made. Talk about whether these were loud, quiet, easy or hard to recognise and make a list of their observations. Tell the children to point to the part of their body they were using to listen with. Compare the sounds they enjoy hearing with those they don't and talk about how sounds – such as alarm bells and pedestrian crossing bleepers – might help to keep us safe.

Group work
1. Provide small groups of children with a selection of percussion instruments and ask them to investigate how to produce sounds on them. When they have had some time to try out each instrument, tell them to sort them according to whether they require a tap or a shake to make a sound.

2. Ask each group in turn to demonstrate different ways of playing their instruments and to talk about the sounds they make. Identify the loudest and quietest ones and compare the percussion sounds with those made by recorders and whistles, or a stringed instrument such as a guitar.

Whole-class work
3. Take the class into the school grounds to hear outdoor sound levels. Begin by standing quietly and listening for a minute, then talk about the variety of sounds the children can hear. Use audio equipment to record examples to listen to in the classroom later.

4. Draw children's attention to natural sounds such as birdsong or barking dogs and compare them with traffic noises, sirens, planes, and so on. Talk about which sounds are loudest or quietest, and whether the quieter sounds are coming from further away.

5. Show the children one of the percussion instruments used earlier in the classroom and ask them to say what they think will happen to the sound as they walk away from it. Ask one of the children – or an accompanying adult – to carry the recording equipment and record what they hear as they walk away from the sound. You can then play the result of this investigation back in the classroom.

6. Begin by making a gentle sound and tell the children to walk quietly and slowly away from you and, if the school grounds are large enough, to stop when they can no longer hear the instrument. At a signal, they should walk slowly back towards you, noticing that the sound gets louder as they approach the instrument again.

Science in the wider world
Sounds are measured in decibels (dB). A whisper would be around 15dB, while a jet engine would be in the region of 120dB. People who work in noisy environments using very loud machinery or tools have to wear ear defenders to prevent damage to their hearing.

Review
Children could listen to the recordings taken outside and list or draw the sounds they recognise. Children could also be assessed on drawings they make of their investigation to find out how sounds change in volume as you move away from them.

Objectives
● To know that we see with our eyes.
● To observe similarities and differences in each other's eyes.
● To investigate and record eye colour.

Resources
Images of road signage and high street brands; mirrors; enough copies of photocopiable page 71 'Eye templates' for each child to be able to colour one eye shape to indicate their eye colour; a large sheet of plain paper; A3 sheets of card in a variety of colours

Speaking scientifically
pupil, iris

Lesson 2: Sense of sight

Introduction

Start with a game of 'I spy' to introduce the idea that we use our eyes to see objects around us. Allow the children the opportunity to identify various items in the classroom. Next, display some pictures of road signage and images of common high street brands. Talk about how the use of colour, shape and lettering make these easy to recognise. Play a 'Who am I'? guessing game, giving clues as appropriate to help the children work out which images you are describing.

Whole-class work

1. Ask the children to use mirrors to look closely at the shape and colour of their eyes and to then compare them with a partner's. Check that they have recognised some similarities and differences, including shape and colour. Explain that the coloured part is called the iris and that the dark circle in the middle is the pupil.

2. Tell the class to complete an eye template cut from photocopiable page 71 'Eye templates' by colouring the iris with their own eye colour.

3. Ask all the children with brown eyes to attach their template onto a large sheet of plain paper to form a column. Repeat for other eye colours to produce a large, simple bar chart. Ask children to use this to identify the most and least common eye colours in the class.

4. Explain that the pupil in the centre of our eyes can get bigger or smaller depending on how bright the light around us is. Talk about children's experiences of being in a dark room where a light is suddenly turned on, or going outside into bright sunlight.

5. Tell the children to try putting their hands over their eyes and counting to 30, then quickly looking at each other's eyes to see if they can spot the pupils changing size.

6. Conduct an investigation on colour in the school grounds. Ask the children to list colours around them and talk about which are the most common and stand out best.

7. Lay out a line of coloured cards at one end of the playground and talk about which ones are most visible from a distance. Compare the children's observations.

Differentiation
● Support children to count the number of eye templates in each column of the class bar chart and talk about how many there are in the highest and lowest columns.
● Challenge children to interpret their bar chart data further: *How many more of one eye colour are there than another? How many children are there altogether?*

Science in the wider world

We see objects when light reflects off them and travels into our eyes through the pupils. The retina at the back of the eye receives these images, which are actually upside down, but our brains unscramble the messages so that we see everything the right way up! Traffic warning signs are generally red because it is easily seen.

Review

Children could be assessed on the information they are able to derive from the eye-colour bar chart and their observations on the use of colour.

Objectives
• To know that skin is sensitive to touch.
• To identify and describe objects by touch.
• To identify which parts of their bodies are most ticklish (sensitive).

Resources
Paper and pencils; feely bags (drawstring gym bags, or similar); selections of objects with a range of textures; images of these objects and some 'red herrings'; craft feathers

Speaking scientifically
texture, rough, smooth, soft, hard, spongy, temperature, vibration

Lesson 3: Sense of touch

Introduction
Begin by recapping the four senses covered so far, and where on the body the related sense organs are located. Point to the tongue, nose, ears and eyes and ask children to say which part of the body they think is necessary for the final sense, touch. Take several suggestions and then explain that we are able to feel things all over our bodies, as skin is sensitive to touch. Make a class list of objects that are pleasant to touch, such as soft cuddly toys, smooth pebbles and furry pets, and talk about ways in which touch can help keep us out of danger – for instance, if something feels sharp or too hot.

Group work
1. Ask the children to draw around one of their hands on a sheet of paper. Explain that they will use this later to record what they think is inside their feely bag.

2. Provide groups of children with feely bags filled with a selection of objects of differing textures. Challenge them to identify the contents using only their sense of touch. Encourage them to describe what they can feel to other group members and to compare the textures. Ensure each group member takes a turn feeling the contents of each bag and is involved in the discussion.

3. Display the images of possible contents and ask the children to decide which ones they think are inside their bags. Tell them to record their guesses with drawings or words around the outline of their hand.

Whole-class work
4. Compare each group's ideas and then reveal the contents of the feely bags. Talk about how accurate the children's guesses were and which objects were the easiest or hardest to identify.

5. Talk about what it feels like to be tickled and whether some parts of the body are more sensitive to touch than others. For example, some children might have very ticklish feet, but people who often walk around barefoot may be able to tolerate hot sand and rough stones.

6. Ask children to say whether they think the palms or backs of their hands will be more sensitive to touch. Ask them to investigate in pairs, using craft feathers on each other's hands, as well as on the inside of their arms and the back of their necks.

7. Talk about which area the children found the most sensitive and whether everyone agrees.

Differentiation
• Support children with image banks of pictures they can cut out and glue around their hand outlines.
• Challenge children to list textures as well as objects which they identify inside the feely bags.

Science in the wider world
Contact and temperature are perceived through the nerves that are present in our skin and throughout our bodies. For example: braille texts are composed of sequences of raised dots which the visually impaired can access through touch; without hearing sound, people may still feel vibrations of it inside their bodies.

Review
Children could be assessed on their recognition of objects through touch and their observations about sensitive parts of the body.

Objectives
● To name some common animals.
● To sort animals according to their characteristics.
● To make predictions about animals in the school grounds.

Resources
Cards for 'animal snap' from photocopiable pages 'Animal images' from the CD-ROM; clipboards; paper; pens and pencils; cameras; interactive activity 'Animals around us' on the CD-ROM; photocopiable page 72 'Animals around us'; gardening or disposable gloves

Speaking scientifically
mammal, reptile, amphibian, fish, bird, minibeast, skeleton, backbone, fur, feather, scale

Lesson 1: Identifying animal families

Introduction
Begin with a class thought-shower activity to list as many types of animal as possible. Talk about characteristics different animals might have in common, such as number of legs or type of skin. Introduce children to the idea of family groupings with a game of animal snap, using cards cut from the photocopiable page 'Animal images' from the CD-ROM. Hold up one image and ask a child to turn over the cards, one at a time. When the children see another member of the same animal family, they should shout 'snap'. Continue to play until all the images have been matched.

Whole-class work
1. Talk about which of the animals from the snap game the class might expect to find in the school grounds. Make a list of the most likely. Ask children to suggest where they would find them.

2. Explain that it is important to treat wildlife with respect. Establish some ground rules, which could include not making loud noises, and handling minibeasts with care and returning them to the same spot they were found in. Cats and dogs which happen to be in the area should be left alone.

3. Take a walk around the school grounds or local park, or a similar environment to look for wildlife. Encourage children to look up at the trees to spot birds and squirrels and gently lift stones and fallen logs to discover minibeasts such as woodlice and slugs. Look out for spiders' webs and birds' nests and any other signs of particular animals. Record findings with photographs and drawings, and simple notes.

4. Back in the classroom, ensure the children wash their hands, and then make a list of all the animals they have observed. Talk about the similarities and differences between them and decide which family groups they could belong to. Encourage children to think of simple questions they could ask about their findings, such as: How many birds did we see? Where did we find the most woodlice? Collate your findings and create a classroom display.

5. Show the children the interactive activity 'Animals around us' on the CD-ROM and complete it. Make comparisons with the children's observations.

Independent work
6. Ask the children to complete photocopiable page 72 'Animals around us'.

Differentiation
● Support children by reducing the number of animals on the photocopiable sheet.
● Challenge children to write in animals' names and group together those they think are in the same animal family.

Science in the wider world
The main animal families are:
● mammals: give birth to live young, bodies are usually covered with fur or hair
● birds: have feathers and lay eggs
● reptiles: have dry scaly skin and lay eggs on land
● amphibians: have moist skin and lay eggs in water, where the young will develop
● fish: have fins and gills and mainly lay eggs
● invertebrates: minibeasts that do not have an internal skeleton; including insects, molluscs and arachnids.

Review
Children could be assessed on whether they can give examples of animals from each of the main families they have learned about.

Objectives
- To compare animal characteristics.
- To group animals by their characteristics.
- To discover the characteristics of mammals.
- To identify humans as mammals.

Resources
Images of a variety of animals (from photocopiable pages 'Animal images' from the CD-ROM); trays or PE hoops labelled: mammals, birds, reptiles, amphibians, fish, insects; photocopiable page 73 'What are mammals?'

Speaking scientifically
mammals, live young, warm blooded, body temperature, breathing, air, lungs

Lesson 2: Mammals

Introduction
Remind the children of the animal families focus in the previous lesson and ask them to recall some of the animals they found out about or discovered in the school grounds. Display images of a variety of animals and use these for a game of 'odd one out'. Begin by comparing features such as the number of legs or whether an animal has wings or not, before focusing on specific mammal characteristics. Show a variety of pets, including cats, dogs and hamsters, alongside a fish or stick insect. Challenge children to identify the odd one out and to give reasons for their choice. Use their ideas to build up a list of features that are common to mammals, such as having a backbone, being covered with hair or fur, giving birth to live young, producing milk to feed babies and using lungs to breathe air. Link these with further images of mammals displaying specific characteristics. Check that the children also recognise that humans belong to the mammal group by including images of them in a final round of 'odd one out'.

Group work
1. Provide small groups of children with image banks displaying a variety of animals. Place trays or PE hoops labelled for each animal family (mammals, birds, reptiles, amphibians, fish and insects) within easy reach and tell the children to sort their images into the correct group. Encourage them to talk about their choices as they do so. Include domestic and farm animals, as well as both familiar and more exotic wildlife examples.

Whole-class work
2. Collect in the animal images from each group and compare the animals they have identified. Talk about similarities and differences between a range of mammals, such as dogs, sheep, squirrels and giraffes. Remind children of the list of mammal characteristics you built up earlier in the lesson and challenge them to give simple reasons for including a particular animal in their set of mammals.

3. Pool all the mammal examples together into one large set to display in your classroom.

Independent work
4. Tell the children to complete photocopiable page 73 'What are mammals?' adding the labels 'fur or hair', 'live young', 'provide milk for young', 'backbone' and 'breathe air into lungs' to different mammals, including humans.

Differentiation
- Support children by reducing the number of animals on the photocopiable sheet.
- Challenge children to make a list of as many mammals as they can.

Science in the wider world
While most mammals give birth to live young, there are a few unusual egg-laying exceptions, such as the platypus. Marsupials – including the kangaroo and koala bear – give birth to tiny live young who then continue to develop and grow inside their mother's pouch. The largest mammal is the blue whale, which reaches a length of around 30m, while the smallest is the bumblebee bat, at around 30mm!

Review
Children could be assessed on how accurately they worked to complete the group task on mammal identification, as well as the independent task to identify features of mammals.

Objectives
• To identify a variety of meat- and plant-eating animals.
• To sort animals according to their diet.
• To correctly use the terms 'omnivore', 'carnivore' and 'herbivore'.

Resources
The story of 'Little Red Riding Hood'; images of mammals which are carnivores, herbivores and omnivores; headbands labelled with the names of a variety of mammals; chalk

Speaking scientifically
carnivore, canine, herbivore, omnivore

Lesson 3: Mammals: carnivores, herbivores and omnivores

Introduction

Read your class the story of 'Little Red Riding Hood' and ask the children to suggest which animal group the wolf belongs to. Remind them of the mammal characteristics they listed in the previous lesson and establish that a wolf is fur coated, breathes through lungs, gives birth to live cubs and produces milk to feed them – so is therefore a mammal. Explain that 'Little Red Riding Hood' is just a fairy tale, but that real wolves *do* have big teeth! Display an image of some wolves where their mouths are clearly visible and draw the children's attention to the large canine teeth. Ask them to think of other animals that have similarly long, pointed teeth and encourage them to give examples, such as dogs, lions and tigers. Explain that some animals need large teeth because they belong to a meat-eating group called 'carnivores'. Other animals – such as horses, cows and sheep – have short, blunt teeth for eating and grinding up grass and other plants. Animals that eat only plants are called 'herbivores'. Creatures that eat both plants and meat are called 'omnivores'.

Group work

1. Display images or video of a range of mammals and ask the children to identify those that they think are meat-eaters. Encourage them to talk about their ideas, put all the carnivores they can find into one group and then look at the animals that are left. Ask them to compare the teeth of the animals that are not in the carnivore group and draw their attention to species, including humans, that have canine teeth and others, such as sheep, that do not. Make groups of herbivores and omnivores from the remaining animals.

Whole-class work

2. Talk about the groups the children have divided the animals into. Ask them to suggest why humans fit into the omnivore group and talk about the types of food they like to eat.

3. Explain that other omnivore mammals include hedgehogs, pigs and bears. Use the interactive whiteboard to demonstrate how to make a Venn diagram with overlapping circles. Begin by placing images of carnivores in one circle and herbivores in the other. Ask the children to suggest where to place animals that eat both meat and plants. Move the omnivores into the overlap created by the two circles.

4. Using masks or labelled headbands, give children animal roles to act out in a 'live' Venn diagram. Ask children to say what each animal needs to eat and talk about where they should stand on large overlapping circles chalked on the floor. Encourage them to identify the animals as 'carnivores', 'herbivores' or 'omnivores'.

Science in the wider world

In addition to mammals, members of other animal groups may also be omnivores. Many garden birds will eat insects or worms as well as berries, and some species of reptile, insects and fish have an omnivorous diet. In the wild, carnivores are predators, while the animals they hunt are the prey.

Review

Children could be assessed on their contribution to the Venn diagram activities; successfully identifying meat- or plant-eaters; and how accurately they can use the terms 'carnivore', 'herbivore' and 'omnivore'.

■SCHOLASTIC

Objectives
- To identify some of the characteristics of birds.
- To know and name some common birds and their habitats.
- To observe and suggest similarities and differences between birds.

Resources
Images of a variety of birds (from photocopiable page 'Animal images: birds' from the CD-ROM); images of a variety of habitats (UK garden, chicken run, African savannah, Antarctica, sub-tropical forests); name labels for each species; bird factfile templates – individual sheets of paper, headed with bird names blackbird, robin, ostrich, penguin, peacock and chicken; photocopiable page 'Bird facts' from the CD-ROM

Speaking scientifically
feather, beak, bill, wing, egg, habitat

Lesson 1: Birds

Introduction
Remind the children about their work in week 3, lesson 1 on animal families. Ask them to list as many different groups as they can recall, then display images of a variety of both familiar and more exotic birds, including garden birds, ostriches, penguins, peacocks and chickens. Talk about characteristics they have in common, such as feathers, beaks, wings and two legs, and ask the children if these animals give birth to live young like mammals, or if they do something different instead (lay eggs). Establish that this lesson's animal family is birds. Ask the children if they can name any of the examples you have displayed. Support them, as appropriate, to identify the images and talk about where they might see each one. Display the habitat images and match the birds to each one. Leave this in view for them to refer to if they need.

Group work
1. Provide groups of children with images of a variety of habitats, pictures of birds and name labels for each species. Tell the children to attach a name label to each bird and then place it on the habitat picture they think is its home. Encourage them to talk about their ideas and work cooperatively.

Whole-class work
2. Ask each group to present their ideas to the rest of the class and display the correctly labelled species and habitats. Talk about the birds that the children have been unable to identify and practise repeating names.

3. Check children's learning by playing a 'Who am I?' game. Describe a bird's appearance and habitat to the children and ask them to name it. Repeat several times to ensure their knowledge and identification skills are firmly embedded.

4. Once children can name all the birds correctly, ask them to look closely at the images and suggest similarities and differences between the birds. Encourage the children to compare beak length, type of feet, and wing and leg size.

Paired work
5. Provide pairs of children with the bird factfile templates and photocopiable page 'Bird facts' from the CD-ROM. Tell them to cut out one bird at a time, match it with the correct name and glue it onto their factfile. By each image they should then add a fact about that particular bird.

Differentiation
- Support children with initial letter clues for the identification of species activity.
- Challenge children to add more information to their bird factfiles.

Science in the wider world
Birds have evolved into thousands of species, all of which have feathers. Feathers protect the skin and keep the bird warm. A film of oil over the feathers makes them waterproof, so waterfowl are able to swim and other birds can stay dry in wet weather. The long tail of the male peacock is called a 'train' and contains around 150 feathers, often over a metre in length. In addition to feathers, chickens have hanging flaps of skin on either side of their beaks called 'wattles'. These, together with a fleshy 'comb' on the head, help keep the birds cool.

Review
Children could be assessed on the accuracy with which they have been able to identify a variety of birds and describe similarities and differences between them.

Objectives
• To think about some characteristics of birds.
• To compare the structure of a bird with the structure of a human.
• To identify the main body parts of a bird.

Resources
Video of different birds in flight; large images of a bird in flight and another with wings folded; bird body-part labels (head, body, legs, feet, wings, beak); photocopiable page 'Bird misfit cards' from the CD-ROM; bird photos (including some in which body parts of different birds have been mixed up); photocopiable page 74 'Bird bodies'

Speaking scientifically
skeleton, backbone, beak, bill, wing, webbed feet

Lesson 2: Bird structure

Introduction
Recap on the previous lesson's focus – naming birds and making a factfile – and ask the children to recall as many names and facts as they can. Talk about characteristics that all birds have in common, as well as similarities and differences between various species. Watch video footage of different birds in flight and ask the children to describe how birds move. Explain that, while all birds have wings, some, like ostriches and emus, are not able to fly. Domestic chickens may be able to fly for short distances. Remind the children of the main human body parts they identified in week 1, lesson 1. Display a large picture showing a bird in flight and another showing it with folded wings. Thinking about what they learnt about the human body, ask the children to place labels on the bird pictures for the head, body, legs, feet, wings and beak.

Paired work
1. Provide pairs of children with a set of jumbled cards from the photocopiable page 'Bird misfit cards' from the CD-ROM. Ask them to spread these out and select one with a head on it. Next, they should find the matching body, leg and feet cards and lay these out in order to make a complete bird, then repeat to make the other birds.

Whole-class work
2. Display some photographs of real birds and some made-up birds, made by mixing up body parts. Ask the children to say which are real and which are made-up. Encourage them to say which body parts are incorrect.

3. Show the correctly completed misfit pictures and challenge children to identify the birds (mallard duck, cockerel, barn owl).

Independent work
4. Provide the children with photocopiable page 74 'Bird bodies', containing the outlines of an ostrich, penguin, heron and duck. Ask them to label the head, body, legs, feet, wings and beak of each one.

5. Tell the children to look closely at the birds and then answer questions about them, such as: Which has the longest legs/biggest beak/longest neck? Also ask the children to identify which birds have webbed feet and to explain why they think these are important.

> ### Differentiation
> • Support children with initial letter clues or body-part labels that can be cut and glued into place.
> • Challenge children to make comparisons between different birds.

Science in the wider world
Some fossil evidence suggests that birds may have evolved from dinosaurs. They share similar skeletal features, including the leg and foot structure that enables them to stand upright. Living species of birds vary immensely in scale: the largest wingspan is that of an albatross, measuring around 3m, while the smallest bird in the world is the bee hummingbird, approximately 6cm in length. Peregrine falcons can drop into a steep dive when they spot their prey, flying at speeds of up to 200mph. With an annual round trip to Antarctica, the arctic tern flies about 40,000 miles each year.

Review
Children could be assessed on how accurately they can identify the main body parts of different birds, fit them together correctly and answer questions about each bird.

Objectives
● To name some varieties of fish.
● To identify some of the characteristics of fish.
● To identify similarities and differences between fish and mammals.
● To begin to group fish.

Resources
Video of different species of fish; large fish outline (on board or sheet of paper); blue paper for an aquarium display; images of a variety of fish (from photocopiable page 'Animal images: fish' from the CD-ROM); fish name labels; sets of fish images for sorting; aquarium outlines; glue

Speaking scientifically
skeleton, backbone, breathe, gills, fin, tail, scale, freshwater, saltwater

Lesson 3: Fish

Introduction
Arrange to make a class visit to an aquarium or a large garden centre or pet store that stocks fish for ponds and tanks. Alternatively, show your class video footage of a variety of tropical fish, as well as some examples of local freshwater and coastal species. Ask the children if they recognise any of the fish they have seen and whether they can name any species. Perhaps some children will have an aquarium at home. Make a list of any fish names they know and ask them to explain what makes a fish a fish! Write their ideas onto a large fish outline and prompt them, as appropriate, to ensure they have considered characteristics of fish such as that they have a skeleton, live in water, breathe through gills, move through the water using fins and a tail, lay eggs and generally have bodies that are covered in scales.

Whole-class work
1. Cover a board or display area with a blue background and tell the children that you are going to make a 'class aquarium'. Share out images of a wide variety of saltwater fish and name labels among the children.

2. Begin by asking the children to pass you the name label for a clown fish. Place this on the aquarium board and then tell them that you are looking for a picture of a fish that likes to live inside sea anemones. It is bright orange and has three white stripes on its body. Allow the children time to find the correct image and then place it next to the name label in your 'aquarium'.

3. Continue to fill up the aquarium board with further fish name labels and images that the children have identified through clues you have given them. Aim to include examples that children may be familiar with, as well as unusual ones such as trumpet fish, manta rays and seahorses.

4. Finally, add a shark to the aquarium board and explain that sharks belong to the fish family, while whales and dolphins are mammals. Ask the children to recall some facts about mammals and identify similarities and differences between the two animal groups.

Paired work
5. Provide pairs of children with further images and tell them to divide these into sets according to shape, size, colour or number of fins. Ask each child to record their groupings on a simple aquarium outline on a landscape-orientated sheet of paper. They should glue on their images and write an appropriate heading for their group.

6. Invite pairs of children to show their work to the rest of the class and talk about the similarities and differences between the fish they have sorted into groups.

Science in the wider world
There are over 25,000 known species of marine and freshwater fish in the world. The earliest fish-like creatures appeared over 500 million years ago – well before the age of dinosaurs – and are thought to be the oldest group of vertebrates on Earth. They are cold-blooded, which means that their body temperature changes according to the surrounding water temperature.

Review
Children could be assessed on the groupings they make on their aquarium sheets, the characteristics they can confidently compare and the number of fish they can identify by name.

Objectives
• To know the main external parts of fish.

Resources
Chalk; metre sticks; plastic straws cut into 1cm strips; images of a variety of fish

Speaking scientifically
whale shark, plankton, filter feeding, dorsal fin, pectoral fin, tail, gills, pelvic fin

Lesson 1: Fish structure

Introduction
Take your class into the playground or large hall and tell them to lay 12 metre sticks end to end. Use chalk to map out a basic fish shape around these sticks, with a tail at one end and head at the other. Ask the children to stand inside the fish shape. Pass around the 1cm plastic straw strips so that every child can hold one in the palm of their hands. Tell the children that they are now standing inside the largest fish in the world – a whale shark – and holding the smallest fish in the world in their hands. Ask the children to turn and face the whale shark's head and, while they watch, use metre sticks to draw a mouth about 1.5m wide. Explain that, although the shark has such a large mouth, it doesn't hunt animals or attack humans. Instead, it lives on tiny plants and animals called plankton, which it catches by swimming around with its mouth open. The smallest fish in the world are less than 1cm long and have been found living in swamps in Indonesia.

Whole-class work
1. Back in class, remind children of the previous lesson, when they found out about different types of fish. Recap on some of the species they looked at and ask them to suggest some common body parts. Draw a simple fish shape on the board and label the head, gills, fins and tail.

2. Ask the children if they think that fish have a skeleton. Perhaps they have experienced eating a fish with bones in it, or watched an adult peel meat away from a fish's backbone. Encourage them to talk about their observations.

3. Show the class some images of different fish. Begin with commonly shaped ones like trout, cod and sardines, but also include some more unusual examples such as blobfish, boxfish and hammerhead sharks. Count the fins on each example and compare their shape and position on each fish. Explain that fish use dorsal fins – the ones on the back of a fish – to balance in the water and move quickly, and that there may be up to three of them. A pair of pectoral fins can be found on the sides of a fish and a pair of pelvic fins towards the tail. Fish tails are also fins. Fish use gills on the sides of their heads to take oxygen out of the water.

Independent work
4. Ask children to draw and label some fish shapes.

> **Differentiation**
> • Support children with fish templates and body-part labels that can be cut and glued into position.
> • Challenge children to write a sentence by each body part to explain how the fish uses it.

Science in the wider world
Most fish have a skeleton made of bone but some, like sharks, have one made of cartilage. The sailfish can reach speeds of 68mph, while seahorses are thought to be the slowest moving fish in the world. Mudskippers are able to 'walk' on their pectoral fins.

Review
Children could be assessed on how accurately they have identified fish body parts and/or described what they do.

Objectives
● To identify the characteristics of an amphibian.
● To identify some common amphibians.
● To compare some common amphibians.

Resources
The story of 'The Frog Prince'; images of frogs, toads, newts, salamanders and caecilians; images of rainforest frogs; frog outline templates; crayons or coloured paper; glue

Speaking scientifically
amphibian, frog, toad, newt, salamander, caecilian

Lesson 2: Amphibians

Introduction
Tell your class the story of 'The Frog Prince', or a similar tale about frogs and humans. Invite some children to take on the roles of the frog, princess and king and act out some scenes, including where the frog first helps the princess and when he comes to the palace expecting the princess to fulfil her promise. Talk about why the princess did not want to keep her side of the bargain and ask the class to describe what a frog looks like and how it differs from a human. Make a list of the main body parts and explain that a frog belongs to the amphibian family. These animals begin life in water, using gills to breathe just like fish, but gradually they change and grow into adults with legs and lungs and can survive on dry land. Toads, newts and salamanders are all members of the amphibian family, as are legless caecilians.

Whole-class work
1. Display some images of adult frogs, toads, newts, salamanders and caecilians and ask the children to identify similarities and differences between them. Encourage children to notice that newts and salamanders have tails, while frogs and toads do not. Explain that amphibians are cold blooded and lay eggs in water.

2. Tell your class that in the UK frogs and toads are the most common types of amphibian and ask the children if they have come across any in local gardens or parks. Frogs tend to have smooth, moist skin and longer back legs than toads. They jump rather than make small hops. The children may also have seen newts, although these are much less common than frogs and toads. Talk about the colours of frogs they have seen in the wild and then show the class some images of brightly coloured rainforest species.

Independent work
3. Ask the children to look closely at the rainforest frog images and then to use crayons or collage to complete a brightly coloured frog in the outline provided.

Whole-class work
4. Play a game of 'What am I?' Encourage the children to ask questions to which the answer can only be 'yes' or 'no' until they have deduced which amphibian you are thinking of. Allow them to ask each other questions, to embed names and differences between amphibians.

Science in the wider world
Although water is still integral to their life cycle, amphibians are thought to have been the first vertebrates to move from an entirely aquatic habitat and begin to live on land. Cold-blooded amphibians generally have skin that is permeable to water, so they are often found by water sources or in damp places. They lay jelly-like eggs in water, where the young hatch and grow and develop into adults. Great crested newts have become quite rare in the UK and are heavily protected. Caecilians may look more like worms or snakes, but are actually legless amphibians.

Review
Children could be assessed on how accurately they are able to recognise differences and similarities between frogs, toads, newts, salamanders and caecilians.

Objectives
- To recognise that amphibians have skeletons.
- To understand the life cycle of a frog.
- To correctly order the life cycle of a frog.

Resources
Images of a frog and a toad (from photocopiable page 'Animal images: amphibians' from the CD-ROM); large outlines of a frog and a newt; body-part labels: head, back, legs, feet, tail; images of the life cycle stages of a frog; photocopiable page 75 'Frog life-cycle stages'; frog outlines on green card

Speaking scientifically
frogspawn, tadpole, froglet, adult frog, gills, lungs

Lesson 3: Amphibian structure

Introduction

Recap on the work carried out in the previous lesson on identifying the characteristics of amphibians and looking at similarities and differences between frogs, toads, newts, salamanders and caecilians. Ask the children to recall which of these have tails and which one does not have legs. Talk about what frogs, toads and newts would look like in X-ray pictures. Ensure the children recognise that amphibians have skeletons. Show the children images of a toad and a frog and challenge them to tell the difference. Remind them that frogs have longer back legs and so can jump further than toads.

Display an outline of a frog and a newt and ask the children to place labels on them, identifying the head, back, legs, feet and – in the case of the newt – tail. Explain that some types of frog have webbed feet, like ducks, while tree frogs have small discs on their toes that help them grip onto trees as they climb up. Other types of frog have claws on their back feet to help them burrow into the ground.

Whole-class work

1. Show the children jumbled images of the stages in a frog's life cycle. Tell them that you dropped them on your way to school and can't remember which order they should go in. Deliberately start displaying them incorrectly and allow children the opportunity to tell you that you are getting it wrong. Ask them to help you put them into the correct order, supporting as appropriate to ensure that they do suggest the right order. Make sure, for instance, that the frog grows back legs before its front ones appear.

Paired work

2. When you have successfully completed the frog's life cycle together, ask the children to work in pairs to un-jumble the images from photocopiable page 75 'Frog life-cycle stages'. Tell them to glue their images in a circle inside an outline of a frog on green card.

3. Ask the children to complete their work on the frog's life cycle by adding labels to each stage.

4. Tell the children in each pair to take turns holding the life-cycle work where their partner can't see it and asking questions such as, 'Which stage comes before the tadpole?' or 'What does a froglet look like?'

> **Differentiation**
> - Support children with first-letter clues for the life-cycle labelling activity.
> - Challenge children to write an account of the frog's life cycle in their own words.

Science in the wider world

The largest amphibian in the world is the Chinese giant salamander, which can grow up to 180cm in length. They have small eyes and poor eyesight, but can sense the vibrations of prey moving around them. A species of frog discovered in Papua New Guinea measures 7mm in length and is thought to be the smallest frog in the world. Not much is known about caecilians as they spend a great deal of time underground and are very rarely seen.

Review

Children could be assessed on their recognition of amphibian body parts and how they complete the life-cycle stages activity.

Objectives
- To recap the characteristics of mammals, birds, fish and amphibians.
- To establish the differences between reptiles and amphibians.

Resources
Images of a lizard, snake and tortoise; video of different reptiles; laminated pictures of lizards and other reptiles, cut into pieces to make jigsaws; photocopiable page 'Reptile body parts' from the CD-ROM

Speaking scientifically
camouflage, skeleton

Lesson 1: Reptiles

Introduction
Recap on all the animal families the children have found out about so far and check that they can describe characteristics of each group, as well as similarities and differences between them. Remind them that mammals, birds, fish and amphibians all have a skeleton and explain that they are now going to learn about one last group of animals which has a skeleton.

Display images of a lizard, snake and tortoise and check that the children recognise these as members of the reptile family. Ask them to describe ways in which reptiles are different from amphibians and establish that they lay their eggs on land and have dry, scaly skin. Like amphibians, however, they are cold blooded and can vary widely in appearance for example, snakes do not have legs, while tortoises and turtles have shells that are permanently attached to their backbone and rib cage.

Whole-class work
1. Show your class some video footage of reptiles. Ask the children to watch carefully to see how the different animals move.

2. Talk about their observations and make a class list of reptiles and their movements. Some reptiles such as turtles, crocodiles and certain snakes are good swimmers. Many lizards are good climbers and geckos have specialised toe pads that enable them not only to climb vertical surfaces, but even to walk across indoor ceilings without falling off!

Paired work
3. Provide pairs of children with a set of lizard jigsaw pieces and ask them to put these together to complete a reptile. Check that they can do this successfully and point to specific body parts as you call them out.

4. Next, give each pair a selection of jumbled reptile jigsaws and challenge them to create three complete animals. Display the whole pictures and ask the children to compare these with their jigsaw.

Independent work
5. Give each child a copy of photocopiable page 'Reptile body parts' from the CD-ROM, showing a snake, lizard, turtle and crocodile. Ask them to label the main body parts of each reptile.

Differentiation
- Support children by giving them fewer jigsaw pieces and creating body-part labels for them to glue in place on the photocopiable sheet.
- Challenge children to make simple comparisons between their reptile pictures and record their observations in sentences.

Science in the wider world
The largest lizard in the world is the komodo dragon, which can grow up to 3m in length. The chameleon is able to hide from predators by changing body colour to blend into its surroundings. Tortoise and turtle shells are part of their skeletons: the top is called the 'carapace', and the bottom is the 'plastron'. Some turtles can pull their heads, legs, and feet inside their shells. The leatherback turtle is covered with a leathery skin supported by tiny bones. This enables it to make deep ocean dives. It can also swim at speeds of up to 6mph, while land tortoises move at a sedate half-mile per hour.

Review
Children could be assessed on how successfully they can complete the reptile jigsaws and describe characteristics of a variety of reptiles.

Objectives
● To know the names of common minibeasts.
● To identify that minibeasts have no backbone.
● To begin to group minibeasts into subgroups.

Resources
Songs about minibeasts; images of a variety of minibeasts, including insects, spiders, slugs, snails and woodlice (from photocopiable page 'Animal images: minibeasts' from the CD-ROM); sets of envelopes addressed to different minibeasts (include a description of each minibeast on the envelope); photocopiable page 76 'Minibeast invitations' 'personalised' with a picture and description of a different minibeast on each one; interactive activity 'Minibeast hunt' on the CD-ROM

Speaking scientifically
minibeast, insect, arachnid, mollusc, crustacean

Lesson 2: Minibeasts

Introduction
Teach the children some songs about minibeasts – there are various nursery rhymes and songs from films that could be used to introduce a wide range of minibeast species. List those mentioned in your songs and ask the children to add as many more minibeasts as they can think of to a large class list. Talk about similarities and differences between the examples given and explain that, although there are many differences between minibeasts, they are all part of a large family, and none of them have a backbone. This makes them very different from the other animal groups the children have been finding out about.

Whole-class work
1. Display images of a variety of minibeasts, including insects, spiders, slugs, snails and woodlice. Explain that these all come from different minibeast families and that insects are minibeasts that have six legs and bodies in three distinct parts. Show some large images of beetles and ants; ask the children to count the number of legs and point out the head, thorax and abdomen. Compare a spider and check that the children recognise a spider is not an insect because it has eight legs. Complete interactive activity 'Minibeast hunt' on the CD-ROM.

2. Tell the children that the beetles are having a big party and have invited all the other minibeasts along. They have worked hard to make personal invitations for their guests, with a picture of each one, but unfortunately, the invitations have somehow got mixed up and are not in the correct envelopes.

Group work
3. Ask the groups to take all the jumbled invitations out of the envelopes, look at them closely and then try to match each guest with the correct envelope. The picture clues and descriptions will help the children to choose the correct envelope for each guest.

Whole-class work
4. When every group has had some time to sort through their jumbled pile, check through these together, taking one minibeast family at a time. Display the correct pairs of named envelopes and picture invitations on a large board.

5. Role play going to the party. Tell the children they will each be a minibeast and must introduce themselves to another guest at the party. Make this into a guessing game by telling children they can only describe their characteristics to a guest, who must then try to work out what they are!

> ### Differentiation
> ● Support children with first letter clues on the invitations.
> ● Challenge children by covering up images and providing clues instead.

Science in the wider world
There are about 900,000 known species of insect in the world, the largest of any animal group. The most common family of insects are beetles. There are over 40,000 known species of spider, one of the largest being the Goliath bird-eating spider, whose leg span is almost 30cm across. Slugs and snails belong to the mollusc group, which also includes squid and cuttlefish, while woodlice are crustaceans, related to crabs and shrimps.

Review
Children could be assessed on how successfully they matched the descriptions and images of minibeasts with their names and introduced themselves at the minibeast party.

Objectives

- To investigate and record common minibeasts and their habitats.
- To identify the characteristics of insects.

Resources

Clipboards; paper; pencils; cameras; large image of a beetle; dice; containers to use as shakers; colouring pencils or crayons; photocopiable page 'Beetle drive' from the CD-ROM; interactive activity 'Minibeast hunt' on the CD-ROM; garden or disposable gloves

Speaking scientifically

habitat, minibeast, insect, arachnid, mollusc, crustacean, head, thorax, abdomen, antenna

Lesson 3: Invertebrate structure

Introduction

Remind the children of the minibeast party invitations activity that they completed in the previous lesson and ask them to recall as many guests as possible. Make a new list of minibeasts, adding as many examples as the children can think of. Remind the children that, while they put all the invitations into the correct envelopes, these haven't actually been delivered to the guests! Ask the children to suggest where each of the minibeasts might live and add their ideas to the class list.

Whole-class work

1. If you are not following these sessions in strict seasonal order, you may well be able to go on a real minibeast hunt around your school grounds. If you do this, remind the children to wear gloves, handle minibeasts with care, put them back where they were found, be aware that black and yellow insects can sting, and wash their hands thoroughly after their investigations. They could record their findings by drawing or taking photos of the creatures they find, and their habitats. If you are doing this lesson at the end of the autumn term, when minibeasts are hard to find, use the interactive activity 'Minibeast hunt' on the CD-ROM in pairs.

2. When you have completed your minibeast hunt, recap on the differences between insects and other minibeasts. Remind the children that insects have six legs and three distinct body parts. Display a large image of a beetle and point to the head, thorax and abdomen.

Group work

3. Give each child the photocopiable page 'Beetle drive' from the CD-ROM. Explain that this is a variation on a traditional parlour game. Each child takes a turn at rolling the dice. They should colour in each body part when they roll the matching number on the dice. They must roll a six to start their beetle. They need to roll six ones to get all the legs, two threes and two twos for the eyes and antennae, and so on. Encourage the children to use the correct terminology for the different body parts. The first child to have completely coloured their beetle is the winner.

Science in the wider world

Insects' bodies are divided into three distinct parts. The head is where the eyes, mouth, brain and antennae are located. Legs and wings are attached to the thorax, and the abdomen is where digestion and the reproductive organs are situated.

Review

Children could be assessed on the drawings, notes and photographic observations they made during the minibeast hunt and their contribution to the class discussion following this.

Objectives
- To recap the various different animal families.
- To make models of creatures from all the different animal families studied.
- To correctly classify creatures from all the different animal families studied.
- To label the body parts of creatures from all the different animal families studied.

Resources
Images of animals from each animal family (mammals, birds, fish, amphibians, reptiles, minibeasts); coloured modelling clay; board; simple tools, such as lolly sticks; body-part labels (back, legs, feet, head, beak, wings, fin, tail); a large sheet of cardboard divided into boxes labelled: mammals, birds, fish, amphibians, reptiles, minibeasts

Working scientifically
- To identify and classify.

Animal body parts

Revise
- Use photographs and examples of the children's work from this topic to recap on the animals they have been finding out about. Remind the children of the animal families they have looked at and encourage them to list as many as they can remember before you fill in any gaps. Children should be able to list mammals, birds, fish, amphibians and reptiles. Talk about what these animals all have in common (a skeleton and backbone) and ask children to describe some of the similarities and differences they noticed between these vertebrate groups. Compare their observations with images of animals from each group and clear up any misconceptions the children may have. Challenge them to remember which group of animals do not have a skeleton or backbone. Recap the work on minibeasts and ask the children to give examples of invertebrates, such as insects, spiders and molluscs.

Assess
- Provide each child with a selection of coloured modelling clay, a board to work on and some simple tools, such as a lolly stick. Tell them to begin by making a model of a human out of the clay, and to lay it carefully in the correct box on their large sheet of cardboard.
- Next, ask them to select some of the body-part labels and gently attach these to their human model.
- Check that the children have made a recognisable human model and attempted to label the major body parts.
- Tell the children to now use their clay to make a model of a bird, placing it in the correct box on their sheet of card and selecting some more body-part labels to attach to it.
- Check that the children have identified wings and beaks on their bird models.
- Carry on with the modelling clay activity, until the children have completed models for the remaining vertebrate groups and have labelled appropriate body parts. Check each time to assess how accurately they can identify specific characteristics, such as fins and tails.
- For the final box, ask the children to make models of at least two different minibeasts and label the appropriate body parts.
- Review each child's models and labels to assess their knowledge and understanding of the main body parts of a variety of animals.

Further practice
- Support children by limiting the number of models you ask them to make and by providing fewer boxes for them to fill. You could also limit the number of body-part labels you ask them to attach, or ask them to point out features on their models and talk about differences between them.
- Challenge children to demonstrate their knowledge and understanding of animal body parts further by asking them to attach labels for specific features, such as dorsal fins, thorax, abdomen and antenna. Encourage them to describe similarities and differences between the animal groups using simple scientific vocabulary. These children could also write sentences about their animal family models.

Objectives
- To recap animal families.
- To correctly classify various animals.
- To assign animals to the correct diet group.

Resources
Images of animals from the different families, in envelopes with clues written on the outside; photocopiable page 'Animal families' from the CD-ROM; images of a wide variety of animals; glue sticks; photocopiable page 'Animal diet' from the CD-ROM; interactive activity 'What animal family am I?' on the CD-ROM

Working scientifically
- To identify and classify.

Animal families

Revise

- Play a 'lost animals' revision game with the children to help them recall the main animal families they have been learning to identify. Begin by dividing a board or screen into six empty boxes and asking the children to help you label them with the names of the animal families: mammals, birds, fish, amphibians, reptiles and minibeasts. Show the class a stack of envelopes and explain that each one contains an image of a 'lost' animal. On the outside of the envelope is a clue. The children must listen carefully to the clue and then suggest which family the particular animal is part of. Practise the game by reading the class a simple clue such as: 'I spend all my life in water and I do not have legs.' Talk about possible answers and make sure the children are clear that the animal could not be a tadpole, as these grow into frogs with legs and adult amphibians do not live in water. Ensure the children can suggest that the most likely animal is a fish and then remove the image from the envelope, show it to the class and attach it to the correct family box. Carry on playing until all the animal groups have examples in them. You could also play interactive activity 'What animal family am I?' on the CD-ROM.
- Play another round of 'lost animals' to practise identifying carnivores, herbivores and omnivores. This time, display a Venn diagram with two overlapping circles and read out clues that describe what particular animals eat. Allow the children time to practise assigning different animals according to diet.

Assess

- Tell the children they are now going to do their own sorting activity, putting lost animals into the correct family boxes.
- Provide each child with photocopiable page 'Animal families' from the CD-ROM, a wide variety of animal images covering all the main groups and some glue sticks. Ask them to look carefully at the pictures, identify each animal and attach it to the correct animal family box.
- Once all the animals have been allocated to boxes, give the children the photocopiable page 'Animal diet' from the CD-ROM, along with further animal images representing examples of carnivores, herbivores and omnivores.
- Tell the children that they now need to attach the animals to boxes to show what sort of food they eat.
- Review each child's completed photocopiable sheets to assess how accurately they can assign examples of animals to different family or diet groups.

Further practice

- Support children by limiting the number of animals you ask them to assign to each family. Provide pictures of animals eating a particular food to help them decide whether they belong to the carnivore, omnivore or herbivore groups.
- Challenge children to demonstrate their knowledge and understanding of animal families by including some more unusual examples. For example, you could include a salamander (an amphibian) and a gecko (a reptile) and check to see if children can correctly distinguish between them. Children could also write additional labels naming particular animals in each family group and use an overlapping Venn diagram template to independently place animals according to diet.

Objectives
- To correctly link senses to sense organs across a variety of animals.
- To identify the characteristics of the animal groups studied.
- To correctly sort insects from other minibeasts.

Resources
A large image of a human face; senses labels; images of mammals, birds, fish, amphibians and reptiles; photocopiable page 'Animal senses' from the CD-ROM; wallets containing five A4 images of different vertebrate animals (one from each family) and smaller images of eggs, live young, fur, scales, feathers, slimy skin and life-cycle stages; glue sticks; photocopiable page 'Which are insects?' from the CD-ROM

Working scientifically
- To identify and classify.
- To observe closely.
- To use their observations to suggest answers to questions.

Animal characteristics

Revise

- Display a large image of a human face and ask the children to tell you what parts of the body they can see that are associated with senses. Identify the eyes, ears, nose, mouth and tongue and match these to labels for the four related senses. Remind children of the investigation they carried out to find out which parts of the body were sensitive to touch. Show the class some images of other animals and talk about which senses these use, encouraging the children to consider similarities and differences with humans. For example, many birds have very keen eyesight to help them spot possible food, while other animals may rely on their sense of smell or hearing to either help find food or keep them safe from predators. Quite often, animals that spend most of their lives underground do not have sight – can the children explain why?
- Recap the main animal families and display examples from each one. Ask the children a series of questions such as *What makes a bird a bird?* and *What do fish have that mammals don't?* Gradually build up a large class list of the main characteristics of each group. Prompt children, as appropriate, to include: body coverings such as fur, feathers or scales; egg-laying or giving birth to live young; body temperature; and whether animals breathe using gills or lungs.

Assess

- Ask the children to complete the photocopiable page 'Animal senses' from the CD-ROM by linking the label for the main sense illustrated to the appropriate part of each animal's body. (The elephants are illustrating the sense of touch rather than smell!)
- Provide every child with a wallet containing a jumbled selection of five A4 images representing each vertebrate animal family – such as a cat, penguin, trout, frog and snake. The wallet should also contain smaller images of eggs, live young, fur, scales, feathers, slimy skin and life-cycle stages. Tell the children to sort out the contents of their wallet by finding characteristics for the mammal, bird, fish, amphibian and reptile. Once they have identified these, they should glue them onto the appropriate animal image.
- Ask children to look carefully at images of various minibeasts on the photocopiable page 'Which are insects?' from the CD-ROM and identify all the insects by circling them with a coloured pencil.

Further practice

- Support children in the senses assessment activity by providing just one image of a human head, rather than images of different animals. Limit the number of jumbled images and characteristics in the wallets; ask children to select just the characteristics that relate to mammals. Provide a smaller range of minibeasts for the children to select insects from.
- Include speech bubbles for children to allocate to various animals in the senses assessment. These could include statements like 'I smell with my tongue. I flick it in and out to find out what's close by' (to link with the snake) and 'I have eyes on the side of my head so that I can see what's happening all around me' (frog, penguin, snake, trout). Tell children to find and circle molluscs and arachnids with different coloured pencils on the minibeast photocopiable sheet.

Body parts

■ Choose the correct word to write in each box.

arm   leg   head   face   hand   foot   chest   knee   elbow
ankle   wrist   hip   thigh   shoulder

I can name parts of the human body.

How did you do?

Tasty surprise

■ Write the name of foods you have tasted around the picture.

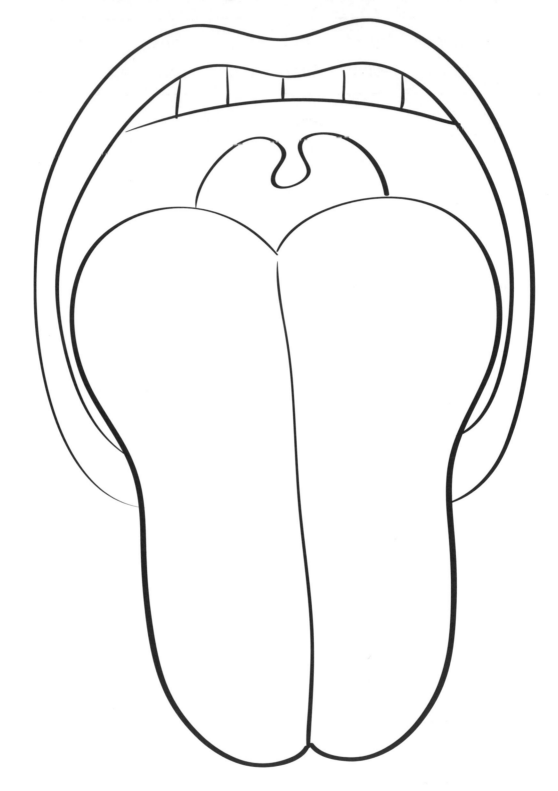

I can list foods with different tastes.

How did you do?

PHOTOCOPIABLE

SCHOLASTIC
www.scholastic.co.uk

Name: _____   Date: _____

Eye templates

- Colour in an eye to match your eye colour.

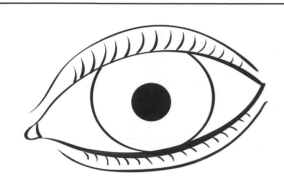 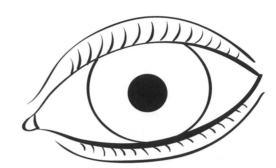

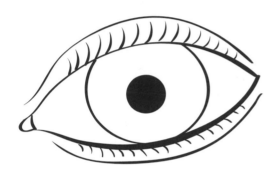 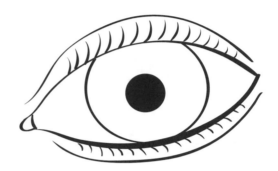

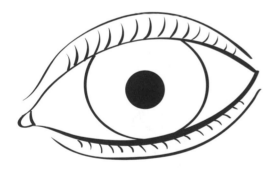 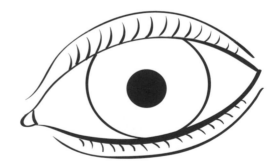

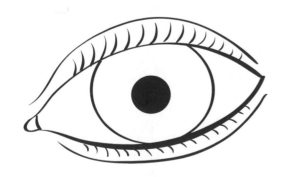 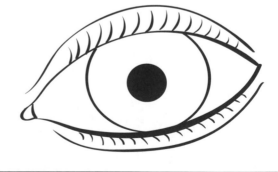

I can show what colour my eyes are.

How did you do?

PHOTOCOPIABLE

Animals around us

■ Cut out and stick the labels in the correct spaces, or choose the right word and write it in the box by each picture.

goldfish	dog	frog	cat	robin	horse	rabbit	mouse	human	sheep	fly	squirrel

How did you do?

I can name some animals that live nearby.

Name: _____   Date: _____

What are mammals?

■ Add labels to these pictures. Use these words to help you.

fur – hair

live young

breathe air
into lungs

I can describe what mammals look like.

How did you do?

Bird bodies

■ Add labels to show the body parts of each bird.

head   body   legs

feet   wings   beak

I can name the body parts of birds.

How did you do?

PHOTOCOPIABLE

SCHOLASTIC
www.scholastic.co.uk

Frog life-cycle stages

■ Cut out these pictures and stick the stages of the frog's life cycle in the correct order. Add labels to each stage.

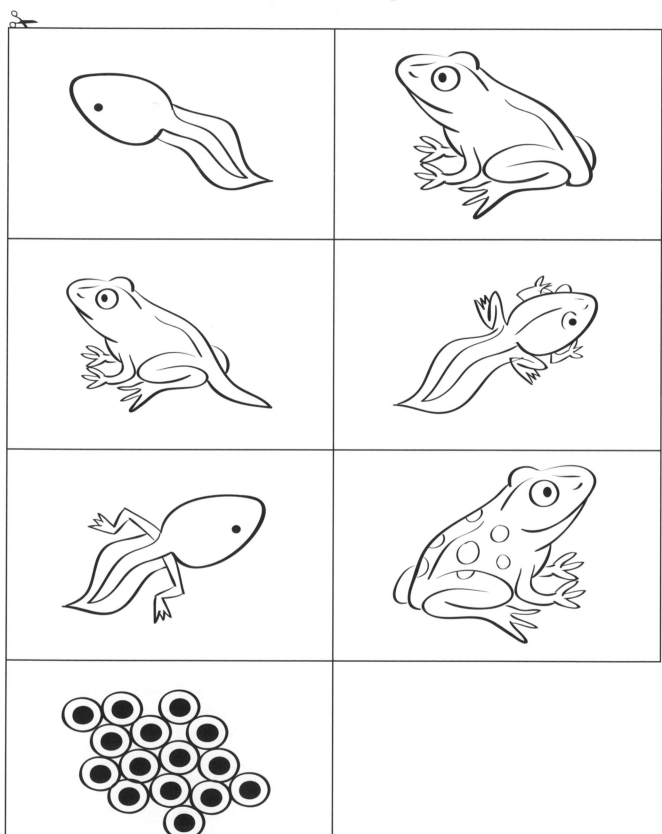

Name: _____ Date: _____

Minibeast invitations

 Dear _____

You are invited to our party in the long grass under the hedge this Saturday. We hope you can come.

Love from

The Beetles

 Dear _____

You are invited to our party in the long grass under the hedge this Saturday. We hope you can come.

Love from

The Beetles

 Dear _____

You are invited to our party in the long grass under the hedge this Saturday. We hope you can come.

Love from

The Beetles

 Dear _____

You are invited to our party in the long grass under the hedge this Saturday. We hope you can come.

Love from

The Beetles

 Dear _____

You are invited to our party in the long grass under the hedge this Saturday. We hope you can come.

Love from

The Beetles

 Dear _____

You are invited to our party in the long grass under the hedge this Saturday. We hope you can come.

Love from

The Beetles

Seasons: winter and spring

Expected prior learning
- Observations about some changes in weather and day length.
- Names of some common plants and animals.
- How seasonal change can affect plants and animals.

Overview of progression
After completing this chapter the children should know about:
- weather associated with winter and spring
- some changes in day length
- how plants, animals and humans are affected by seasonal changes associated with winter and spring

Creative context
- This topic provides many opportunities for children to make observational drawings and use images to present their findings.
- Children will be required to deploy their design and technology skills when making snowflakes, bird feeders, cotton-wool penguins and sunrise–sunset models.
- The natural environment lends itself to various forms of creative writing, song, music and dance.

Background knowledge

Seasonal changes
The winter solstice, the shortest day in the northern hemisphere, occurs around 21 December, when the Earth's axis leans furthest from the Sun. The summer solstice occurs around 21 June, when the Earth's axis leans furthest towards the Sun.

Hibernating animals
Some animals, such as hedgehogs, hibernate over the winter. This means that they go into a very deep sleep, during which their body temperature drops and their breathing slows down. Most hedgehogs begin to hibernate November and wake up in March or April when temperatures start to rise again.

Snowflakes
Snowflakes start when water vapour in clouds sticks to grains of dust and freezes. Temperature, air currents and humidity affect snowflake formation. The lower the temperature, the sharper the tips of the snowflakes.

Speaking scientifically
- In this chapter, the children will have opportunities to work scientifically and observe changes across winter and spring, observe and describe the weather at the particular time of year and observe the apparent movement of the Sun and how daylight varies. A simple scientific vocabulary will enable the children to comment on their observations and could include: temperature, thermometer, weather vane, rain gauge, rainfall, wind speed, deciduous, evergreen, dormant, migration, hibernation, habitat, insulation, sunrise, sunset, sunlight, solstice and horizon.

Preparation
You will need to provide: simple thermometers with a comparative scale for 'cold', 'colder', 'warm' and 'warmer'; simple temperature-monitoring fridge thermometer; craft and construction kit materials for model making; images of wintery scenes; clock faces; photographs and cameras; gardening gloves

On the CD-ROM you will find: photocopiable pages 'Timeline image sheet', 'What's the time Mr Wolf?', 'Our tree'; interactive activities 'Changing seasons', 'Wind', 'Autumn and winter', 'Day and night', 'Signs of spring'

Chapter at a glance

Week	Lesson	Curriculum objectives	Lesson objectives	Main activity	Working scientifically
1	1	• To observe changes across the four seasons.	• To observe seasonal changes. • To compare changes in winter with autumn. • To observe and record daily temperatures. • To know that the environment is affected by seasonal change.	Visiting an indoor snow centre/local park/school grounds if covered in snow. Identifying wintery weather, taking temperature readings. Making snow sculptures, looking at icy puddles.	• Asking simple questions. • Identifying and classifying. • Observing closely. • Making comparisons.
	2	• To observe and describe weather associated with the seasons.	• To know that the environment is affected by seasonal change. • To observe and record changes in temperature. • To compare and discuss temperatures in different places. • To be able to suggest winter weather activities.	Discussing winter weather and looking at photos of wintery conditions. Identifying advantages/ disadvantages of winter weather and recording ideas with drawings.	• Identifying and classifying. • Observing closely. • Making comparisons.
	3	• To observe how day length varies.	• To know that there is less daylight in winter. • To observe the hours of daylight before and after school. • To observe and classify 'light' and 'dark' activities.	Talking about getting up/ going to bed in the dark. Listing and classifying which activities can be done in daylight/ require lights.	• Asking simple questions. • Identifying and classifying. • Observing closely. • Making comparisons.
2	1	• To observe and describe weather associated with the seasons.	• To know that temperatures are lower outside in winter. • To observe and record changes in blocks of ice kept inside and outside on a winter's day.	Comparing what happens to 'icy hands': one outside the classroom window, the other inside the classroom. Recording with photos and drawings.	• Asking simple questions. • Identifying and classifying. • Observing closely. • Making comparisons. • Recording and communicating findings in a range of ways.
	2	• To observe and describe weather associated with the seasons.	• To know that smooth surfaces slide on ice. • To distinguish between 'slippy' and 'grippy' shoe soles. • To know that icy weather can be fun, but also dangerous.	Identifying objects that slide on ice and objects that prevent sliding. Talking about how to stay safe on the ice.	• Asking simple questions. • Identifying and classifying. • Observing closely. • Making comparisons.
	3	• To observe and describe weather associated with the seasons.	• To observe the structure of a snowflake. • To know that snowflakes are a feature of winter weather.	Talking about what snow looks/feels like. Making a snowflake display.	• Observing closely. • Making comparisons.
3	1	• To observe and describe weather associated with the seasons.	• To know that winter weather makes it hard for birds to find food. • To identify some common birds. • To observe and record birds visiting bird feeders.	Looking at video/photos of garden birds visiting bird feeders. Making bird feeders and feeding birds in the playground.	• Identifying and classifying. • Observing closely. • Making comparisons. • Gathering and recording data to help in answering questions.
	2	• To observe and describe weather associated with the seasons.	• To know that winter weather makes it hard for animals to find food. • To think of ways of preventing squirrels from raiding bird feeders.	Looking at video footage of squirrels. Creating a model squirrel baffle.	• Observing closely. • Making comparisons.
	3	• To observe and describe weather associated with the seasons.	• To observe and compare animal tracks closely. • To identify specific animal tracks.	Looking at pictures of animal tracks in the snow. Matching footprints to animals.	• Identifying and classifying. • Observing closely. • Making comparisons.

Chapter at a glance

Week	Lesson	Curriculum objectives	Lesson objectives	Main activity	Working scientifically
4	1	• To observe and describe weather associated with the seasons.	• To know that animals need to find ways of staying warm in winter. • To perform a simple test to investigate insulation. • To use a thermometer to check and record temperatures.	Watching video footage of huddling penguins Establishing they live in very cold conditions so need to keep warm. Making models of penguins. Observing changes in temperature.	• Asking simple questions. • Performing simple tests. • Observing closely, using simple equipment. • Making comparisons. • Gathering and recording data to help in answering questions.
	2	• To observe changes across the four seasons (winter/ spring).	• To know that some animals sleep during the winter months. • To identify some animals that hibernate. • To understand why some animals hibernate.	Reading about the Mad Hatter's tea party and talking about the dormouse sleeping. Identifying animals that hibernate, matching them to the places they hibernate in.	• Asking simple questions. • Gathering and recording data to help in answering questions.
	3	• To observe and describe weather associated with the seasons (winter/ spring).	• To measure and record weather conditions. • To know that in spring the weather begins to get warmer, but can still be cold.	Watching weather reports and looking at weather measurements. Making and recording weather measurements.	• Asking simple questions. • Observing closely, using simple equipment. • Making comparisons. • Gathering and recording data to help in answering questions.
5	1	• To observe how day length varies.	• To observe the apparent movement of the Sun during the day. • To create models showing the apparent movement of the Sun. • To understand the position of the Sun at different times of day.	Reminding children of 'winter light' lesson/talking about what happens when it gets dark. Making a model to demonstrate the apparent movement of the Sun.	• Asking simple questions. • Observing closely. • Making comparisons.
	2	• To observe how day length varies.	• To know that the Sun appears to move across the sky. • To know the difference between sunrise and sunset.	Playing 'What's the time Mr Wolf?' for times between sunrise and sunset, linking to time of day and year.	• Using simple scientific language.
	3	• To observe changes across the four seasons.	• To recognise that spring follows winter. • To know that plants begin to grow as winter ends. • To identify some of the changes that take place as spring begins.	Talking about plants that shut down for winter. Looking at images of snowdrops, crocuses, catkins/tree blossom.	• Asking simple questions. • Observing closely. • Making comparisons.
6	1	• To observe changes across the four seasons (winter/ spring).	• To identify and record signs of spring. • To compare spring with winter and autumn.	Revisiting same park as in autumn term and discussing changes that have occurred. Predicting how the park will have changed.	• Asking simple questions. • Observing closely. • Making comparisons. • Gathering and recording data to help in answering questions.
	2	• To observe changes across the four seasons (winter/ spring).	• To suggest seasonal changes that may have happened to a tree. • To make scientific observations of a tree. • To identify and record changes to a tree in spring.	Revisiting the tree observed in the autumn term to look for signs of seasonal change and record further observations.	• Asking simple questions. • Observing closely. • Making comparisons. • Gathering and recording data to help in answering questions.
	3	• To observe changes across the four seasons (winter/ spring).	• To identify that there are different weather conditions in different seasons. • To identify which weather conditions will produce shadows. • To match weather sayings to the conditions they describe.	Telling American groundhog folktale. Shadow hunting in playground. Using groundhog tradition to make weather predictions.	• Observing closely. • Making comparisons. • Gathering and recording data to help in answering questions.
Assess and review					

● To observe seasonal changes.
● To compare changes in winter with autumn.
● To observe and record daily temperatures.
● To know that the environment is affected by seasonal change.

Resources
The seasons mobile from autumn 1, week 1, lesson 2; photographs from visits made in autumn 1, week 1, lesson 1 and autumn 1, week 6, lesson 1; large thermometer with a comparative scale for 'cold', 'colder', 'warm' and 'warmer'; photographs of 'winter wonderland' visit site; cameras; clipboards and paper; photocopiable page 102 'Wintery scene'; the weather chart from autumn 1, week 4, lesson 1

Speaking scientifically
temperature, ice, snow, frost, frozen, slide, speed, deciduous, evergreen, migration, hibernation

Lesson 1: Winter wonderland

Previous knowledge
During the Early Years Foundation Stage, children will have had opportunities to develop their understanding about similarities and differences between living things. They should have found out about different features of their immediate environment compared to others. They will also have made observations on how animals and plants occur or change. In addition to this, the children should have completed the Year 1 seasons topic on autumn/winter, where they began to observe seasonal changes, weather associated with different seasons and how day length varies over the year.

Introduction
Look at the seasons mobile from the previous term and talk about which months have passed since you set it up in the autumn. Check that the children are able to name and order the seasons and that they are aware that winter has started and spring will follow. Remind the class of all the work they did previously on seasons and display some of this, along with photographs from any off-site visits that they made to observe changes in the environment. Make a list of what they found out about changes in autumn and challenge them to suggest questions about how the environment is changing through the winter and what will happen next. Show the children the thermometer they used to take temperature readings as part of their weather observations in the autumn term and recall how it works.

Whole-class work
1. Plan to visit an indoor snow centre – or use the school grounds or a local park if there is a covering of snow – to introduce the children to a 'winter wonderland'. If you are making an off-site educational visit you will need to prepare by carrying out a thorough risk assessment and obtaining permission from parents and carers. Consider details such as transport, food, clothing, medical requirements (including any allergies) and an appropriate level of adult support.

2. Tell the children that you are going on a visit to a 'winter wonderland'. Show them some photographs of where they will be going and ask what they might expect to see there. Make a list of their ideas. Explain that they will be finding out about winter weather and establish some ground rules for staying safe and warm, such as dressing appropriately, wearing robust footwear to cope with slippery conditions and staying with their group and accompanying adults.

3. If visiting an outdoor location, begin by looking at the trees and asking the children to notice which ones have lost all their leaves and which are still green. If visiting an indoor snow centre, encourage the children to play 'I spy' on the way, looking for signs of winter. Take photographs of general scenes and anything particular from the children's initial observations.

Group work
4. Divide the class into small adult-led groups and direct them to different locations around the park or indoor snow centre. If outside: tell the children to look carefully at the trees and plants in their area, as well as on the ground, to find evidence of winter. Ask them to take photographs and temperature readings and be ready to report back to the rest of the class on what they have seen. If there is enough snow, challenge them to build snow sculptures and take photographs of these. At various points during the visit, bring the whole class back together and talk about what they have noticed. Compare each group's observations about winter and send the children out to new locations to repeat their investigations.

Checkpoint
● What are the months of the year?
● What are the names of the seasons?
● Which season has just ended?
● Which season is just beginning?
● What happens in winter?
● How do trees change during the year?
● What will change between now and spring?

If at an indoor snow centre: arrange for small groups to spend time observing the skiing, sledging and ice skating areas, as well as having their own opportunities to play in the snow. Take the thermometer with you so that children can take readings during their visit and make a record of these. Collect the class together at various points and talk about their observations on temperature, travelling through snow and ice and moulding snow into shapes.

5. At the end of the visit, collect the whole class together again and review all their findings. Collate their temperature readings, photographs of trees, snow sculptures, icy puddles and any other evidence, for a classroom display.

Whole-class work

6. Back in class, remind children of their visit to the indoor snow centre or outdoor location and invite them to recall what they saw. Display the photographs and other evidence of winter they collected and challenge them to start noticing and reporting their observations on wintery conditions as they travel to and from school or are out and about at weekends.

Independent work

Provide the children with photocopiable page 102 'Wintery scene' and ask them to label the signs of winter and shade it using appropriate colours.

Introducing the new area of study

Teach your class to sing 'Walking in a Winter Wonderland' and other songs about wintery weather and talk about the lyrics. Display the weather chart the children used in the autumn term and explain that they will carry on with their temperature measurements over the next few weeks. Show them pictures of animals such as garden birds and dormice and explain that they will be finding out about how animals cope with the cold, dark winter months and watching out for signs of spring.

Differentiation
● Support children with the photocopiable sheet by giving first-letter clues or labels to glue onto their wintery scene.
● Challenge children to label their wintery scene in more detail and write sentences about their visit.

Science in the wider world

In winter in the UK, deciduous trees have shed their leaves and entered a period of dormancy which will last until spring. Evergreen trees shed their leaves on a gradual basis, so branches will not be completely bare at this time of year. Animals such as swallows will have migrated south for the winter, while others, like dormice, will be hibernating until temperatures warm up in the spring.

Review

Children could be assessed on the observations they have made about signs of winter and any evidence they have collected from their visit. They could also be assessed on their completion of the photocopiable sheet and inclusion of relevant detail, such as colour, labels and sentences about their observations.

Objectives
- To know that the environment is affected by seasonal change.
- To observe and record changes in temperature.
- To compare and discuss temperatures in different places.
- To be able to suggest winter weather activities.

Resources
Photographs from 'winter wonderland' visit in previous lesson or images of wintery scenes; temperature readings from 'winter wonderland' visit; large thermometer with comparative scale for 'cold', 'colder', 'warm' and 'warmer'; large chart for recording daily temperature readings; sheets of paper divided into two boxes

Speaking scientifically
thermometer, temperature, cool, cooler, warm, warmer, freezing, ice, snow, frost

Lesson 2: Winter weather

Introduction
Display the photographs taken during the 'winter wonderland' visit in the previous lesson or general images of wintery scenes. Remind the children of how they dressed to go outside or visit the indoor snow centre and show them the large thermometer with the comparative scale for 'cold', 'colder', 'warm' and 'warmer' which they used to record temperatures. Talk about how the thermometer works and what it measures.

Whole-class work
1. Talk about what is meant by 'warm' and 'cold' weather and how we can check whether the temperature changes on different days. Place the large thermometer outside and – once it has been in place for a few minutes – take a first reading.

2. Back in class, add the information on temperature to a large chart and explain to the class that they will carry on measuring the temperature and recording it on a daily basis for the next few weeks.

3. Look at the temperature measurements taken during the 'winter wonderland' visit. List the various locations where the thermometer was used and record the children's observations alongside each one. Ask them to say what the most common temperature was and why this might have been. Encourage the children to describe the places that felt the warmest and coldest during their visit and talk about some of the factors that could have affected the temperature in these locations.

4. Tell the children to suggest activities that can only happen when there is ice or snow, as well as some that have to be postponed in these sorts of conditions. Make a list of their ideas.

Independent work
5. Provide each child with a sheet of paper divided into two boxes. In one section, ask them to draw a picture of an activity that is fun to do in the ice and snow. In the second box, tell them to draw a picture of something that could not happen if it is very icy and snowy.

Science in the wider world
Water freezes at 0°C, but a range of atmospheric conditions can affect how it falls to the ground. Snow is formed when water freezes around specks of dust. If enough ice crystals stick together they become too heavy for the clouds to hold and fall to the ground. Sleet is generally considered to be a mixture of snow and rain and occurs as snow begins to melt before it touches the ground. When drops of rain move up and down inside thunderclouds, ice balls form due to the low temperatures at the top of the clouds. These grow in size until the clouds can no longer support them and they fall as hailstones.

Review
Children can be assessed on the observations they make about winter temperatures and their drawings about suitable and unsuitable activities for winter weather.

Objectives
• To know that there is less daylight in winter.
• To observe the hours of daylight before and after school.
• To observe and classify 'light' and 'dark' activities.

Resources
Sunrise–sunset timelines created by the children in autumn 1, week 2, lesson 2; photographs or video of people's activities in the winter; photocopiable page 103 'Light and dark'; a large clock face for display and smaller ones for children to use; sorting templates – sheets with two shapes large enough to contain cut-out images from the photocopiable sheet

Speaking scientifically
sunrise, dawn, sunset, dusk, higher, lower, sunlight, shortest, longest, time, solstice

Lesson 3: Winter light

Introduction
Recall autumn 1, week 2, lesson 3, where the children talked about the activities they had been able to do on summer evenings, such as barbeques, camping trips, or simply playing out before bedtime. Establish that there was enough daylight to do these activities then. Question whether it would still be possible to do them in the winter. Display some of the sunrise–sunset timelines the children made during their work on autumn. Remind them about some of the activities and times of day they logged on their timetables and ask them to suggest what might be different now that it is winter.

Whole-class work
1. Tell the children to think about what it is currently like when they are getting up in the morning on a school day and going home again in the afternoon, and talk about when lights are switched on or off and curtains are drawn. Ask them to describe what happens if they go to any after-school activities or on other occasions when they are later returning home than usual. Are street and car lights on? Establish that the lights are switched on because the sun has set and that this has happened before bedtime.

2. Show video footage or display images of people going about their daily business, working, shopping and travelling on short winter days. Encourage the children to make observations about how dark it is outside on these occasions, though there are still lots of people about.

3. Display a large version of photocopiable page 103 'Light and dark' alongside a big clock face. Point to each activity and ask the children to describe what they can see and suggest what is happening. Draw their attention to the clocks and set the corresponding time on the clock face for each activity. Give the children smaller clock faces and encourage them to practise setting the times with you. Talk about which activities would take place in the daylight and which would take place in the dark, and ask if this would be different in the summer.

Independent work
4. Provide each child with the photocopiable sheet and ask them to cut out the pictures of daylight activities and stick them onto their sorting template. They should do the same for those that occur in darkness during winter, then colour them appropriately.

> ### Differentiation
> • Support children by pre-labelling the sorting template with 'light' and 'dark' and limiting the number of images you ask them to put in each shape.
> • Challenge children to add their own labels and write sentences to describe what is happening in the pictures.

Science in the wider world
The winter solstice occurs around 21 December each year at the point in the Earth's orbit where the northern hemisphere is leaning most fully away from the Sun. Following the summer solstice, the day length shortens, but after the winter solstice it begins to increase gradually.

Review
Children could be assessed on their observations about light and dark during the winter months and the detail they can add to their 'light' and 'dark' pictures.

• To know that temperatures are lower outside in winter.
• To observe and record changes in blocks of ice kept inside and outside on a winter's day.

Resources
'Icy hands' (fill rubber gloves with coloured water, freeze and carefully peel away the gloves); a camera; trays; clock faces; sheets of paper divided into four equal boxes

Speaking scientifically
temperature, icy, freezing, melting, cool, cooler, warm, warmer, ice, snow, frost

Lesson 1: Icy hands

Introduction

Remind the children of the ice balloon investigation they did in autumn 1, week 4, lesson 1 and talk about what they found out. Recall how they left one balloon outside overnight and kept the other in the classroom. The following morning, the outdoor balloon was much bigger than the indoor balloon because it had been cold in the night. Ask them to think about what might happen if they were to do something similar now it is winter and encourage them to recognise that, as temperatures are lower, the ice outside would take even longer to melt. Explain that this time the class will watch what happens to the ice during the day.

Whole-class work

1. Display the two 'icy hands' and explain that these are what the class will use to test out winter temperatures. Take some photographs and place each one on a tray to catch any drips as they melt.

2. Decide on suitable locations inside the classroom and outside in the playground where the icy hands can be safely left and observed over the course of the school day. Use the clock faces from the previous lesson and set them to show three or four times over the school day, for example 11am, 12 noon, 1pm and 2pm. Explain that when the classroom clock reaches each of these times, the children will look at both icy hands, take photographs and compare how they are melting.

3. Collect your information throughout the day. In the afternoon, bring the icy hand back in from the playground and place it next to the one that has been in the classroom. Encourage the children to make comparisons and take some final photographs. Make a display of the photographs alongside the times they were taken and the children's observations.

Independent work

4. Provide the children with sheets of paper divided into four boxes. In the top left-hand box, ask them to draw the inside icy hand at the beginning of the day and then, in the box alongside it, what it looked like by the afternoon. Repeat this in the bottom two boxes for the outdoor icy hand.

> **Differentiation**
> • Support children by suggesting they draw around their own hands and record any changes by rubbing fingers out.
> • Challenge children to write in times and descriptions of the icy hands.

Science in the wider world

The freezing point of water is the temperature at which it changes from a liquid to a solid. Ordinarily the freezing point of water is 0°C or 32°F. If you add salt to ice, however, the temperature at which it freezes drops by several degrees. This means that you can melt ice on paths or roads by sprinkling salt over them. The salt dissolves into liquid water in the ice and lowers its freezing point.

Review

Children could be assessed on their observations on the icy hands over the course of the day and what these told them about indoor and outdoor winter temperatures.

Objectives

- To know that smooth surfaces slide on ice and snow.
- To distinguish between 'slippy' and 'grippy' shoe soles.
- To know that icy weather can be fun, but that there are also dangers.

Resources

Photographs and video footage of people participating in winter sports; images of a selection of footwear showing a variety of soles (such as ballet shoes, PE pumps, hiking boots); photographs of tractor and mountain bike tyres; image of a red warning triangle; sheets of paper with a large triangle shape drawn on

Speaking scientifically

temperature, freezing, icy, smooth, sliding, melting, grip, dangerous

Lesson 2: Slipping and sliding

Introduction

Display some photographs of winter activities that were taken during your visit to the indoor snow centre in week 1, lesson 1, or general images of skiing, sledging and ice skating. Talk about what the people are doing in these pictures and whether skiers and skaters need to be able to slide quickly on the ice and snow. Ask the children about their own experiences of moving in slippery conditions and to say whether these were enjoyable or not. Encourage them to think about what happens when they are walking to school on paths that haven't been treated with salt or when cars are driving down icy roads. Establish that it can be fun to play in the ice and snow, but that there are dangers too.

Whole-class work

1. Look at the winter activity photographs again and ask the children to describe the equipment that is being used. Encourage them to recognise that the bottoms of skis, skates, toboggans and even curling stones are all very smooth. Talk about why this should be the case and watch some video footage of winter sports action to reinforce the idea that smooth surfaces slide on ice and snow.

2. Remind the class that, while sliding can be fun, it can sometimes be dangerous. Display some images of different types of footwear with the soles visible. Ask the children to choose the ones which they think would be best for walking to school on icy mornings and to say why. Establish that the shoes with the deepest tread will give more grip in slippery conditions. Tell the children to check the soles of their shoes and select ones that would be 'slippy' or 'grippy' on the ice. Talk about the footwear that they may be changing into for their journey home from school. Display some photographs of tractor and mountain bike tyres and ask the children to suggest why they have such a deep tread.

3. Return to the pictures of ice skaters and talk about where they are skating. Encourage the children to recognise that the people are on ice that has been specially prepared for the sport and that this has to be very thick so that there is no danger of it melting enough for anyone to fall through. Talk about how difficult it can be to gauge how thick the ice is on local ponds and canals and ensure that the children are aware that this can be very dangerous.

4. Display a red warning triangle and explain that this is often used in traffic signs to warn drivers about dangers. Tell the children that they are going to use this symbol to make a poster about staying safe on ice.

Paired work

5. Provide pairs of children with a large sheet of paper with a blank triangle on it. Ask them to make a poster warning people that they should never play on frozen water and to colour the warning triangle red.

Science in the wider world

In some parts of the world, winter temperatures drop low enough to freeze water in lakes and rivers to a depth that is safe to skate on. In the UK, this very rarely happens and children should be aware that it is unsafe to step onto ice on local stretches of water, even if it looks solid.

Review

Children can be assessed on their observations about sliding and grip in slippery conditions and the posters they make on the dangers of ice.

Objectives
● To observe the structure of a snowflake.
● To know that snowflakes are a feature of winter weather.

Resources
Video footage of falling snow; magnifiers and a camera or close-up images of snowflakes; squares of blank white paper and scissors

Speaking scientifically
snowflake, ice crystal, water vapour, frozen

Lesson 3: Snowflakes

Introduction

Show the class some video footage of falling snow and teach the children to sing 'Let It Snow'. Display the photographs taken during the 'winter wonderland' visit in week 1, lesson 1, or general images of wintery scenes, and ask the children to describe what snow looks like when it is falling. Encourage them to think about how the snow would look if they could see it through a magnifier. If there is a covering of powdery snow in the playground, you could take the children outside to look at it with some magnifiers and take close-up photographs. Otherwise, find some images of snowflakes to display in the classroom. Talk about the conditions that are necessary for snow and ensure the children recognise that it occurs when it is very cold and is generally a feature of winter weather.

Whole-class work

1. Tell the children to look closely at the snowflakes. Talk about how they all look different from each other and count how many sides each snowflake has. Explain that although no two snowflakes are exactly the same, they generally have six sides.

2. Demonstrate to the children how they are going to make snowflakes. Begin with a square sheet of white paper and fold it diagonally into a triangle. Fold again to make a smaller triangle and then fold over again lengthways from the apex so that the longer edges are flush with each other. Snip off the points protruding from the bottom of this new triangle. Now begin cutting into the sides, apex and bottom of the shape. Cutting at the top will create a hole in the middle of your snowflake, while cuts along the bottom edge will increase the number of points it has.

Independent work

3. Provide each child with a square sheet of white paper. Tell them to carefully fold these into triangles and to follow your instructions on further folds and cuts. This method will produce a six-pointed star, but if children are struggling with the triangles, make simpler shapes by folding the paper in half into an oblong and then in half again. Tell the children to draw a zigzag line between the folded sides, which they can then cut around. They can cut into the folds to create holes inside the snowflake. Once the children have completed their cuts, they can carefully open out the sheet of paper to reveal a completed snowflake for your classroom display. Challenge the children to count how many different snowflakes they have created.

Science in the wider world

Snowflakes occur as water freezes around grains of dust floating in clouds. Environmental conditions affect the structure of each snowflake so that no two are exactly identical – although some may look alike. The light-reflecting surfaces of snowflakes act like a prism, scattering light into all its colours, so that snow appears white.

Review

Children could be assessed on their observations about what snow looks like and the snowflakes they design and make for your classroom display.

Objectives
● To know that winter weather makes it hard for birds to find food.
● To identify some common birds.
● To observe and record birds visiting bird feeders.

Resources
Video footage of garden birds feeding; images of common garden birds, such as blue tits, great tits, robins and blackbirds; sticks – approx 20cm long, with holes drilled through; string; disposable gloves; trays; newspaper; aprons; honey; spoons; birdseed; binoculars

Speaking scientifically
wildlife, food, winter, ice, snow, nest, habitat, climate

Lesson 1: Feed the birds

Introduction
Show your class some video footage of common species of wild bird visiting garden bird tables and feeders. Talk about what the birds are doing and why they are eating food that has been put out for them rather than catching insects for themselves, or eating berries. Establish that it is often difficult for birds to find enough to eat when the weather is icy and there is snow on the ground, so humans can help them survive through the winter by putting food out for them. Before involving any children in work with foodstuffs, check for allergies. Peanuts and seeds are both common allergens and common ingredients in bird foods.

Whole-class work
1. Identify an area in the school grounds where you will be able to hang bird feeders. Explain to the children that this should be somewhere quiet and off the ground and away from other places accessible to cats. Preferably it should also be within view of your classroom window so that the children can keep an eye on who is visiting!

2. Show the class images of some common garden birds to watch out for, which might include: blue tits, great tits, robins and blackbirds.

Paired work
3. Tell the children to put on aprons and disposable gloves before beginning work on their bird feeders. Lay out the equipment in trays and place it on tables covered with old newspaper. Provide pairs of children with sticks that are between 10 and 20cm long. Prepare these beforehand by drilling a hole in each one through which string can be threaded to make a handle, or attach the string with a wall stapler.

4. When they are ready, the children need to smear honey around their sticks and then roll them in bird seed.

5. Carefully collect the sticks together and hang them in your chosen area.

6. Tits will hang off the sticks to feed, but species like robins and blackbirds need a flat surface, so lay some more seed out for them in a safe place. All birds will also need water to drink, especially when the weather is icy.

7. Keep some binoculars by the classroom window and tell the children to watch out for their visitors. Record how many birds, or how many of a particular type of bird, visit each day or over a week.

Science in the wider world
While birds most often experience food shortages during the autumn and winter, these can also occur at other times of the year, particularly during adverse weather. If this happens when birds have nesting young, be aware that they may need to supplement their diet from the bird table and feeders. It is important that loose peanuts or large chunks of bread that could be a choking hazard to chicks are not left out at these times.

Review
Children could be assessed on their observations about why birds often need food in winter and which kinds of birds they can help in the playground.

Objectives
● To know that winter weather makes it hard for animals to find food.
● To think of ways of preventing squirrels from raiding bird feeders.

Resources
Video footage of squirrels raiding bird feeders; images of commercially produced 'squirrel-proof' bird feeders; model construction kit equipment; story such as the *What Squirrels Do Trilogy* by Hazel Nutt

Speaking scientifically
wildlife, food, winter, cold, ice, snow, red squirrel, habitat

Lesson 2: Squirrels in action

Introduction

Tell your class that birds might not be the only wildlife eating food that has been left out in winter; grey squirrels are common visitors to gardens in the UK and have become very adept at accessing many types of bird table and feeder. Show some video footage of squirrels by-passing most deterrents put up by people who try to keep them away from bird food. Ask your class what they think of the squirrel visitors: are they stealing food that was meant for the birds, or do the children think that it is not just birds, but any wild animal who could be in need of extra food in winter and so the squirrels should be allowed it too? Grey squirrels are the most common visitors to gardens in the UK, but native red squirrels also need food in winter – although it is much rarer to see these in the wild.

Whole-class work

1. Explain to the children that squirrels do not know the bird food is not meant for them. There are lots of differently designed bird feeders that are meant to keep them away, but very often they are able to work out how to use these. Show your class some images of commercially produced 'squirrel-proof' bird feeders (sometimes called 'baffles') and ask the children if they think these would work.

Paired work

2. Provide pairs of children with an assortment of model construction kit equipment, including assorted lengths of piping and gears. Challenge the children to construct their own squirrel baffle model that could be placed near their bird feeders to prevent the squirrels getting to the birds' food. Invite the children to explain how their model works to the rest of the class. (The emphasis here is on allowing the children's creativity to flow, rather than necessarily creating the most effective baffle!)

Whole-class work

3. Recap on the ingenuity of squirrels in overcoming baffles to access bird feeders. Talk about why squirrels might become hungry during the winter and whether humans should put food out for them. Hold a class discussion and encourage the children to explain their ideas.

4. Read the children a story such as *The Squirrel Olympics* – from the *What Squirrels Do Trilogy* by Hazel Nutt. Talk about the events that feature in the story and compare these with the children's observations – or video footage – of real ones.

5. Ask the children to draw pictures of their favourite squirrel Olympic event.

Science in the wider world

Red squirrels are an indigenous species in Britain, but since the arrival of grey squirrels from America during the 19th century their numbers have greatly declined. Grey squirrels are much larger than red ones and – although they are not thought to attack the reds – there is often not enough food to support both species. Greys are better equipped to access whatever food is available. Their greater body weight means that they can store more fat in the winter and they produce more young than the reds. It is estimated that there are over 2.5 million greys but only about 140,000 wild red squirrels left in Britain – mainly confined to large wooded areas of Scotland and the north of England.

Review

Children could be assessed on their observations about wild animals such as squirrels and their squirrel baffle models.

■SCHOLASTIC

Objectives
● To observe and compare animal tracks closely.
● To identify specific animal tracks.

Resources
Images of animal and human footprints in snow; images of the animals that made the footprints; camera; photocopiable page 104 'Animal footprints'

Speaking scientifically
footprints, hind legs, digits, round pads, webbing, cloven hoof, alternating tracks

Lesson 3: Tracks in the snow

Introduction
Display images of animal and human tracks in the snow. Talk about the shapes that have been made in the snow and ask if it is possible to tell which direction the animal or person was walking in. Encourage the children to think about whether their tracks would look much different if they were walking over a beach with bare feet, or whether anyone would be able to tell if they were taking their dog for a walk. Establish that different animals leave different footprints in soft surfaces like sand and snow because their feet are different shapes and sizes. If there is snow on the playground, take the children outside. Find an area for them to walk over and take photographs of their footprints. Ask them to look around the edges of the playground where children have not been walking to see if they can spot animal tracks. Photograph any they come across to look at back in the classroom.

Whole-class work
1. Show the class some images of different tracks and challenge the children to identify which animals have made them. Include the tracks of a variety of mammals and birds and encourage the children to consider clues such as whether the animal has webbed feet.

2. Reveal photographs of the animals that made the tracks. Talk about their size and how many legs they have. Ask the children to count the number of toes and notice details such as the cloven feet of deer and cattle or the webbed feet of water birds like ducks and geese.

Independent work
3. Provide children with photocopiable page 104 'Animal footprints'. Tell them to look at the pictures of animals and draw lines to match these with the correct footprint. Ask them to find the names of the animals at the bottom of the sheet and to write them next to the correct pictures.

Differentiation
● Support children by limiting the number of animals to match with their footprints and by providing labels that they can glue directly into the name boxes.
● Challenge children to identify a wider range of animal tracks and to describe differences between them.

Science in the wider world
Badgers' feet consist of five digits with a large central pad. Fox tracks are similar to those of dogs, with two outer digits curving towards two inner ones. Deer such as fallow and red deer have cloven hooves with two toe digits. Some birds alternate their feet like humans, while others hop with both feet together. With duck and geese tracks, it is usually possible to spot the webbing between their toes.

Review
Children could be assessed on their observations about how animal tracks have been made and their work on matching various animal footprints with their owners.

Objectives

• To know that animals need to find ways of staying warm in winter.
• To perform a simple test to investigate insulation.
• To use a thermometer to check and record temperatures.

Resources

Video footage of emperor penguins huddling in Antarctica; two temperature-monitoring fridge thermometer strips (with a range of –5 to 12°C); a roll of cotton wool; elastic bands; two small hot water bottles; a plastic bag

Speaking scientifically

thermometer, temperature, freezing, dark, insulation

Lesson 1: Huddling penguins

Introduction

Choose a cold day to carry out this investigation – when the temperature is around freezing, if possible. Tell the children that they are going to find out about some animals that live in the coldest place on Earth – Antarctica. Explain that this is a large area of land around the South Pole, where it stays dark for several months during the winter. While most types of penguin move to places that are not quite so cold, the male emperor penguins stay in colonies, huddling together to keep warm and incubating their eggs. Show the class some video footage of emperor penguins gathered in a large group. Explain that it is very important that they stay warm because they are looking after the eggs, and that they take it in turns to stand on the edges and in the middle of the huddle.

Whole-class work

1. Tell the class that they are going to make a group of model penguins and use these to find out more about huddling together to keep warm. Ask them to recall the name of the instrument that measures how warm or cold it is and remind them about the large thermometer used for your weather observations. Show the children the temperature-monitoring fridge thermometer strips and tell them that these are used to measure how warm or cold it is inside a fridge. Explain how the strips change colour as the temperature rises or falls and that the fridge needs to be cool to store food in safely.

2. Tell the children that they are going to make some penguin models to huddle around one of the hot water bottles and use the fridge thermometers to see if that bottle stays warmer than the other one when they take them both out to the playground.

3. Show the children how to create penguin models by rolling up a strip of cotton wool to about the width of an adult's finger and securing it with a rubber band. Draw on eyes and a beak with felt pen. Allow the children time to make two each.

4. Fill the hot water bottles with tepid water and place a fridge thermometer on top of each one. Check that the children notice it is too warm to store food safely in your classroom! Collect all the 'penguins' and put them inside a bag containing one of the hot water bottles and a thermometer to make a snug fit.

5. Take both bags out into the playground and leave them long enough for the unprotected one to drop in temperature. Explain that you are going to check the one the penguins have been looking after, but will have to be quick because as soon as you take the penguins away, the hot water bottle will start to get cold. Tell the class to huddle together like the emperor penguins so that they can all see the thermometer as you slide it out. The hot water bottle should still be warm as the cotton wool has acted as an insulator.

6. Talk about the difference the cotton-wool penguins have made and relate this to the children's own need to wrap up warm on cold days.

Science in the wider world

Female emperor penguins lay a single egg, pass it to their partner to look after and head back out to sea. They will spend the next two months feeding on fish and krill while the male emperor looks after their egg by balancing it on his feet and covering it with his thick feathers.

Review

Children could be assessed on their observations about temperature and the difference huddling together can make.

Objectives
- To know that some animals sleep during the winter months.
- To identify some animals that hibernate.
- To understand why some animals hibernate.

Resources
A copy of *Alice in Wonderland*; images of dormice, hedgehogs, bats, frogs; photocopiable page 105 'Hibernating animals'

Speaking scientifically
hibernating, body temperature, dormouse, hedgehog, bat, frog

Lesson 2: Hibernating dormice

Introduction

Read your class the section of *Alice in Wonderland* that describes the Mad Hatter's tea party. List all the characters at the party and talk about the strange conversation they have and how sleepy the dormouse seems. Invite some of the children to pretend to be the dormouse and make announcements like, 'I breathe when I sleep' and 'I sleep when I breathe.' Tell them to say their lines in a very sleepy voice. Play a game of 'sleeping dormice', where the children start by pretending to eat nuts and berries and then curl up in a ball and try to stay very still while the Mad Hatter attempts to make them laugh! Establish that, in the story, the dormouse is constantly dozing off and ask the children to suggest why the dormouse is so sleepy.

Whole-class work

1. Display some images of real dormice awake and active, on stalks of grass, and curled up fast asleep in their nests. Talk about what they look like and what they are doing in the pictures. Explain that dormice are able to survive cold winters by going to sleep for a few months. This type of very long sleep is called 'hibernation'.

2. Show the class some more images of animals that hibernate over winter in the UK; these include hedgehogs and bats. Animals that hibernate need to eat as much food as they can at the end of the summer, so they won't have to feed over the winter. Hedgehogs crawl under piles of leaves or plant cuttings, while dormice build little nests to curl up in. Bats hibernate in caves, tunnels and even in the lofts of houses. Some other UK animals, such as frogs, do not truly hibernate, but can spend much of the winter asleep in a safe and cosy place.

Independent work

3. Provide the children with photocopiable page 105 'Hibernating animals'. Ask them to identify each animal and match it to the place where it hibernates.

4. Ask the children to make a large drawing of one of the locations from the photocopiable sheet and draw the correct animal snuggled up inside it for the winter.

Differentiation
- Support children with name labels to glue and stick by each animal. Provide enlarged photocopiable sheets so that the pictures of animals and hibernation locations can be cut out and matched.
- Challenge children to add more detail to their pictures and to write sentences to describe the animals that hibernate.

Science in the wider world

Breathing, body temperature and heart rates drop as animals enter a state of hibernation, which enables them to save energy during the cold winter months. For example, a hedgehog's heart rate slows from around 190 beats per minute (bpm) to 20bpm. Depending on when the first frosts arrive, dormice can sleep from October to May, when food becomes available again. Bats are able to come out of periods of torpor if the weather becomes milder but are generally fully hibernating by December.

Review

Children can be assessed on their observations about dormice and their completion of the photocopiable sheet.

Objectives
● To measure and record weather conditions.
● To know that in spring the weather begins to get warmer, but can still be cold.

Resources
Video footage of children's weather reports from autumn 1, week 3, lesson 1; class weather chart from autumn 1; temperature chart from spring 1; enlarged photocopiable page 38 'Weather chart'; weather measurement instruments from autumn 1; interactive activity 'Changing seasons' on the CD-ROM; interactive activity 'Wind' on the CD-ROM

Speaking scientifically
temperature, thermometer, weather vane, rainfall, wind speed

Lesson 3: Spring weather

Introduction
Show the class some of the video footage of their weather reports that they made during their work on seasons in autumn 1, week 3, lesson 1. Look at the class weather chart from autumn 1 and list the types of measurement the children made: temperature, wind direction and amount of rainfall. Use this to identify times when there was a lot of rain during the autumn. Display any temperature readings they have taken previously and identify the warmest and coldest days. Ask the children if they think their measurements would be different if they were to take some more now. Encourage them to make comparisons and suggest ways in which early spring weather could be similar or different from that in the autumn or winter; suggest that it may be gradually getting warmer now, although it can still be very cold, with snow often falling in February (and beyond). Do the interactive activity 'Changing seasons' on the CD-ROM together.

Whole-class work
1. Display the thermometer, rainfall gauge and wind measurers which the children used previously and ask them to describe how these work. Tell the children that over the next few lessons they will be using these to make some new weather measurements.

2. Ask the children to look out of the classroom window to see if there are any signs of the wind. Draw their attention to swaying trees or bits of rubbish blowing in the playground. Remind them about the Beaufort scale they found out about in autumn 1, week 3, lesson 3. Use the interactive activity 'Wind' on the CD-ROM to revise how to identify differing wind strengths again.

3. Take the wind measurers, rain gauge and thermometer into the playground and place the latter two back in the same positions as last term. Distribute the wind measurers and tell them to find out where the wind is blowing from. Encourage them to describe the strength of the wind by thinking about which of the plastic strips are moving, how much trees are moving, and so on. Before going back inside, take a temperature reading from the thermometer.

4. Back in class, display an enlarged photocopiable page 38 'Weather chart' and ask the children to suggest how to fill in the information they have just gathered in the playground. Look at the symbols and select the most appropriate ones to go alongside their temperature and wind observations.

Independent work
5. Provide children with the photocopiable sheet and ask them to complete it by drawing in the appropriate symbols for the day. Explain that they will be adding to it over a few weeks to build up their own record of weather measurements.

> **Differentiation**
> ● Support children by enlarging the chart and providing symbols and labels to cut and stick.
> ● Challenge children to think about some of the measurements from autumn and to predict how much rain they might collect in their gauge this time.

Science in the wider world
There is much debate as to when spring officially starts in the UK. As the year is divided between four seasons, the first day of spring could be taken as 1 March, although the vernal (spring) equinox does not occur until around 20 March. February is considered to be the coldest month of the year, so there is no guarantee that mild spring weather will suddenly appear as February ends and March begins.

Review
Children could be assessed on their weather observations and weather charts.

Objectives
- To observe the apparent movement of the Sun during the day.
- To create models showing the apparent movement of the Sun.
- To understand the position of the Sun at different times of day.

Resources
Sunrise–sunset timelines from autumn 1, week 2, lesson 2; completed examples of photocopiable page 103 'Light and dark' from week 1, lesson 3; images or video footage of sunrise and sunset; interactive activity 'Day and night' on the CD-ROM; paper plates cut in half; paints; craft materials; plastic drinking straws; circles of yellow card; split pins

Speaking scientifically
sunrise, sunset, daylight, night, long, short, horizon

Lesson 1: Sunrise and sunset

Introduction

Prior to this lesson, make a sunrise–sunset model to demonstrate to your class (see 2–6 below).

Display completed examples of photocopiable page 103 'Light and dark', which the children worked on in week 1, lesson 3 when they were thinking about what daylight is like in winter. Remind them of some of their observations about having to switch on lights when they got home from school, getting up in the dark, and so on. Ask them if they have noticed anything changing since they filled in the photocopiable sheet. Work through the true or false questions together in the interactive activity 'Day and night' on the CD-ROM. Remind the class of the timelines they completed in the autumn term and compare these with their more recent observations. Draw the children's attention to the sunrise and sunset at the beginning and end of their timelines and ask them to explain what these are and why they added them on. Show some images or video footage of sunrise and sunset and reiterate that these mark the beginning and end of daylight.

Whole-class work

1. Tell the children that they are going to make a model to show where the Sun is in the sky during the day. Show one that you made earlier and talk about what happens to the Sun as you move it in a clockwise direction, encouraging the children to say 'sunrise' as the movement begins and 'sunset' as it ends, at the other side of the plate.

2. Demonstrate how the children are going to make their models. Explain that they will start with half a paper plate each, on which they are going to paint a daytime scene. Encourage the children to suggest ideas about what a suitable picture for this might be.

3. Provide craft materials for them to decorate a yellow circle of card to represent the Sun while their daytime paintings dry. The Sun can then be glued to one end of a drinking straw.

4. When their painting work is dry, the drinking straw arm can be loosely attached with a split pin to the middle of the plate, about 2cm above the 'horizon' (the bottom edge of the plate).

5. Swing the arm to the edge of the plate on the left and tell the children that this is sunrise. Gradually move the Sun away from the horizon, but point out that it is still low in the sky. Continue to move the arm until it is at right angles to the horizon and explain that this is midday, then carry on until the arm reaches the right-hand side of the plate – sunset.

6. Use the models as you might do small clock faces, instructing the children to show you sunrise, midday, late afternoon, and so on, by moving the arm to the correct part of the sky.

Science in the wider world

The Earth takes 24 hours to rotate once on its axis. As it does so, the part of the Earth that is facing towards the Sun experiences daylight. The part that has turned away from the Sun is in darkness. It is this turning that makes the sun *appear* to move across the sky. Sunrise is the time at which the upper part of the Sun becomes visible above the horizon and sunset occurs as the last part of the Sun is about to disappear from view. The times for these are generally based on what is happening at sea level, but if the viewer is surrounded by mountains then sunrise will occur later and sunset earlier.

Review

Children could be assessed on the different times of the day they can show on their model.

Objectives
• To know that the Sun appears to move across the sky.
• To know the difference between sunrise and sunset.

Resources
Children's sunrise–sunset models made in the previous lesson, chalk, a pointer on a long handle

Speaking scientifically
sunrise, sunset, daylight, night, long, short, horizon, summer, winter

Lesson 2: What's the time Mr Wolf?

Introduction

As the main activity will require spending quite a bit of time in the playground, you may wish to choose a mild day for this lesson!

Begin by looking at the models from the previous lesson. Ask the children to move the Sun to show sunrise, midday and sunset. Challenge them to show 11am or 1pm. Talk about what time sunset is currently happening.

Whole-class work

1. Outside, teach your class to play 'What's the time Mr Wolf?' To begin with, you will need to select a 'wolf'. This child stands facing a wall while the rest of the class line up in a long row across the other end of the playground.

2. When everyone is in position, the game begins with the class calling loudly, in unison, *What's the time Mr Wolf?* The 'wolf' then shouts out a time, for example *3 o'clock*, and the children walk forward the same number of steps, counting them out loudly as they do so.

3. The children continue to ask Mr Wolf the time and count out their steps based on the answer. At any point, however, the wolf may shout out *Dinner time*, whereupon he or she turns away from the wall and gives chase to the rest of the class. Whoever is caught becomes the next wolf.

4. Play a variation of the game to link with the Sun's movement across the sky. Draw a large semicircle with chalk on the wall, next to where the wolf will stand. Write '12 noon' at the top of the arch, in the centre. To the left count back to 7am and to the right count forward to 6pm, spacing the numbers along the edge of the semicircle. Give the wolf a large pointer. When everyone is in position at the beginning of the game, the wolf shouts *Sunrise* and points to the far left of the semicircle. Each time the wolf is asked the time, he or she shouts back one of the times on the wall and indicates it with the pointer. Instead of shouting *Dinner time*, the wolf shouts *Sunset* before giving chase to the other children.

5. When the children have played this version a few times, explain that they are going to pretend it is summer. Put new numbers on the semicircle ranging from 5am to 9pm, and ask the children to explain why you have done this. Ensure they understand that sunrise happens earlier and sunset later in summer, and there is daylight for longer.

6. Play the new version a few times. Finish by asking the children to say what the differences were between the two versions – and which one they preferred.

Science in the wider world

In the UK, the Sun is only at its highest point at midday when GMT (Greenwich Mean Time) is in operation. When the clocks are put forward by 1 hour onto BST (British Summer Time), the Sun is actually at its highest point at 1pm. For the purposes of the game, however, stick to midday. The times of sunrise and sunset in the game have also been rounded to the nearest hour. By the summer solstice, in central England sunrise is around 4.45am and sunset is in the region of 9.30pm. By mid-December, the Sun does not rise until around 8.15am and has set again by 4pm.

Review

Children can be assessed on their observations about differences between sunrise and sunset in summer and winter.

Objectives
- To recognise that spring follows winter.
- To know that plants begin to grow as winter ends.
- To identify some of the changes that take place as spring begins.

Resources
Photographs taken during the topic of wintery scenes; seasons mobile from autumn 1, week 1, lesson 2; images of winter and spring: hibernating dormouse, bare tree, frogspawn, snowdrops, icicles, pussy willow trees; photocopiable page 106 'Signs of spring'

Speaking scientifically
season, autumn, winter, spring, summer, temperature, hibernation, growth

Lesson 3: Signs of spring

Introduction
Display some of the photographs of wintery scenes taken during this topic, for example during the 'winter wonderland' visit in week 1, lesson 1 and from investigations in the playground. Encourage the children to talk about all the work they have done on winter, such as how plants and animals are affected and all their wintery weather observations. Prompt their recall as necessary and make a class list about winter, which could include entries about lessening daylight, trees losing their leaves and animals going into hibernation. Ask the children how much longer they think the winter will last and point out where the current month is on your seasons mobile.

Whole-class work
1. Establish that winter will soon be coming to an end and check that the children recognise that the next season will be spring. Point to the class winter list you have just made and ask the children how they think any affected plants and animals might begin to change again. Add their ideas to a second column under the heading 'spring'.

2. Encourage the children to think about what the first signs of spring might be and display images corresponding to those on photocopiable page 106 'Signs of spring', including a hibernating dormouse, a bare tree, frogspawn, snowdrops, icicles and pussy willow trees. Show one image at a time, ask the children to identify it, and then talk about whether it is something that has happened over the winter, or a sign of spring.

3. Challenge the children to start looking out for signs of spring and to be the first child to bring in a picture of something they have spotted out of school!

4. Display an enlarged photocopiable sheet and point out the pictures, the labels and the headings 'winter' and 'spring'.

Independent work
5. Provide each child with the photocopiable sheet and ask them to complete it by looking at the pictures and deciding which heading each one should go under.

Differentiation
- Support children by providing them with an enlarged photocopiable sheet, to cut and paste pictures under the correct headings.
- Challenge children by asking them to write the labels under the correct headings and to add more examples to each column.

Science in the wider world
As daylight lengthens and temperatures begin to rise, plants that have been dormant over the winter start to put out new leaves again. The soft, velvety pussy willow catkins are one of the first signs of spring, as is the appearance of frogspawn in ponds and ditches. Early spring flowers such as snowdrops, crocuses and daffodils begin to appear, hedgehogs emerge from their winter hibernation and squirrels and birds become more active. Farmers, too, are busy with the arrival of lambs at this time of year.

Review
Children could be assessed on the comparisons they make between winter and spring and their completion of the photocopiable sheet.

Objectives
- To identify and record signs of spring.
- To compare spring with winter and autumn.

Resources
Photographs and display work from visit to park in autumn 1, week 1, lesson1; images of winter and spring from previous lesson; examples of completed photocopiable page 106 'Signs of spring'; cameras; paper; clipboards and pencils; disposable or gardening gloves; collecting bags; laminated photocopiable page 36 'Tree identification chart' from previous term; interactive activities 'Autumn and winter' and 'Signs of spring' on the CD-ROM; sheets of paper split into two equal sections

Speaking scientifically
season, autumn, winter, spring, summer, temperature, deciduous, evergreen, dormant, growth, leaf, bud, blossom, catkin, flower, frogspawn

Lesson 1: Seasonal change

Introduction
Remind the children of their 'hunt for autumn' in week 1, lesson 1, autumn 1, when they visited a local park. Encourage them to recall what they did and saw there and show the photographs and display work based on their observations. Recap on the signs of autumn and winter they noticed then and ask the children what will be changing in the park now. Make a list of their ideas and any questions they may have. Talk about their recent work on the signs of spring and display the images you used, such as a bare tree, icicles, frogspawn and snowdrops. Talk about some of their completed photocopiable sheets or use interactive activity 'Signs of spring' on the CD-ROM. Explain that they are going back to the same areas of the park to see if spring has started.

Whole-class work
1. As before, prior to this lesson, you will need to prepare for an off-site educational visit by carrying out a thorough risk assessment and obtaining permission from parents and carers. Consider details such as transport, food, clothing, medical requirements (including any allergies) and an appropriate level of adult support. Once again, establish ground rules for staying safe and remind the children to use gloves to collect natural objects that have fallen (they should not be picked) and to tell an adult if they come across rubbish or dog mess.

2. Provide children with clipboards and paper and begin your visit in the same place as last time. Encourage the children to notice any changes in the trees, such as leaf buds, catkins or blossom appearing, and for signs of flowers such as crocuses and daffodils. Explain that birds are becoming more active again and that the children should listen and watch out for any flying between the trees – possibly with nesting materials in their beaks. They should also make a note of any squirrels and insects they come across.

3. If there is a pond in the park, assess whether it is safe to take supervised groups to look for evidence of frogspawn.

Group work
4. Divide the class into small adult-led groups and direct them to different locations in the park. Tell the children to collect any evidence of spring, such as fallen blossom petals, using gloves and their special collection bags. Ask them to make drawings and to take photographs of any signs of change.

5. At the end of the visit, collect the whole class together again and review all their findings. Collate their drawings, photographs and other evidence of spring for a classroom display. Challenge the children to start noticing and reporting their observations as they travel to and from school or are out and about at weekends.

Paired work
6. Back in class, work through the interactive activity 'Autumn and winter' on the CD-ROM. Then provide children with small photographs of the park from the spring trip and an earlier autumn/winter trip and ask them to put these into groups that show the same area. Tell them to select two and to glue them onto a recording sheet. They could then describe what they notice.

Science in the wider world
The timing and speed with which deciduous trees put out buds and blossom will vary from year to year, depending on the weather. A continuation of low temperatures and ice can mean considerable delay, while an early mild spell will bring out blossom and bulbs, as well as animals that feed on them.

Review
Children could be assessed on the observations they make about spring and their comparison work on seasonal photographs.

Objectives
- To suggest seasonal changes that may have happened to a tree.
- To make scientific observations of a tree.
- To identify and record changes to a tree in spring.

Resources
Autumn/winter photographs of tree 'adopted' in autumn 1, week 6, lesson 2; completed examples of photocopiable page 'Our tree' from the CD-ROM; paper; a length of string or measuring tape; magnifiers; camera; photocopiable page 107 'Our tree in spring'

Speaking scientifically
change, grow, branch, trunk, leaf, root, bud, flower, spring, summer, autumn, winter

Lesson 2: Trees in spring

Introduction
Remind your class that, in addition to their visits to the park to observe what is happening as the seasons change, they have also been keeping an eye on a tree much closer at hand. Display the photographs you took of this tree in the autumn term and talk about what it is called, its location in the playground or local area and how it has changed so far. Show the children some of their completed examples of photocopiable page 'Our tree'. Ask them if they think the tree will have grown over the winter and what they might see under the tree now. Encourage them to explain their ideas and to describe any changes they have noticed since the initial photographs were taken.

Whole-class work
1. Take the class outside to make some observations of their adopted tree. Begin by looking at it from a distance and talking about what the children notice before going closer to the tree.

2. Tell the children to now look carefully and use the magnifiers to make close-up inspections. Encourage them to check whether the tree has started to grow leaf buds or blossom and what these look like, if so. Ask them to see if there are any variations in the colour of the trunk and branches and to try to recall whether this is the same as or different from last time. Remind them that the trunk may be a different colour on one side because the wind and rain come mainly from that direction.

3. Look around to see if any of the roots are visible and talk about anything else the children notice under the tree. Ask them to suggest where the fallen leaves could have gone and to notice whether any plants are starting to grow around the bottom of the tree.

4. Tell the children to measure around the trunk with a length of string or a measuring tape and to take photographs and bark rubbings of their tree.

5. Back in class, collate all their findings and straighten out the length of string that you used to measure the girth of the tree and compare it with the heights of the children, and to the length of string you used to take the trunk measurement in the autumn term.

6. Ask them to describe what they think the tree will look like in the summer.

Independent work
7. Give the children the 'Our tree' work that they did in the autumn term. Ask them to think about what has changed since then and to complete photocopiable page 107 'Our tree in spring', colouring the trees appropriately.

Differentiation
- Support children with the photocopiable sheet by providing labels for them to paste on.
- Challenge children to add in more detail and write further sentences about their tree.

Science in the wider world
Every growth season, trees add a new layer of wood to their trunks and limbs. These appear as rings of concentric circles, making patterns of light and dark. By counting the number of rings, it is possible to work out the age of a tree. Early wood is light and formed when the tree is growing rapidly in the spring and early summer, while the darker portion is the late wood, formed as the growing season begins to slow down again. These light and dark woods together represent a year's growth for the tree.

Review
Children could be assessed on the observations they make about their tree and their recording of how it has changed.

Objectives
● To identify that there are different weather conditions in different seasons.
● To identify which weather conditions will produce shadows.
● To match weather sayings to the conditions they describe.

Resources
Images of groundhogs (woodchucks); a camera; photocopiable page 108 'Weather sayings'

Speaking scientifically
sun, shadow, season, winter, spring, summer, autumn, hibernation, groundhog, weather

Lesson 3: Groundhog Day

Introduction
Remind the children of the work they did previously on hibernating animals and explain that many animals in other parts of the world also sleep through the winter months. Display an image of a groundhog (woodchuck) and tell the children that this animal is a member of the squirrel family and lives in the USA. It hibernates over the winter and its awakening has become the stuff of legends in America! Groundhog Day is held on 2 February each year and the traditional belief is that if a groundhog can see his shadow on this particular day, then winter will last for another six weeks.

Whole-class work
1. Explain to your class that there are many old sayings about the weather and seasons, such as 'Red sky at night, shepherds delight,' and 'March winds and April showers bring forth May flowers.' Another one is 'If Candlemas Day is bright and clear, there'll be two winters in the year.' Ask your class what these sayings might mean and clarify that the latter means that, if the sun shines on Candlemas Day, 2 February, then winter is not over.

2. In the town of Punxsutawney in Pennsylvania, people began to link Candlemas Day with the end of hibernation for groundhogs in the area. Candlemas Day became known as Groundhog Day and a new saying evolved: 'If the sun shines on Groundhog Day, half the fuel and half the hay.' In other words, six more weeks of using up fuel to keep warm and a further delay to crop planting.

3. Over 100 years ago, the town named a local groundhog 'Punxsutawney Phil'. They began to gather outside his burrow on 2 February to see if his body cast a shadow as he emerged. Now every year on this date there are early morning festivals to watch groundhogs emerge from their burrows.

4. Remind your class of the work they did on shadows in autumn 1, week 2, lesson 1 and ask them to describe how shadows are made. Tell the children that you are going on a shadow hunt in the playground and encourage them to say how likely they are to find any.

5. Walk the children around the school grounds, pausing to look for shadows and taking photographs of any that you see.

Independent work
6. Read through the weather sayings on photocopiable page 108 'Weather sayings' and talk about what each one means. Tell the children to complete the photocopiable sheet by matching the sayings to the pictures and colouring it in.

> ### Differentiation
> ● Support children by limiting the number of sayings you ask them to match.
> ● Challenge children to explain what they think each saying means.

Science in the wider world
Groundhogs are the largest members of the squirrel family and, although they are usually seen on the ground, they can also climb trees and even swim. They are often found on the edge of woodlands, in fields or by streams, where they eat grasses and plants as well as fruits and tree bark. The most famous groundhog is Punxsutawney Phil, who has apparently been making predictions for over 125 years – the local explanation for this long life is that Phil is kept alive with a magical potion!

Review
Children could be assessed on their observations regarding the Sun and shadows and completion of the photocopiable sheet.

■SCHOLASTIC

Objectives
● To observe and describe weather associated with the seasons (winter/spring).

Resources
Class weather chart completed during this topic; photographs of icy hands and huddling penguins investigations (week 2, lesson I and week 4, lesson I); photographs of the 'winter wonderland' visit in week I, lesson I; a selection of children's clothes appropriate for different seasons; photocopiable page 41 'Dress for the season'; a list of words associated with winter clothing; swatches of warm and cool fabrics; glue

Working scientifically
● To identify and classify.
● *To make comparisons and decide how to sort and group.*
● To gather and record data.

Dressed for the season

Revise
● Display the class weather chart you made during this topic and talk about what you found out. Ask the children to identify the warmest and coldest days during the observation period, say how much rain fell and how strong the winds have been. Talk about the temperature readings for days when there was ice or snow on the ground and display photographs of the icy hands and huddling penguins investigations. Ask the children to describe what they did and what they found out about wintery weather. Ensure they recognise that the outdoor icy hand did not melt as much as the indoor one because it was colder in the playground than in the classroom; and that the penguins huddling around the hot water bottle kept the water inside warmer than the water in the unprotected bottle. Display some articles of children's clothing appropriate for different seasons, and ask the class to say when they might wear any of these. Talk about the type of clothing the children are currently wearing. Link their observations with photographs of the 'winter wonderland' visit and talk about why they dressed warmly.

Assess
● Show the class a further selection of children's clothing appropriate for different weather conditions. This could include a variety of hats, jackets and footwear, as well as scarves, gloves, tops and trousers. Ask them to feel the clothes and to make observations about how they are similar to or different from each other.
● Provide each child with a model cut from photocopiable page 41 'Dress for the season'. Ask them to draw appropriate winter clothing on the model and to colour it in.
● Tell the children to then draw or paint a suitable seasonal outdoor backdrop for their models on a sheet of plain paper. When their picture is finished, they should decide where to place their model in the scene and glue it on.
● Ask them to select appropriate labels from the list of words you have supplied to describe the clothing they have chosen and to glue these around their models.
● Give the children a selection of fabric swatches and a sheet of paper divided into two sections, or with two circles drawn on it. Tell them to choose some warm winter fabrics to glue in one section and some that they think would keep them cool in the summer to glue in the other. Ask them to label their groups with the appropriate season.
● Tell the children to draw another picture to show how any of the animals they have found out about during this topic cope with wintery conditions (this could be huddling penguins or hibernating animals).

Further practice
● Support children by providing a smaller list of words for them to select labels from, or give them ready-made labels to attach directly to their pictures. Ask them to talk about which fabrics are suitable for winter and which are better for warmer weather.
● Challenge children to demonstrate their knowledge and understanding of seasonal change further, using simple scientific vocabulary to describe weather and fabrics. Ask them to name other animals that hibernate and to make other comparisons between seasons based on what they have covered so far.

Objectives
● To observe changes across the four seasons.

Resources
Images of dormouse, squirrel, blue tit, emperor penguin and human in summer and winter; photographs of pussy willows, frogspawn and daffodils; photocopiable page 109 'What do animals do in winter?'; photocopiable page 107 'Our tree in spring'; photographs from topic work on seasons covering autumn, winter and the start of spring; thumbnails of these photographs for children to label

Working scientifically
● To observe closely, using simple equipment.
● *To make comparisons.*
● To gather and record data to help in answering questions.

Animals and plants

Revise

● Show the class images of a dormouse, squirrel, blue tit, emperor penguin and human involved in a range of activities such as feeding, nesting, looking after young and playing. Ask the children to say whether they think these are activities that the animals have been doing in the winter.

● Encourage them to explain their ideas and then display different photographs of the same animals taken during the winter. How do these compare with what the animals are doing at other times of the year?

● Remind your class of their visit to the park to look for signs of spring. Ask the children to give examples of some of the things they noticed and show them photographs of pussy willows, frogspawn and daffodils to prompt their ideas further.

● Display the photographs you took of your adopted tree and talk about how it has changed so far. Ask them to recall any signs of spring they noticed on their tree.

● Play a game with the children to help them recognise different seasons. Show them images from their work and visits relating to autumn, winter and the beginnings of spring. Tell them to guess which one you are thinking of, by asking questions you will only answer yes or no to.

● Alternatively, show one image at a time and tell the children to call out the season they think it portrays.

Assess

● Give each child photocopiable page 109 'What do animals do in winter?' On the sheet there are images of five different animals: a dormouse, squirrel, blue tit, emperor penguin and human; and there are five statements in a jumbled order. The children need to decide which animal is being described in each statement and draw lines to connect it to the correct picture.

● At the bottom of the photocopiable page, the names of all the animals are displayed. Ask the children to write the correct name by each picture.

● Provide children with photocopiable page 107 'Our tree in spring'. Tell them to complete this independently, adding details about how the tree is changing as spring arrives.

● Show the children a selection of photographs from their topic work on the seasons, covering autumn, winter and the start of spring. Tell them to label these images with the most appropriate season.

Further practice

● Support children by providing labels for them to paste onto the photocopiable pages 'What do animals do in winter?' and 'Our tree in spring'. Supply labels with names of seasons for them to attach to the photographs.

● Challenge children to demonstrate their knowledge and understanding of seasonal change further, by using simple scientific vocabulary to write additional sentences about how animals and trees change as spring arrives. Ask them to make other comparisons between the seasons based on what they have covered so far.

- To observe the apparent movement of the Sun during the day.
- To observe how day length varies.

Resources
Video footage or images of activity on a dark winter's day; sunrise–sunset models from week 5, lesson 1; photographs of groundhogs; sheets of paper with a semicircle on it with room for drawings and labels; photocopiable page 'Timeline image sheet' from the CD-ROM; photocopiable page 'What's the time Mr Wolf?' from the CD-ROM

Working scientifically
- *To use simple scientific language.*

Following the Sun

Revise

- Recap on the work the children did earlier in the term, finding out about activities that happen in the dark during winter. Remind them that sometimes they need the lights on and the curtains drawn when they are getting up in the morning on a school day and when they get home again in the afternoon. Ask the children to describe what happens when they go to after-school activities or on other occasions when they are later returning home than usual, thinking about whether street and car lights are on. Show some video footage or display images of people going about their daily business, working, shopping and travelling, on short winter days. Encourage the children to make observations about how dark it is outside on these occasions, though there are still lots of people about.
- Display some of the sunrise–sunset models the children made with paper plates and drinking straws. Ask them to explain how they work and check that they can identify sunrise and sunset as you show them. They should also be able to say that, when the Sun is in the middle, it is midday. Remind the children of the 'What's the time Mr Wolf?' games they played and ask them to explain the sunset rule and say why it is different in summer and winter. Look at some photographs of groundhogs and ask the children to explain what happens on Groundhog Day in America.

Assess

- Give each child a sheet of paper with a semicircle on it. Below the semicircle write 'In the dark' and in the middle of the semicircle write 'In the daylight'. Tell the children to draw a sunrise at one end. Ask the children also to draw in where they think the Sun would be in the middle of the day.
- Provide children with photocopiable page 'Timeline image sheet' on the CD-ROM. Tell the children that they should next choose from the illustrations of activities and cut and stick one on the morning side of their semicircle and then find one for the afternoon side.
- Ask them to find a third illustration of an activity that happens in the dark and stick that below the semicircle at the bottom of the page.
- Provide each child with photocopiable page 'What's the time Mr Wolf?' from the CD-ROM. This shows two semicircles and a puzzled Mr Wolf. Each semicircle has a sunrise, sunset and midday Sun drawn on, but one has numbers that go from 7am to 6pm and the other has numbers that go from 5am to 9pm. Ask the children to write in 'sunrise', 'sunset' and 'midday' on each of the semicircles.
- Then explain that Mr Wolf is playing a summer game and a winter game and ask the children to label each semicircle with the right season.

Further practice

- Support children by limiting the images and labels you ask them to stick onto sheets.
- Challenge children to demonstrate their knowledge and understanding further by asking them to add in times around their semicircle in the first activity. They could also write some sentences to describe how days are longer in the summer than they are in the autumn and winter.

Name: _____ Date: _____

Wintery scene

■ Look carefully at this wintery scene. Label the signs of winter and colour it in.

| snow | frozen | ice |
| slippery | cold | warm clothes |

I can find signs of winter in the park.

How did you do?

PHOTOCOPIABLE

■ SCHOLASTIC
www.scholastic.co.uk

Name: _____ Date: _____

Light and dark

■ Sort these activities into those that happen in the light and those that happen in the dark in winter.

✂

Animal footprints

■ Identify these animals and match them to their footprints.

squirrel

duck

sparrow

badger

rabbit

fox

I can match animals to their footprints.

How did you do?

Hibernating animals

■ Name these animals. Match each animal to the place it sleeps during winter.

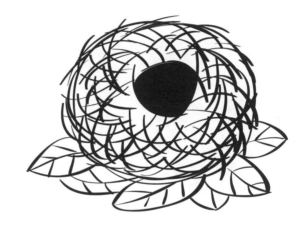

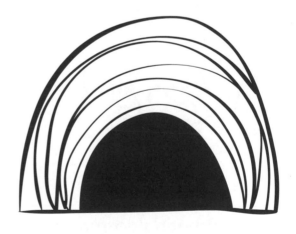

| dormouse | bat | hedgehog |

I can name animals and show where they sleep in winter.

How did you do?

Signs of spring

■ Look at the pictures and link them to the right season.

winter	spring

(hibernating dormouse)   (bare tree)   (frogspawn)

(snowdrops)   (icicles)   (pussy willows)

I can show how some plants and animals change with the seasons.

How did you do?

PHOTOCOPIABLE

SCHOLASTIC
www.scholastic.co.uk

Our tree in spring

■ How has your tree changed since the autumn? Draw in the things you notice have changed.

leaves   branches   trunk

roots   buds   blossom   plants

I can see spring changes in our tree.

How did you do?

Weather sayings

Link each saying to the correct meaning.

Red sky
at night,
shepherds
delight.

It will rain.

The louder
the frog, the
more it will
rain.

Spring will be
late.

If the sun
shines on
Groundhog
Day, half the
fuel and half
the hay.

Tomorrow will
be dry and calm.

I can match weather sayings to weather conditions.

How did you do?

PHOTOCOPIABLE

What do animals do in winter?

**Draw lines to connect each picture of an animal to its description.
Write the correct name by each picture.**

| I huddle up with my friends. |

| I have a nice long sleep. |

_____

| I have a warm hat and coat. |

_____

| I visit gardens to look for food. |

_____

| I'm very good at getting to food that wasn't meant for me. |

_____

_____

(dormouse)   (squirrel)   (blue tit)

(emperor penguin)   (human)

I can say what some animals do in winter.

How did you do?

Plants

Expected prior learning
- Some similarities and differences between living things.
- Features of immediate environment compared to others.
- Names of some common plants and how these are affected by seasonal change.

Overview of progression
After completing this chapter the children should know:
- names of a variety of common garden and wild plants
- the basic structure of a variety of common flowering plants
- names of a variety of deciduous and evergreen trees.

Creative context
- This topic provides many opportunities for children to make observational drawings and use images to present their findings.
- Children will be required to deploy their design and technology skills when making models of flowering plants and designing willow structures.
- The natural environment lends itself to various forms of creative writing, song, music and dance.

Background knowledge

Common garden and wild plants
Annuals, including busy lizzies, pansies and petunias, generally only flower once and are usually added to gardens for a splash of summer colour. Perennials such as lupins and primroses die back in the autumn, but reappear the following year. Daffodils, tulips and lilies grow from bulbs. Wild plants are protected by law and must not to be picked. Be aware that many plants, including sweet peas and foxgloves are poisonous – check thoroughly for toxins and potential allergies before introducing any plants into your classroom.

Common flowering plants
Flowering plants produce flowers for reproduction. Generally, these are brightly coloured and scented to attract insects, who visit to drink a sweet liquid called nectar. In the process, pollen produced on the stamens of the flower rubs off onto their bodies. As the insect visits another flower, the pollen is transferred to the stigma. This is called pollination. Fertilisation occurs when the insides of pollen grains travel down the style to the ovaries and fuse together with ovules to form seeds. These are dispersed from the plant by animals, the wind or flicking out.

Speaking scientifically
- In this chapter, the children will have opportunities to work scientifically and identify and name a variety of common plants and describe the basic structure of some flowering plants. A simple scientific vocabulary will enable the children to comment on their observations and could include: deciduous, evergreen, fruit, coniferous, trunks, branches, stems, leaves, seeds, bulbs, temperature, tropical, arid, annuals, perennials, seedlings, germinate, corm, tuber, rhizome, nectar, pollen, environment.

Preparation
You will need to provide: seeds and bulbs, plant pots and containers, compost, magnifiers, gardening or disposable gloves, cameras; wide selection of plants, flowers, and so on.

On the CD-ROM you will find: photocopiable pages 'Seed diary (1)', 'Seed diary (2)', 'Seed diary (3)', 'Make a flower', 'Deciduous trees'; interactive activities 'Who am I?', 'Plant parts'; media resource 'Record-breaking trees', 'Where do plants live?'

■SCHOLASTIC

Chapter at a glance

Week	Lesson	Curriculum objectives	Lesson objectives	Main activity	Working scientifically
1	1	• To identify and name a variety of common wild and garden plants.	• To know the names of some flowering plants. • To know the main parts of flowering plants. • To observe and record the appearance of plants. • To observe and recount conditions plants grow in.	Inspiring a sense of wonder through a visit to botanical gardens. Observing a variety of plants and looking for signs of growth. Making simple plant observations.	• Asking simple questions. • Identifying and classifying. • Observing closely. • Making comparisons. • Gathering and recording data to help in answering questions.
	2	• To identify and name a variety of common wild and garden plants.	• To know some names of common garden flowering plants. • To compare some common garden flowering plants. • To be able to identify some common garden flowering plants.	Eliciting children's knowledge of plant names. Looking at images of garden plants and identifying similarities/ differences. Linking plant names through games.	• Asking simple questions • Observing closely. • Making comparisons.
	3	• To identify and name a variety of common wild and garden plants.	• To know some names of common wild flowering plants. • To compare some common wild flowering plants. • To identify some common wild flowering plants.	Looking at images of wild plants. Displaying dandelions and asking children to identify different parts. Observing how potted dandelions grow and change in the classroom.	• Asking simple questions. • Observing closely. • Making comparisons and deciding how to sort and group.
2	1	• To identify and describe the basic structure of a variety of common flowering plants including trees.	• To know that flowering plants grow from seeds. • To observe, measure and record carefully the germination process of a bean.	Reading 'Jack and the Beanstalk' and discussing how long it really takes bean plants to grow. Planting beans and observing how they grow and change.	• Asking simple questions. • Identifying and classifying. • Observing closely. • Making comparisons. • Gathering and recording data to help in answering questions.
	2	• To identify and describe the basic structure of a variety of common flowering plants including trees.	• To observe and compare a plant that has been watered with one that has not. • To observe and identify the basic structure of a plant. • To know that flowering plants have roots.	Looking at a dried-out pot plant and comparing with one watered regularly. Discussing the role of roots. Watering the dry plant and drawing 'before' and 'after'.	• Asking simple questions. • Identifying and classifying. • Observing closely. • Making comparisons. • Gathering and recording data to help in answering questions.
	3	• To identify and describe the basic structure of a variety of common flowering plants including trees.	• To know that some flowering plants grow from bulbs. • To recognise some common plants that grow from bulbs. • To observe and record the growth of a hyacinth bulb.	Explaining that some plants grow from bulbs. Playing 'odd one out' game to identify plants that grow from bulbs. Observing the growth of hyacinths from bulbs.	• Asking simple questions. • Observing closely. • Identifying and classifying.
3	1	• To identify and describe the basic structure of a variety of common flowering plants including trees.	• To understand that plants grow from seeds. • To compare seeds from different plants. • To recognise the conditions needed for germination. • To observe and record the germination of seeds.	Looking at examples of common fruit: seeds/conkers/ acorns. Comparing with packs of seeds. Growing cress seeds on damp paper towels and keeping a diary of how they grow.	• Asking simple questions. • Identifying and classifying. • Observing closely. • Making comparisons. • Gathering and recording data to help in answering questions.
	2	• To identify and describe the basic structure of a variety of common flowering plants including trees.	• To carry out an experiment showing the effect of light and dark on plants. • To understand that plants need light for healthy growth.	Comparing two specimens of plant. Identifying differences and recording with drawings.	• Asking simple questions. • Observing closely. • Making comparisons. • Gathering and recording data to help in answering questions.
	3	• To identify and describe the basic structure of a variety of common flowering plants including trees.	• To understand why plants have flowers. • To suggest why flowers are sometimes scented and colourful. • To revise basic plant structure.	Looking at images showing how buds open into flowers and how flowers are visited by insects. Making model flowers.	• Asking simple questions. • Identifying and classifying. • Observing closely. • Making comparisons.

Chapter at a glance

Week	Lesson	Curriculum objectives	Lesson objectives	Main activity	Working scientifically
4	1	• To identify and describe the basic structure of a variety of common flowering plants including trees.	• To observe and compare the roots of two different plants. • To observe and record the roots of some root vegetables.	Planting germinated bean seeds in clear containers filled with pebbles to observe their roots. Looking at examples of roots on vegetables. Making comparisons between different root systems.	• Asking simple questions. • Identifying and classifying. • Observing closely. • Making comparisons.
	2	• To identify and describe the basic structure of a variety of common flowering plants including trees.	• To revise common plant names. • To recount plant investigations • To observe and record plant growth. • To understand the conditions needed for plant growth.	Looking at a collection of flowering plants and identifying visible features, Including roots, stem, leaves and flowers. Making labelled drawings or collages of flowering plants.	• Identifying and classifying. • Observing closely. • Making comparisons.
	3	• To identify and describe the basic structure of a variety of common flowering plants including trees.	• To identify different parts of plants. • To identify which part of a plant various vegetables come from.	Looking at vegetables. Making a model of a composite plant.	• Asking simple questions. • Identifying and classifying. • Observing closely. • Making comparisons.
5	1	• To identify and name a variety of common wild and garden plants, including deciduous and evergreen trees.	• To compare trees with other plants. • To know some names of common trees. • To identify some common trees. • To make some observations of trees.	'Hugging' trees and making bark rubbings, drawings and taking photos. Making some simple comparisons: height, leaf and tree trunk width, and so on.	• Asking simple questions. • Identifying and classifying. • Observing closely. • Making comparisons. • Gathering and recording data to help in answering questions.
	2	• To identify and name a variety of common wild and garden plants, including deciduous and evergreen trees.	• To explore differences between evergreen and deciduous trees. • To know that deciduous trees lose their leaves in autumn. • To identify a number of common deciduous trees.	Displaying images of locally occurring trees from different times of the year and discussing and identifying features. Recording names of trees on appropriate leaf shapes.	• Asking simple questions. • Identifying and classifying. • Observing closely. • Making comparisons.
	3	• To identify and name a variety of common wild and garden plants, including deciduous and evergreen trees.	• To distinguish between evergreen and deciduous trees. • To identify some evergreen trees that produce cones. • To identify some evergreen trees that produce berries.	Using images of evergreen trees and discussing similarities/differences between deciduous trees. Comparing a variety of pine cones and matching cones to trees.	• Asking simple questions. • Identifying and classifying. • Observing closely. • Making comparisons.
6	1	• To identify and describe the basic structure of a variety of common flowering plants, including trees.	• To know that plants grow and change and that some roots, stems, flowers and leaves are edible.	Creating a plot in the school grounds to plant vegetables, salad, herbs. Observing how they grow and change.	• Asking simple questions. • Identifying and classifying. • Observing closely. • Making comparisons.
	2	• To identify and name a variety of common wild and garden plants.	• To know that different plants live in different conditions. • To identify some plants from warmer climates.	Recapping on botanical gardens visit. Listing plants grown outside locally and comparing with food plants from warmer parts of the world.	• Asking simple questions. • Identifying and classifying. • Observing closely. • Making comparisons.
	3	• To identify and describe the basic structure of a variety of common flowering plants, including trees.	• To observe willow plants. • To recognise some parts of plants. • To know that willows can be bent into living structures.	Visiting a garden centre/ local play area with a living willow structure. Designing or making a willow structure.	• Asking simple questions. • Identifying and classifying. • Observing closely. • Making comparisons.
Assess and review					

Objectives
- To know the names of some flowering plants.
- To know the main parts of flowering plants.
- To observe and record the appearance of plants.
- To observe and recount conditions plants grow in.

Resources
Selection of fruits; paper plates and napkins; photographs of gardens children will visit; cameras; paper; clipboards and pencils; disposable or gardening gloves; collecting bags; photocopiable page 135 'Botanical gardens'; photographs of plants shown on photocopiable sheet; songs about plants; posters of flowering plants; packets of seeds; pictures of fruit and vegetables

Speaking scientifically
temperature, tropical, arid, environment, stem, leaves, flowers, seeds, bark, branches, trunk, deciduous, evergreen

Lesson 1: Botanical gardens visit

Previous knowledge
During the Early Years Foundation Stage, children will have had opportunities to develop their understanding of similarities and differences between living things. They should have found out about different features of their immediate environment compared to others. They will also have made observations on how animals and plants occur or change. In addition to this, the children should have completed the Year 1 season topics on autumn, winter and spring and observed how plants are affected by some seasonal changes.

Introduction
Plan a fruit snack time to introduce the idea that we can eat plants. Check for allergies among the children beforehand and provide a selection of fruits such as apples, grapes, strawberries and oranges. As the children are eating, point to any stalks on the fruit, as well as to the pips inside. Ask the children to suggest what the stalks are for and establish that these are where the fruits were once attached to a growing plant. Explain that the pips are seeds that could grow into new plants. Tell the children that they are going to be finding out much more about how plants grow and ask if they know the names of any plants. Make a list of examples that the children may have come across, such as grass, daisies and nettles.

Whole-class work
1. Prior to this lesson, prepare for an off-site educational visit by carrying out a thorough risk assessment and obtaining permission from parents and carers. Consider details such as transport, food, clothing, medical requirements (including any allergies) and an appropriate level of adult support. If you make this visit in early spring, many trees will not be in leaf – although some species blossom at this time of year. Rhododendrons could be in flower, along with many spring bulbs. Check with your local gardens to find out what you can expect to see and whether the children will be allowed to collect fallen petals and so on.

2. Tell the children that you are going on a plant hunt at the botanical gardens. Show them some photographs of where they will be and ask what they might expect to see there. Explain that they will be taking photographs and making drawings of what they find. Establish some ground rules for staying safe: children should use gloves to collect fallen petals (if permitted by the gardens), be aware that some plants are spiky, on no account put plants in their mouths and tell an adult if they come across any rubbish.

3. Begin your visit to the botanical gardens with an initial look at the grounds closest to the entrance. Talk about how large the gardens look and encourage the children to notice the height and colour of the plants around them and whether any of them have flowers. Point out the glasshouses, and talk about what might be growing inside them. Take photographs of general scenes and anything particular from the children's initial observations.

Group work
4. Divide the class into small adult-led groups and direct them to different locations in the gardens. Ensure these include any areas of plants that are currently, or close to, flowering, as well as any tropical and arid glasshouses. Tell the children to look carefully at the trees and plants in their area, and to make drawings and take photographs of plants that they notice. Encourage them to try to find out the names of some of these.

5. At various points during the visit, bring the whole class back together and talk about what they have found out. Compare each group's observations about the plants they have seen and send the children out to new locations to repeat their investigations.

6. At the end of the visit, collect the whole class together again and review all their findings. Collate their drawings, photographs and any other evidence for a classroom display.

Whole-class work

7. Back in class, remind the children of their visit to the botanical gardens and ask them to describe what they saw. Encourage them to recall the names of any plants they learnt about and add these to your class list. Talk about whether these plants were growing in one of the glasshouses or outside in the grounds and what the differences are between these areas. Encourage the children to describe the atmosphere inside various glasshouses compared to outside. Display the photographs and drawings from their visit.

Independent work

8. Provide the children with photocopiable page 135 'Botanical gardens' and ask them to complete and colour it. Show them photos of any plants included on the sheet that they did not see on their visit.

Introducing the new area of study

Teach your class some songs about plants. Various websites provide suggestions for lyrics which can be put to familiar tunes such as 'I'm a Little Teapot' – or have a go at making up your own! Talk about what the lyrics mean. Display posters of flowering plants and packets of seeds and tell the children that they will be finding out how these change and grow. Show them pictures of fruit and vegetables such as apples, strawberries, carrots and beans, and explain that they will be finding out about plants that we can eat.

> **Differentiation**
> ● Support children with the photocopiable sheet by giving first letter clues for labels to glue onto their botanical gardens scene.
> ● Challenge children to label their botanical gardens scene and write sentences about their visit.

Science in the wider world

Many new species of plant were discovered as a result of global explorations during the 18th and 19th centuries. Botanical gardens were set up in various locations around the UK to house new collections of plants and became focal points of great interest to both scientists and the general public. The hot, humid atmosphere of tropical glasshouses enables plants from equatorial regions, including banana, cocoa and rubber trees, to thrive. The arid glasshouses can support plants from climates with low, irregular rainfall, such as cacti and other succulents. Botanical gardens make a vital contribution to plant science and conservation. Kew Gardens' Millennium Seed Bank project has been collecting seed samples from around the world and currently safeguards over 30,000 species.

Review

Children could be assessed on the observations they have made about different plants during their visit to the botanical gardens and any evidence they have collected in the form of drawings, photographs, fallen petals, and so on. They could also be assessed on their completion of the photocopiable sheet and inclusion of relevant detail such as colour, labels and sentences about their observations.

Objectives
● To know some names of common garden flowering plants.
● To compare some common garden flowering plants.
● To be able to identify some common garden flowering plants.

Resources
Class list of plants from previous lesson; images of large floral displays; images of individual plants: lily, rose, busy lizzie, pansy, daffodil, tulip; laminated 'snap' cards displaying images of the flowers introduced in this lesson (created from the photocopiable sheet); photocopiable page 136 'Who am I?'; interactive activity 'Who am I?' on the CD-ROM

Speaking scientifically
daffodil, tulip, crocus, snowdrop, lily, bulb, busy lizzie, pansy, petunia, lupin, primrose, rose

Lesson 2: How does your garden grow?

Introduction
Sing 'Mary, Mary Quite Contrary' with your class. Remind the children of some of the plants they saw at the botanical gardens and draw their attention to the class list of plants. Ask whether they could grow bananas or cocoa beans at home, and if they would want plants like nettles in their garden. Talk about what sorts of plant people like to have in their gardens and encourage them to name some more. Display images of large floral displays and explain that you are going to find out more about some of these.

Whole-class work
1. Explain that many girls' names come from flowers and that you are going to introduce the class to some of these. Show them images of individual common garden flowers and talk about their shape, colour and size. Practise saying the name of each one before moving on to the next image. Go back several times to previous images to ensure that the children are beginning to connect the names with how each plant looks.

2. Once the children are reasonably secure with a number of common garden plant names, display a few of them together and play a 'Who am I?' game. Begin by describing the flower you are thinking of and gradually move on to yes/no answers as the children become more proficient at recognising them. Gradually add more flowers to the game and give individual children the opportunity to answer questions and give clues.

3. Next, display pairs of flowers from different species and ask the children to make comparisons by describing similarities and differences between them. Draw their attention to colour and shape, but also encourage them to look at the number of petals and what they can see inside the flower.

Group work
4. Provide groups of children with a pack of cards (created from photocopiable page 136 'Who am I?') containing a card for each flower introduced. Tell them to play a game of 'snap'. Each child begins with a pile of six cards placed face down and takes it in turn to put one card, face up, in the middle. As soon as there are two consecutive cards the same, the first player to shout 'snap' wins all the cards in the middle. The game continues until one player holds all the cards.

Independent work
5. Ask children to complete the photocopiable sheet by linking plant name labels to the correct drawings (or use interactive activity 'Who am I?' on the CD-ROM).

> **Differentiation**
> ● Support children with an initial letter clue next to each flower on their photocopiable sheet to help them match name labels. Limit the number of plants that you ask them to identify.
> ● Challenge children to identify a wider range of flowers and to write in the names on their photocopiable sheet.

Science in the wider world
In addition to the common names we use for plants, they have scientific names that enable scientists to study species properly without confusion. These scientific names are a combination of the genus and the species names. For example, the scientific name for busy lizzie is *Impatiens walleriana*.

Review
Children could be assessed on the number of garden flowers they can identify and how accurately they can match labels to examples on their photocopiable sheet.

Objectives
• To know some names of common wild flowering plants.
• To compare some common wild flowering plants.
• To identify some common wild flowering plants.

Resources
Images of bluebells, poppies, buttercups, daisies, dandelions, nettles and thistles; images of garden flowering plants from previous lesson; two complete dandelion plants with open flowers: one that has been carefully unearthed, the other potted up to grow on in the classroom; an image of a dandelion clock; camera; sheets of paper divided into two sections

Speaking scientifically
wild flower, bluebell, poppy, weed, buttercup, daisy, dandelion, nettle, thistle, root, stem, leaf, flower

Lesson 3: Buttercups and daisies

Introduction

Recap on the garden flowers you looked at in the previous lesson and check that children can recall the names of these. Explain that the types of plant that grow at the botanical gardens and in people's own gardens are generally well looked after, but that plants can grow healthily in the wild too. Display some images of bluebell woods and fields full of poppies. Name these for the children and explain that, as in parks and botanical gardens, we can enjoy looking at them, but are not allowed to pick them.

Tell the children that there are other plants which gardeners don't usually want in their gardens because they don't look so nice and take up space and nutrients where other plants might grow. These plants are generally known as 'weeds' and gardeners spend a lot of time trying to get rid of them!

Whole-class work

1. Display some images of common weeds such as buttercups, daisies, dandelions, nettles and thistles. As with the garden flowers, show the children images of individual weeds and talk about their shape, colour and size. Practise saying the name of each one before moving on to the next image. Go back several times to previous images to ensure that the children are beginning to connect names with how each plant looks.

2. Play another 'Who am I?' game with the weeds and wild flowers and, as the children become proficient at recognising them, add in the garden flowers the children learnt about previously. Give children opportunities to compare different flowers and recognise similarities and differences between them.

3. Show the class a dandelion plant that you have carefully unearthed and ask if the children recognise it. Point to the roots, stem, leaves and flowers and ask the children what each part is called. Ask children if they know how dandelions change and display an image of a dandelion clock.

4. Explain that the dandelion which is growing in a pot is going to stay in the classroom so the children can watch how it changes. Take a photograph of the potted dandelion and ask the children to suggest what the plant will need to keep it healthy and what might happen to it after the flowers have died back.

Independent work

5. Provide the children with sheets of paper divided into two sections and tell the children to draw what the dandelion currently looks like in the first box and write in the date. Explain that they will make another drawing to record what the dandelion looks like once it has changed.

Science in the wider world

Dandelions produce yellow flowers, which die back to reveal fluffy seed heads. The seeds are carried on the wind and germinate quickly once they settle onto soil. Dandelions grow long, deep roots that can be hard to pull up, which makes them difficult to eradicate from gardens and lawns.

Review

Children can be assessed on the number of wild flowers they can identify.

Objectives
- To know that flowering plants grow from seeds.
- To observe, measure and record carefully the germination process of a bean.

Resources
'Jack and the Beanstalk' story; pots; compost; runner bean seeds; labels; sticks; canes or 'wigwams'; trays or saucers; camera; magnifiers; lengths of string; photocopiable page 137 'Bean diary' enlarged to A3 cut into individual weeks and made into booklets; gardening or disposable gloves

Speaking scientifically
seed, root, seedling, stalk, leaf, flower, bean, magnifier, germinate

Lesson 1: Growing beans

Introduction
Read your class the story of 'Jack and the Beanstalk' and talk about how Jack's beans grow and change. Show the children some real bean seeds and explain that, while you are fairly certain they are not magic and won't grow up to the sky, you hope that they will be able to grow some bean plants in the classroom! Talk about how long real beans might take to grow and what the children should do to look after them and help the plants grow healthily.

Group work
1. Provide groups of children with pots, compost and seeds. Check for legume allergies before providing children with pots, compost, bean seeds and gardening or disposable gloves. The children could either each plant their own seed in a small pot, or put three or four seeds into a much larger container. Ensure the pots are labelled clearly and place sticks or wigwams for the seedlings to cling onto as they start to grow.

2. Place all the pots onto trays or saucers in a light position in the classroom (but out of direct sunlight) and ensure that they are watered regularly. Explain to the children that over the next few weeks they will be watching to see how the seeds grow and taking photographs of their progress.

3. Show the children an enlarged photocopiable page 137 'Bean diary' and demonstrate how to begin filling it in.

Independent work
4. Provide magnifiers and more bean seeds and tell the children to look at them carefully. Ask them to lay a piece of string next to a seed and carefully cut the string to the same length.

5. Tell the children to make a drawing of a seed on the first page of their 'Bean diary' and to attach the first measuring string so that it hangs from the bottom of the page. As the seeds germinate and start to grow the children can take a string measurement each week and attach it to the relevant page in their diary. As the weeks go on, they should see that the strings are getting progressively longer; the children can compare the lengths to see how much their plants have grown.

> **Differentiation**
> - Support children by adapting the diary so that it is a series of larger pages and provide labels for them to stick onto each sheet.
> - Challenge children to use a ruler to measure the lengths of string and record bean growth in centimetres.

Science in the wider world
There are many types of bean, including French, broad, soya and kidney beans, all of which belong to the legume family, as do peas and lentils. Runner beans are sometimes known as 'string beans' because of the fibre that runs along one side of the pod, although many versions have now been successfully cultivated without this 'string'. The plants bear pink, red, white or bi-coloured flowers, which are followed by pods which can grow up to 25cm in length and 2cm in width.

Review
Children can be assessed on their observations about how their bean plants grow and the drawings and measurements they make to record this.

Objectives
- To observe and compare a plant that has been watered with one that has not.
- To observe and identify the basic structure of a plant.
- To know that flowering plants have roots.

Resources
Two busy lizzie plants – one that has been watered regularly and one that has been allowed to dry out (but is still alive); image of busy lizzie from week 1, lesson 2; a beaker with a drinking straw; camera; photocopiable page 138 'Plant parts'; interactive activity 'Plant parts' on the CD-ROM; images of healthy plants and plants that haven't had enough water; sheets of paper divided into two equal sections

Speaking scientifically
root, stem, leaf, flower

Lesson 2: Thirsty plants

Introduction
Display the healthy busy lizzie plant and challenge the children to identify it from their earlier lesson on garden plants. Show the class an image of the plant to remind them and recap on the names of all the garden plants they found out about. Present the other busy lizzie plant that has not been watered for a few days and has begun to dry out. Ask the children to say what is the same and what is different about the two plants and what might have happened to the one that doesn't look healthy. Encourage them to make comparisons and describe the differences they notice in the stems and leaves. Remind the children about the dandelion plant they looked at previously and talk about the part of the plant under the soil. Establish that the roots hold the plant in the soil and take in water from the ground, so if the soil dries out the plant is going to get very thirsty. Show the children the beaker with the drinking straw. Explain that plants' stems are a bit like straws; the water travels up inside them from the roots.

Whole-class work
1. Ask the children what they think will happen if you start to water the second busy lizzie plant again. Explain that you will take a photograph of the plant while it looks dried out and then take more photographs to record any changes over the next few days, as it starts to receive water again. Display the two plants together and encourage the children to make further comparisons during the week.

2. Display some images of other plants that either look healthy or like they have not been watered and challenge the children to say which ones are which. Encourage them to recognise that water is important to all living things.

Independent work
3. Provide each child with photocopiable page 138 'Plant parts' (or the interactive activity on the CD-ROM) and ask them to label the parts of the plant correctly.

4. Tell the children to draw both the busy lizzie plants on a sheet of paper divided into two sections, labelling the one that has been watered and the one that hasn't. Once the thirsty plant has recovered, they can make further drawings to record the changes.

Differentiation
- Support children with initial letters for labels indicating each plant part.
- Challenge children to make detailed drawings of the busy lizzies and label the plant parts on each one.

Science in the wider world
Plants collect moisture from the soil through their roots and lose it through their leaves in a process called transpiration. The roots are covered with tiny hairs that absorb water and dissolved nutrients, which then travel up inside the stem to every part of the plant above soil. Once in the leaves, the water evaporates through tiny holes called 'stomata'.

Review
Children could be assessed on their observations and comparisons of the two plants and their completion of the photocopiable sheet.

Objectives
● To know that some flowering plants grow from bulbs.
● To recognise some common plants that grow from bulbs.
● To observe and record the growth of a hyacinth bulb.

Resources
Images of garden plants used in previous lessons; examples or images of bulbs, such as lily, daffodil, hyacinth, snowdrop, tulip (note that crocuses grow from corms rather than bulbs); hyacinth bulbs; images of hyacinths in flower; transparent plastic containers with a narrow top where the hyacinth bulb will fit; disposable or gardening gloves; camera

Speaking scientifically
bulb, corm, tuber, rhizome, root, stem, leaf, flower, poisonous

Lesson 3: What grows underground?

Introduction
Show the class the images of the garden plants that you have used in previous lessons and challenge them to recall the names of these again. Ask the children to identify the plant parts they can see on the images and remind them about the one they can't see: recap on the importance of roots and ask if they know anything else that grows underground. Explain that some of our vegetables, like potatoes and carrots, grow in the roots of their plants, but that some other types of plant grow from an underground ball-like lump called a 'bulb'. Display some images or examples of bulbs and compare the sizes and shapes. Some of them may look a bit like onions, but ensure the children understand that bulbs could make us very poorly if we tried to eat them and are best handled with garden or disposable gloves.

Whole-class work
1. Tell the children that you are going to play a game of 'odd one out'. Explain that you will show them the garden flower pictures again, and this time they are going to guess which of the plants has grown from a bulb. Say that you will give clues as necessary.

2. Arrange the images so that only one bulb plant appears in the group each time. When the children have identified it, move the image into a set for plants that grow from bulbs. Continue until you have collected the images of the lily, daffodil, hyacinth, snowdrop, tulip and crocus. Explain that one of the wild plants the children looked at – the bluebell – also belongs to this group.

3. Display the bulbs again and talk about their shapes and sizes. Ask the children to try to match the correct bulb with each plant image.

4. Show the class some hyacinth bulbs and display some flowering examples. Explain that bulbs are usually planted underground, but that there is a way of growing hyacinths so that we can see how the roots develop.

5. Fill your containers with water and place a hyacinth bulb in each so that the water is just below the bottom of the bulb. Use gardening or disposable gloves when handling the bulbs. The bulbs and containers should then be placed in a cool, dark area and topped up with water as necessary. When the stems are about 6–8cm high, gradually introduce the hyacinths into light, but aim to keep them as cool as possible and out of direct sunlight.

6. Take photographs to record how the hyacinths grow and change, and ask the children to make regular observations. Compare the hyacinth roots with the dandelion roots they observed in a previous lesson.

Science in the wider world
Bulbs are compacted layers of leaves that store food for the developing plant. The roots, growing from the bottom, anchor the plant in the ground and absorb water and nutrients, while the stem emerges from the top. Corms, from which some irises grow, contain stem tissue rather than leaves. Rhizomes are stems that grow horizontally.

Tubers, such as potatoes, are the swollen underground stems; while dahlia tubers develop from the roots.

Bulbs mature and grow larger, providing a store of new food each year. They often develop 'bulblets', which can grow into new bulbs.

Review
Children could be assessed on their identification of flowering plants and their observations about how the hyacinths change and grow.

Objectives
- To understand that plants grow from seeds.
- To compare seeds from different plants.
- To recognise the conditions needed for germination.
- To observe and record the germination of seeds.

Resources
Plant pots; trays; compost; plant labels; a variety of seeds: coconut, avocado stone, conkers, apple pips; white paper plates; packets of commercially produced annual seeds; cress seeds; kitchen roll; plastic saucers; magnifiers; digital microscope or camera; disposable or gardening gloves; photocopiable pages 'Seed diary (1)–(3)' from the CD-ROM

Speaking scientifically
grow, plant, seed, germinate, root, poisonous

Lesson 1: Seed diary

Introduction
Display a variety of seeds, such as a coconut, an avocado stone, conkers and apple pips, as well as some tiny ones like cress seeds. (Be aware of nut and seed allergies in the class; use photos instead, if necessary.) Ask the children if they know what the seeds might grow into.

Group work
1. Put a variety of seeds on white paper plates so that they can be seen easily. Provide a plate for each group. Make sure the children understand they must not eat any of the seeds.

2. Talk about the different types of seed and compare the pictures of mature plants on the seed packets. Ask how they should be planted.

3. Provide each group with a suitable container (ensure that it has drainage holes). Tell them to wear the gloves and to fill their container with compost, until it is 1–2cm below the top edge. They should then sprinkle some seeds over the soil and loosely cover these with compost.

4. The seeds will need watering in, but advise the children to water gently so as not to wash out their seeds. You could dampen the compost before they start working to limit the amount of water they will need to add at this stage.

5. Finally, the children will need to label their containers and put them in a suitable place (avoid window sills, as the temperature varies too much).

Paired work
6. Ask pairs of children to put cress seeds on a damp kitchen towel spread over a plastic saucer. Say that they could use a magnifier to watch for the first signs of the root and shoot over the next few days. Explain that this is the seeds 'germinating' – they are becoming plants.

7. A digital microscope, suitable for use in primary schools, or a camera could also be used to observe and record how the seeds change and grow. Tell the children to take daily snapshots and build a class slideshow.

Independent work
8. Ask children to complete the photocopiable page 'Seed diary (2)' on the CD-ROM.

Differentiation
- Support children by providing them with the simple writing frame in 'Seed diary (1)' from the CD-ROM.
- Challenge children to make booklets using photocopiable page 'Seed diary (3)' from the CD-ROM to record the progress of their plants.

Science in the wider world
Some seeds, such as cress and mung beans, germinate very quickly – within a few days. Most annuals germinate quite quickly, but will take several weeks to produce flowers and seeds. French marigolds will produce seeds before the summer holidays, if started off in a warm place in February or March. This will allow the children to see the whole life cycle of a plant, from seed to adult plant producing seeds.

Review
Children could be assessed on their observations on how seeds change and grow, in discussion and on the photocopiable sheet.

Lesson 2: In the dark

Introduction

You will need three sessions for this activity: one to set up the investigation and the others to observe the results. Look at two trays of healthy green plants in the classroom and ask the children to say where they are greenest (the leaves). Talk about how healthy the plants are and recap on the names of different parts. Ask the children to suggest what plants need to grow healthily and to say what they think might happen if they put one tray in a dark cupboard. Talk about why it would be a good idea to only put one of the plant trays in the cupboard and keep the other one in the classroom. Encourage the children to recognise that they will then be able to compare the one that has had light with the one that hasn't. Decide how long you are going to leave the plant in the cupboard (a week should be long enough).

Whole-class work

1. Begin the next session by reminding the children about the healthy plants they looked at previously and ask them to say what they think might have changed. Take the tray of plants out of the cupboard and compare it with the tray that has been in the light all week.

2. Encourage the children to notice how the plants that have been in the dark are now yellow, and may have grown longer and straggly in their search for light. Talk about which plants look healthier and what might happen if you leave both trays in the light again.

Independent work

3. Provide the children with sheets of paper divided into thirds on which to record their observations. In the first box, ask them to draw what the two trays of plants looked like before one of them went in the cupboard.

4. In the middle box, they should draw both trays again, showing the differences that being in the dark has made. They should then complete their recording after both plants have been in the light again for a few days.

Differentiation
- Support children with headings on the recording sheet to reduce the writing task.
- Challenge children to write sentences to describe how the plants in the dark changed.

Science in the wider world

There is often confusion over the difference between growing plants and germinating seeds. Seeds do not generally need light to germinate. They are usually in the soil, where it is dark. The initial germination uses the food reserves in the seed. However green plants need light if they are to grow. They do this through the process of photosynthesis in the leaves. Plant leaves are green because of the presence of chlorophyll, a pigment that traps light energy and so allows photosynthesis to take place. Water is absorbed through the roots; carbon dioxide is absorbed through the leaves. Using these in the presence of light energy, plant cells synthesise sugars, which are then stored as starch.

Review

Children could be assessed on the observations they make about light and dark and on their recording of how the plants in the dark changed.

Objectives
- To carry out an experiment showing the effect of light and dark on plants.
- To observe and record plant growth under different conditions.
- To understand that plants need light for healthy growth.

Resources
Two trays of healthy plants – cress or similar; sheets of paper divided into three equal sections

Speaking scientifically
light, dark, healthy, colour, grow

Objectives
● To understand why plants have flowers.
● To suggest why flowers are sometimes scented and colourful.
● To revise basic plant structure.

Resources
Images of garden and wild flowers from the previous lessons; images of insects visiting flowers; time-lapse photography or slow-motion video footage of buds opening into flowers; photocopiable page 'Make a flower' from the CD-ROM; art straws; string or wool; crayons; coloured paper

Speaking scientifically
bud, petal, nectar, insect, scent, root, stem, leaf, flower

Lesson 3: From bud to bee

Introduction
Show the class some time-lapse photography or slow-motion video footage of buds opening into flowers. Talk about why plants have flowers and what the brightly coloured parts are called. Encourage the children to think about why petals are so brightly coloured and why flowers often smell nice too. Show some further footage of insects visiting flowers and explain that stored inside at the base of the petals is a sweet liquid called 'nectar' which the insects like to drink. The colour and smell of the flowers attract the insects to the plant. Show the images of garden and wild flowers that you have used in previous lessons and challenge the children to recall the names of these. Compare the number, size, shape and colour of the petals on each of the examples and use these characteristics as clues in a guessing game to further reinforce the names.

Whole-class work
1. Remind the class of photocopiable sheet 138 'Plant parts' that they completed previously, and recap on the main parts of the flowering plant with them. Check that they are able to identify the roots, stem, leaves and flower as you point to them and can describe the jobs that some of these parts do.

Independent work
2. Provide the children with photocopiable page 'Make a flower' from the CD-ROM, an art straw, string and glue. Explain that they are going to cut out the petals and centre and stick them together to make a flower, which they will then glue onto an art-straw stem, along with the leaves. They will also attach some string or wool to the other end to represent the roots. Explain that they will need to decide on the number of petals and that they can add more than on the photocopiable sheet if they wish.

3. First, they should decide on colours for their petals, centre and leaves and shade these with crayons before cutting them out.

4. Ask the children to glue their flowers onto a background sheet and to label each part carefully.

Differentiation
● Support children by providing ready-cut templates and labels that can be added to the appropriate parts.
● Challenge children to add to their labels with short descriptions about what jobs each part of the plant does.

Science in the wider world
At this stage, the children do not need to know about pollination or the life cycle of flowering plants, but it is worth reinforcing that many insects are attracted to the flowers to consume nectar – not pollen (although honey bees do require pollen as part of their diet). Plants rely on insects to collect pollen on their bodies as they drink the nectar. When they visit another flower, they transport this pollen, which then rubs off on the stigma and the contents leave the pollen grain and go down a pollen tube in the style to the ovaries, where it fuses with the ovules to form seeds. The nectar is the plant's reward to the insects for pollinating them.

Review
Children could be assessed on their identification of plant parts and description of what each part does.

Objectives
● To observe and compare the roots of two different plants.
● To observe and record the roots of some root vegetables.

Resources
Hyacinths in clear plastic containers from week 2, lesson 3; images of plants with intact roots; germinated runner beans; clear plastic containers; gravel or small stones; black paper and elastic bands; disposable or gardening gloves; name labels; carrots, parsnips and other root vegetables with roots still attached; magnifiers

Speaking scientifically
root, shoot, absorb

Lesson 1: Roots

Introduction

About a week before this session, germinate some more runner beans on damp kitchen roll.

Begin the lesson by looking at the hyacinths that you planted previously in clear containers and display some images of plants that have been lifted out of the soil with roots still attached. Encourage the children to make comparisons and observations about the different plants and to notice that not all plants have the same kind of roots. Remind them of the beans they planted earlier in the topic and ask them to suggest what the roots might be doing under the soil. Show the children the germinated beans you have prepared and compare these with any bean seeds left over from when they did their planting. Explain that they are going to plant these germinated runner beans in clear plastic containers, this time filled with pebbles rather than soil.

Group work

1. Provide each group with gloves, a clear plastic container and some gravel or pebbles. Tell the children to fill their container with the stones and then pour in enough water to come to just below the top of the stones.

2. Next, the children should place four or five germinated beans on top of the pebbles, around the edge of the container, making sure that the beans do not become waterlogged. The final step is to wrap black paper around the container, secure it in place with an elastic band and attach a name label. The containers can then be kept in a safe location and topped up with water as required. After a week, the children can carefully remove the paper and make some observations about how the roots have grown.

3. Give each group a selection of root vegetables from a supplier such as a market stall or organic greengrocer, which still have some roots attached. Tell the children to use their magnifiers to see the smaller roots coming from the central 'tap root'.

4. Cut the tap roots lengthways and widthways so the children can look inside and ask them to make drawings of what they can see.

Science in the wider world

Not all plants have the same root systems. Some plants develop a strong main root, or tap root, that grows deeply into the ground, while others may have many fine roots that spread out just below the surface. A tap root anchors the plant firmly in the ground. Common plants with this type of root are carrots and parsnips. Dandelions also have a long tap root, which explains why they are so difficult to pull up. Roots usually grow downwards, towards water and in the dark. Their job is to absorb water and nutrients from the growing medium, usually soil or compost. They also play a part in helping to prevent soil erosion by holding the soil together and stopping it being blown or washed away.

Review

Children could be assessed on their comparisons of different root systems and the observational drawings they make of root vegetables.

Objectives
• To revise common plant names.
• To recount plant investigations.
• To observe and record plant growth.
• To understand the conditions needed for plant growth.

Resources
Plants in the classroom from previous lessons: planted dandelion, bean plants, busy lizzie plants, hyacinths in water, cress trays, runner beans in clear containers; any 'before' and 'after' photographs of plants in the classroom; children's recording work on the plants in the classroom; old magazines and seed catalogues

Speaking scientifically
root, bulb, stem, leaf, flower, petal, seed, nectar, pollen, insect, light, dark, water

Lesson 2: From root to flower

Introduction
Many of the activities suggested in this topic involve setting up an investigation and then having to wait for the plants to change over the course of a week or so. This lesson is intended as an opportunity to bring together all the plants that have been growing in your classroom to allow the children to review their work, observe the plants closely and make comparisons. Remind your class of their initial visit to the botanical gardens to see all the plants growing there and observe that the classroom has become something of a mini botanical garden! Tell the children that you are going to take a 'tour' of their plants and ask them to explain what each exhibit tells us about how plants grow.

Group work
1. Provide each group with one of the specimens you have looked at during the topic: the planted dandelion, beans, busy lizzie plants, hyacinths in water, cress trays and runner beans in clear containers. Also give each group any photographs that were taken of their plants 'before' and 'after' the investigations.

2. Allow the children time to look carefully at their exhibits and photographs, recalling what they looked like at the start and observing any recent changes.

3. Announce that you are beginning your tour and visit each group in turn. Ask the children questions to elicit their understanding about what the plants have needed to grow well. Begin by asking for the names of the plants and which parts can be seen and identified. Ask the children to explain the nature of the investigation carried out, and describe how their plants have changed and what this has told them about the conditions plants need to grow well.

4. Invite the rest of the class to comment on each exhibit before you move on; draw their attention to all the growth that has occurred and remind them about the plants that were deprived of light or water, but have since recovered.

5. Carry on visiting each group in turn to complete your mini botanical tour.

Independent work
6. Use this lesson as an opportunity for children to complete all their photocopiable sheets, such as the bean and seed diaries, and observational drawings they have made to record how their plants have grown and changed.

7. Provide the children with old magazines and seed catalogues and ask them to make flowering plant collages from the pictures, and to label the parts of the plants.

Differentiation
• Support children by asking them to complete their recording activities by adding in some of the photographs you have supplied for the mini botanical tour.
• Challenge children to complete their labelling with as many plant parts as they know and to write about their latest observations on plant growth.

Science in the wider world
Plants are essential to all life on Earth. Large forests are often called 'the lungs of the Earth' because they can absorb vast quantities of carbon dioxide, which is produced by animals and by many of our power stations, vehicles and manufacturing processes. As they photosynthesise, plants give off oxygen, which animals need to sustain life. All green plants, including green algae floating near the surface of the world's oceans, carry out this process.

Review
Children can be assessed on their plant presentations during the mini botanical tour and identification of plant parts, as well as on the completion of all their diary activities and observational drawings.

Objectives
● To identify different parts of plants.
● To identify which part of a plant various vegetables come from.

Resources
A selection of vegetables and vegetable images to construct a composite plant: flowers – cauliflower, broccoli; stem – celery; leaves – spinach, lettuce, cabbage; roots – carrots, radishes; fruit – tomatoes; seeds – loose sweetcorn or peas; a large plant outline; plant outlines drawn on large pieces of card; camera

Speaking scientifically
root, stem, leaf, flower, petal, fruit, seeds

Lesson 3: Food from plants

Introduction
Display your selection of vegetables and ask the class to identify each one. Establish that vegetables come from different parts of plants and talk about how they are eaten and what they taste like. Challenge the children to say which part of the plant each of the examples is from. Show them a large outline of a complete plant along with images of each vegetable. Explain that you are going to use the vegetables to make a giant (but pretend) vegetable plant!

Whole-class work
1. Take each of the vegetable images in turn and encourage the children to look carefully at it and suggest which part of the plant it is. Start with the carrots, reminding the class that they have already looked closely at these in a previous lesson. Establish that carrots are from the roots of the plant, as are radishes, and move these into the root part of the large plant outline.

2. Continue to build up the plant by selecting other vegetables, such as celery for the stem, spinach for the leaves and cauliflower or broccoli for the flowers, talking about which part of the plant they are and moving each image to the corresponding part of the plant outline. Add on tomatoes for fruit and peas or sweetcorn to represent seeds.

3. Once the outline is complete, check that the children can identify each plant part and write labels by these on the board. Ensure that the children realise that vegetables come from different plants, and not one super vegetable plant!

Group work
4. Provide groups with a plant outline drawn on a large piece of card and further images of each vegetable.

5. Tell the children to make their own giant vegetable plants by selecting pictures to represent roots, stems, leaves, flowers and seeds and gluing them onto the outline.

6. Ask the children to label their giant plants by writing in the plant parts and the names of the vegetable they used for each section. Provide wordbanks to support this, as appropriate.

7. If you have enough examples of each vegetable, the children could build plant models using these – or you could make a large class model. Find a large floor space where you can lay everything out and take photographs of the completed 'plants'.

Science in the wider world
Many plants are edible, or have parts of their structure that can be eaten, from root ginger, the rhizome of the ginger plant, to the dried camomile petals used in herbal tea. However, while some parts of plants are safe to eat, others may not be, for example rhubarb stalks can be cooked and eaten, but the leaves of this plant are poisonous. Birds and other animals are often able to eat plant parts that would make humans very ill, for example koala bears live on a diet of highly toxic eucalyptus leaves. Ensure the children understand that they should never pick or taste plants that grow in the wild.

Review
Children could be assessed on their identification of edible plant parts, building of composite plants and labelling of vegetables and corresponding plant parts.

Objectives
- To compare trees with other plants.
- To know some names of common trees.
- To identify some common trees.
- To make some observations of trees.

Resources
Photocopiable page 36 'Tree identification chart'; media resource 'Record-breaking trees' on the CD-ROM; a camera; paper; crayons; clipboards

Speaking scientifically
root, trunk, branch, leaf, flower, fruit, nut, berry, seed

Lesson 1: Tree expedition

Introduction

Tree hugging may be possible in your school grounds, otherwise you will need to organise an off-site educational visit for this activity (see autumn 1, week 1, lesson 1 for the necessary considerations).

Remind the class of their visit to the botanical gardens earlier in this topic, as well as any trips they have made to a local park to observe seasonal change. The children may also have 'adopted' a tree in the school grounds as part of their work on seasons. Establish what they already know about trees. Talk about how trees differ from other plants the children have been finding out about in this topic and make a class list of their ideas, encouraging them to suggest details such as that trees are much taller, have thick trunks covered in bark, sometimes drop their leaves in autumn and can live for a very long time. Challenge the children to recall any tree names they know.

Whole-class work

1. Display an enlarged photocopiable page 36 'Tree identification chart' and recap on the names of common trees and what they look like. These could include oak, sycamore and horse chestnut. Compare their outline shape, as well as what their leaves look like and any distinguishing features, such as sycamore keys.

2. Show the class the media resource 'Record-breaking trees' on the CD-ROM: the Methuselah, one of the oldest trees in the world; the Hyperion, thought to be the tallest in the world; the General Sherman, reputed to be the largest living organism on Earth; and the Árbol del Tule, a cypress tree in Mexico that is thought to have the widest trunk in the world.

Group work

3. Find an area of parkland that has a grassy space in the middle and some mature trees within easy reach. Collect all the children together on the grass and ask them to point to the tallest and shortest trees they can see.

4. Next, ask them which tree they think is the widest. Explain that they are going to investigate by forming a circle around one tree at a time and counting how many children are needed to hug it. Send each group off to a different tree and rotate until all the trees in the sample area have been measured.

5. Compare the results and take photographs, bark rubbings and drawings of the class's record-breaking trees.

Science in the wider world

A redwood known as Hyperion is considered to be the tallest tree in world, standing 116m high. A giant sequoia called the General Sherman tree is believed to be the largest living organism on Earth. It stands around 84m tall, with a base circumference of 31.3m, and only begins to grow branches nearly 40m above the ground. A bristlecone pine tree nicknamed Methuselah is thought to be the oldest tree in the world, at almost 5000 years old. The Árbol del Tule is a cypress tree in the Mexican state of Oaxaca. It is thought to be around 1400 years old and to have the widest tree trunk in the world, with a girth of around 50m.

Review

Children can be assessed on their identification of common trees and their observations during the tree-hugging activity.

■SCHOLASTIC

Objectives
- To explore differences between evergreen and deciduous trees.
- To know that deciduous trees lose their leaves in autumn.
- To identify a number of common deciduous trees.

Resources
Images of deciduous and evergreen trees; conkers (images if no real ones available); images of horse chestnut tree, monkey puzzle, weeping willow and spruce (Christmas) tree; a series of images to show how a horse chestnut changes over the year; photocopiable page 139 'Horse chestnut tree story'; photocopiable page 36 'Tree identification chart'; enlarged leaf outlines of examples given on the tree identification chart

Speaking scientifically
deciduous, evergreen, root, trunk, branch, leaf, flower, fruit, nut, berry, seed

Lesson 2: Deciduous trees

Introduction
Recap on the names of trees the children have become familiar with so far and talk about some of the similarities and differences between trees and smaller plants. Remind them of the record-breaking trees they found out about in the previous lesson – as well as the trees they came across during their work on seasons in Chapters 1 and 3. Display images of deciduous and evergreen trees and compare these with the trees which they came across during their tree expedition. Play a game of 'odd one out' to distinguish between deciduous and evergreen trees, encouraging the children to recognise that some trees lose all their leaves in autumn and grow new ones in the spring. Explain that you are going to focus on this sort of tree in this lesson.

Whole-class work
1. Show the children examples or images of conkers. Ask them to say what these are called and where they might have come from. Establish that they are the seeds of a horse chestnut tree and are what the trees grow from. Display an image of a mature horse chestnut tree in leaf, alongside a monkey puzzle, weeping willow and spruce tree, and ask the class to help you match the conkers to the right tree.

2. Ask the children to describe how the horse chestnut tree will look in autumn and show images of examples displaying coloured leaves. Talk about what eventually happens to all the leaves and display another image of the tree in winter. Encourage the children to continue the horse chestnut story, recognising that new leaves grow in spring and the tall candle-like flowers then appear in late spring or early summer, followed by the conkers in September.

3. Display an enlarged photocopiable page 139 'Horse chestnut tree story' and explain to the children how they should complete it by either drawing the leaves, flowers and conkers on the horse chestnut tree for the correct times of year, or using the templates on the worksheet. Show how the leaves change at different times of year with different coloured crayons.

Independent work
4. Provide children with the photocopiable sheet to complete the story.

5. Tell the children to look at enlarged leaf outlines prepared from those on photocopiable page 36 'Tree identification chart' and ask them to match these to the correct tree on their identification chart. They should write the name of the tree onto each leaf (lime, sycamore, oak, horse chestnut, beech and ash).

Differentiation
- Support children by providing initial-letter clues or complete name labels to attach to each leaf on the tree identification chart.
- Challenge children to write about how the horse chestnut tree grows from a conker to a mature tree.

Science in the wider world
Horse chestnut trees can grow up to 35m high and live for over 300 years. They are usually in leaf from early spring, and long candle-like flowers appear between May and June. The leaves are divided into 5–7 leaflets, pointed at the tip and tapered towards the base. The seeds (conkers) are encased within green prickly shells, which are the fruit walls.

Review
Children can be assessed on their completion of the 'Tree identification chart' photocopiable sheet, the order in which they have put in the leaves, flowers and conkers on the horse chestnut and whether they have identified the differences in leaf colour between spring/summer and autumn.

Objectives
- To distinguish between evergreen and deciduous trees.
- To identify some evergreen trees that produce cones.
- To identify some evergreen trees that produce berries.

Resources
Completed examples of photocopiable page 139 'Horse chestnut tree story' from previous lesson; images of deciduous trees, including: horse chestnut, lime, sycamore, oak, ash; images of evergreen trees, including: Scots pine, spruce, holly, privet, laurel; close-up images of leaves of these evergreens; a variety of pine cones; images of holly, privet and laurel in flower or with berries; images of Scots pine and spruce with cones; photocopiable page 140 'Evergreen trees'

Speaking scientifically
evergreen, coniferous, root, trunk, branch, leaf, cone, berry, seed, poisonous

Lesson 3: Evergreen trees

Introduction
Recap on the deciduous trees you looked at in the previous lesson and ask the children to list the names of those they remember. Show them some completed examples of photocopiable page 139 'Horse chestnut tree story' and talk about how this sort of tree changes over the year. Ensure the children recognise that losing all the leaves in autumn is an important characteristic of deciduous trees. Display some images of evergreen trees and challenge the children to explain what the difference is. Explain that these trees do not lose all their leaves in one go, but shed and replace them continuously, so that they always look green. Replay the 'odd one out' game to distinguish between deciduous and evergreen trees and make a list of evergreen trees together, including Scots pine, spruce, holly, privet and laurel.

Whole-class work
1. Tell the children to look closely at the close-up pictures of evergreen tree leaves and describe any similarities and differences they notice. Guide them to recognise that not all evergreen leaves look the same: the Scots pine and spruce have thin, needle-shaped leaves, while those on the holly, privet and laurel are wider and look waxy.

2. Ask the children to talk about where they may have seen any of these trees: the spruce is often used as a Christmas tree, for instance, while sprigs of holly are made into Christmas wreaths; privet is a common hedging plant in the UK.

3. Show the class some pine cones and ask them to suggest which tree they think they might belong to. Show the images of each deciduous tree first and ensure that the children understand that the pine cones do not belong to any of those before focusing on the evergreen ones. Look at each one in turn, using images that show the holly, privet and laurel with flowers or berries and the Scots pine and spruce with cones. Encourage the children to notice that the only trees with cones are the spruce and Scots pine.

4. Talk about the flowers and berries they can see on the holly, laurel and privet and explain that 'coniferous' trees do not grow these, but instead develop their seeds inside cones.

5. Provide the children with photocopiable page 140 'Evergreen trees', which contains outline images of a holly, Scots pine, spruce and privet. Talk about the shape of each tree. The triangular shape of the spruce tree helps to stop heavy snow building up on its branches. Tell the children to think about which tree they should draw berries on and which one needs pine cones. Ask them to complete the trees, write in their names and colour them in appropriately.

Differentiation
- Support children with pictures of trees bearing cones and berries for them to compare with the outlines on their photocopiable sheet and provide them with a name label for each tree.
- Challenge children to name each tree and write a sentence to describe it.

Science in the wider world
Evergreen trees can survive in cooler climates because their leaves are tough and waxy; or thin and needle shaped with a reduced surface area, which enables them to resist the cold and retain moisture. Not all evergreens are conifers; those that are include firs, spruces and pines. The seeds develop inside the cones and fall out as the scales open.

Review
Children can be assessed on their identification of differences and similarities between deciduous and evergreen trees and their completion of the photocopiable sheet.

Objectives
● To know that plants grow and change and that some roots, stems, flowers and leaves are edible.

Resources
The Tale of Peter Rabbit by Beatrix Potter; an area of the school grounds suitable for a vegetable garden; bean plants grown by children previously; garden tools – spades, forks and rakes – for adults and children; compost; edging and paving materials, if appropriate; seedlings grown in plugs; watering cans; examples of mature vegetables – beans, lettuces, radishes; canes and string; vegetable seeds (fast-growing varieties where possible); organic fibre pots that can be planted directly into the ground; disposable or gardening gloves; labels; camera

Speaking scientifically
compost, shelter, sunlight, water, root, stem, leaf, flower, seed

Lesson 1: Make a vegetable garden

Introduction
Prior to this lesson, you will need to identify a suitable site in the school grounds that your class can use as a vegetable garden, if you don't already have one. Look for an area that is level and not overshadowed by buildings or trees or exposed to strong winds. Plan a bed that the children will be able to access from all sides, without having to walk through it. If possible, enlist the support of adult volunteers who can help clear the space and do some of the initial heavy digging, although involve the children where possible, especially in the later stages of preparation. Record this work with photographs and keep your class up to date with all the work in progress. (If you are short of space, investigate siting some window boxes or large flower pots in a suitable location.)

Read the children *The Tale of Peter Rabbit* and ask them to list all the vegetables Peter comes across in Mr McGregor's garden, such as lettuces, beans and radishes. Show examples of some these vegetables and talk about which parts are edible.

Whole-class work
1. If the bean plants the children began growing earlier in this topic still look healthy, they could be planted out directly into the vegetable bed. Check the advice on the seed packets for the best time to do this and harden the plants off by leaving them outside in their pots for a few days before planting them in the ground. Make supports for the beans to climb up using canes and string and ensure that their position in the vegetable patch won't cast a shadow over the rest of your emerging crop.

2. Display the packets of vegetable seeds and remind the children of the work they did earlier in this topic on growing plants in the classroom. Explain that you will start some of your crop off in pots in the classroom and sow others directly into the vegetable bed.

Group work
3. Provide groups of children with small organic fibre pots (cut-down kitchen roll or newspaper tubes would also work), radish, lettuce or other fast-growing seeds and gloves to wear. Tell the children to fill the pots with compost, sprinkle on two or three seeds, cover these lightly with more compost, place the pots in a plastic tray and carefully water in. Allow the seeds time to germinate and tend the seedlings in the classroom, following the seed packet instructions about when to plant out. Alternatively, rake over an area of your vegetable patch, sprinkle seeds directly onto it, lightly cover over and water in. Ensure the children label each part of their crop so that they can easily identify plants once they start to grow.

4. Organise groups of children to take turns weeding and watering their vegetable garden, and taking photographs to record how the plants grow. Encourage the children to inspect their garden regularly and talk about their observations.

5. Harvest the crops as and when they are ready and hold a vegetable party for your class.

Science in the wider world
Be aware that you may have to take steps to guard against garden pests destroying the children's efforts. Slugs and snails can make short work of tender seedlings, so consider ways in which you could limit the damage. Avoid using pellets where children are gardening, but organic solutions could include laying broken egg shells or coffee grounds around the base of the young plants.

Review
Children can be assessed on their observations about how their vegetables grow and their identification of which parts of the plants they can eat.

Objectives
• To know that different plants live in different conditions.
• To identify some plants from warmer climates.

Resources
Photographs and drawings from visit to the botanical gardens; photocopiable page 141 'Where do plants live?'; media resource 'Where do plants live?' on the CD-ROM; images of tropical and desert environments featuring plants on the photocopiable sheet; images or a selection of fruits such as apples, pears, strawberries, mangos, bananas and oranges (but be aware of allergies)

Speaking scientifically
temperature, warm, cold, environment, tropical, arid, temperate, rainfall

Lesson 2: Where do plants live?

Introduction

Remind the children of the visit to the botanical gardens they made at the beginning of this topic. Display the photographs and drawings they made and identify the parts of the gardens they visited and the names of some of the plants they saw growing in each place. Ask the children to describe the glasshouses and challenge them to recall the names of some of the plants they saw growing in tropical or arid environments. Talk about what the temperature was like inside the glasshouses and how that compared with the temperature outside. Encourage the children to think about why the plants inside the glasshouses have to be kept so warm. Show the class some images of tropical rainforests and desert environments and encourage the children to describe what these look like and what they might be like to visit. Compare these conditions to their own environment.

Whole-class work

1. Display an enlarged photocopiable page 141 'Where do plants live?' (or the media resource on the CD-ROM) and ask the children to help you complete it. Begin by identifying the plants in the pictures: cactus, banana tree, aloe vera, vines, horse chestnut tree. Challenge them to identify the odd one out and explain that the horse chestnut tree can survive outdoors in the UK, whereas the others come from much warmer parts of the world.

2. Point to the labels on the photocopiable sheet and ask the children to suggest which one goes with which picture.

Independent work

3. Provide each child with the photocopiable sheet and ask them to link the labels to the pictures.

Group work

4. Ask groups of children to look at images or real examples of a selection of fruits, such as apples, pears, strawberries, mangos, bananas and oranges. Challenge them to sort them into those that can be grown in the UK and those that come from warmer climates. Compare each group's ideas and clear up any misconceptions.

Differentiation
• Support children with initial-letter clues or by providing them with complete labels to stick onto the sheet.
• Challenge children to write sentences to explain why some plants only grow in certain parts of the world.

Science in the wider world

Bananas grow in the humid, tropical conditions of Africa, South East Asia, the Caribbean and Central and South America. The average temperature in these regions is around 27°C, with an annual rainfall of over 200cm. Succulent plants such as cacti and aloes survive in desert areas where temperatures can rise to 55°C during the day and fall below 0°C at night, while rainfall can be as low as 100mm per annum. The temperate maritime climate in the UK means that temperatures average around 3–6°C in the coldest months and 16–21°C in summer. Average annual rainfall varies between 800mm and over 1000mm.

Review

Children can be assessed on their observations on conditions in the botanical gardens' glasshouses and their completion of the photocopiable sheet.

Lesson 3: Willow structures

Introduction

This lesson could serve as a simple focus on the living and growing element of willow structures, or as an opportunity to employ a specialist company who will work with your class to design and erect one of these structures in your school grounds.

Plan an off-site educational visit to a garden centre or local play area that has examples of living willow structures for the children to explore. If possible, arrange to meet with a specialist who can explain how the shapes have evolved and show photographs of each construction stage. Encourage the children to look inside the willow tunnels, domes or dens and talk about how the plants have been trained to grow into these shapes and how they will continue growing and putting out fresh shoots and leaves.

Whole-class work

1. Gather the children inside one of the larger shapes and explain how the willow shoots have been pushed into the ground and woven together. Ask them to look carefully at the stems and leaves and talk about which part of the plant is keeping it alive, and where it is. Tell the children to take photos and make some observational drawings and encourage them to describe what it feels like when they are inside these structures, as well as which shape they like the best.

2. Back in school, display the photographs and drawings the children made and recap on the construction stages they found out about. If you have invited a specialist company to work with the class to create a structure in the school grounds, present the children's observations during the initial consultation with them.

Paired work

3. Whether as a prelude to creating a real structure in the school grounds or as an activity to reinforce further aspects of the children's learning on plants, ask them to work in pairs to design a willow structure. Encourage them to think about how it will look, whether it will be tall enough for them to stand up in and how many children would fit inside at once.

4. Provide pairs of children with photographs from your visit to see the living willow structures and tell them to look carefully at how the stems, or 'whips', have been woven together.

5. Ask them to try weaving some willow whips into different shapes, or – if you are unable to source real willow – use long pipe cleaners which can be threaded through and across each other and then bent into model domes or tunnels. Tell the children to cut out paper leaves and attach these to their mini-structures.

Science in the wider world

Willow is a tough plant that tends to grow roots easily – even from a cut stem that has been pushed into the ground. It also produces very flexible stalks that can be bent and woven together to create hedges or three-dimensional structures that can be used in the school's play area or as an outdoor living classroom.

Review

Children could be assessed on their observations about willow structures, their recognition of plant parts, their designs and their weaving work.

Objectives
● To identify and describe the basic structure of a variety of common flowering plants.

Resources
Pipe cleaners; coloured fabrics; card; paper, wool; large sheets of card; glue; a selection of plant-part labels

Working scientifically
● To identify and classify.

The basic structure of flowering plants

Revise
● Use photographs and examples of the children's work from during this topic to recap the basic structure of flowering plants. Remind the children of all the plants they have watched growing and changing, such as the dandelions, runner beans, busy lizzie plants, hyacinths and cress seeds, and talk about what has been happening to these. Prompt the children to think about the jobs done by different parts of the plant in anchoring it into the ground, collecting water and attracting insects. Ask them to describe the giant vegetable plant they made, with its carrot roots, celery stem, spinach and lettuce leaves and cauliflower and broccoli flowers, and encourage them to name as many plant parts as they can remember. Talk about why the roots are important and why flowers need to attract insects. Check their learning and fill in gaps as appropriate.

Assess
● Provide each child with a selection of pipe cleaners, coloured fabrics, card, paper and wool. Tell them to begin by making a pipe-cleaner model of a plant stem and laying it carefully on a large sheet of card.
● Next, ask them to select some of the coloured fabric, paper or card to cut into leaf shapes and to find another material suitable for roots. Tell them to attach these to their pipe-cleaner stem and then add the appropriate labels for the plant parts to their model.
● Tell the children to use more coloured fabric, paper or card to make a flower for their plant. Advise them to think carefully about the types of flowers they have observed during this topic and to try to show individual petals and possibly what it might look like inside the flower.
● Ask the children to select and add any further labels they think their model needs.
● Check that the children have made a recognisable representation of a flowering plant and have attempted to label the main parts of it. Also check that they have selected suitable colours for the leaves, stem, roots and flower.
● When the children have completed their flowering-plant model, ask them to draw an insect on their sheet, showing it flying towards the plant. Encourage them to think about which part of the plant the insect might be heading for and why.
● Review each child's model, drawing and labelling to assess their knowledge and understanding of the basic structure of flowering plants.

Further practice
● Support children by pre-labelling their sheets of card with 'root', 'stem', 'leaves', and 'flower' and provide pre-cut leaf and petal shapes from appropriately coloured materials, or blank templates for them to colour in. Ask them to point out features on their models and name them.
● Challenge the children to further demonstrate their knowledge and understanding of the structure of flowering plants by asking them to add on and label seeds and fruit. Encourage them to describe how the plants grow and change using some simple scientific vocabulary. These children could also write sentences about the jobs that the roots, stem and flowers do.

Objectives
● To identify and name a variety of common wild and garden plants deciduous and evergreen trees.

Resources
Images of all the focus plants covered during the topic; photocopiable page 142 'How does your garden grow?'; photocopiable page 'Deciduous trees' from the CD-ROM; photocopiable page 140 'Evergreen trees'; plant image 'snap' cards and plant identification charts for plants children have looked at this term

Working scientifically
● To identify and classify.
● *To make comparisons and decide how to sort and group.*

Naming common plants

Revise
● Remind the children of the visits they have made to the botanical gardens and the park as appropriate, to look at flowering plants and trees. Display photographs and examples of their work from this topic and challenge them to list as many plants as they can remember. Sing 'Mary, Mary Quite Contrary' to prompt their memories about garden plants and remind them that quite a few of these had girls' names. Ask if they can name any of the garden plants that grow from bulbs and remind them of the hyacinths they grew in class. Next, tell the children to recall as many wild plants as they can and write these in a list. Continue adding to the list with the names of deciduous and evergreen trees. Play some 'odd one out' and 'I spy' games to help reinforce the children's learning and practise linking names with specific plant images.

Assess
● Provide each child with photocopiable page 142 'How does your garden grow?' Tell them to match the garden plants with their names (lily, rose, busy lizzie, pansy, daffodil, tulip) and then try to answer the extension question: 'Can you name a plant that gardeners would not want in their gardens?'
● Give children the photocopiable page 'Deciduous trees' from the CD-ROM and explain that on the left-hand side of page there are outline drawings of lime, sycamore, oak and ash trees. On the right-hand side of the page, there are drawings of their leaves, but these have been jumbled up. Ask the children to draw lines to connect each tree with its leaf and then to select the correct name from the choice at the bottom to write onto the leaf.
● You could also assess how well the children can recall the names of evergreen trees using photocopiable page 140 'Evergreen trees'. Remind the children that these were trees they learnt about in a previous lesson. Ask them to look carefully at the trees again and try to remember which ones had berries and which had cones. Tell the children to draw these on the right trees and to write in the names of the trees.
● Make playing-card-size images of all the plants covered in this topic and challenge the children to use them to play games of 'snap', but add in an extra rule that, before the child who has shouted 'snap' can pick the cards up, they have to say what the plant is called. (Provide the children with plant identification sheets to help them check.)

Further practice
● Support the children by providing ready-made labels for them to attach to pictures in the plant identification assessment activities. You could also enlarge the photocopiable sheets or limit the number of plant images that you ask them to identify to one or two.
● Challenge the children to list the names of other plants they know and add in information about whether they grow from bulbs or seeds, or produce berries or cones, for example.

Objectives
● To identify and describe the basic structure of a variety of common flowering plants.

Resources
Large outline of entire plant from week 4, lesson 3; hyacinths (or photographs of them) from week 2, lesson 3; bean plants grown in pebbles (or photographs of them) from week 4, lesson 1; photographs of busy lizzies from week 2, lesson 2; photographs of plants in trays from week 3, lesson 2; photocopiable page 138 'Plant parts'; small images of the dry busy lizzie and tray of plants that was kept in the dark printed onto sheets of paper with space for the children to write on; sheets of paper with two plant outlines; selection of torn coloured papers; glue

Working scientifically
● To identify and classify.
● *To make comparisons and decide how to sort and group.*
● To gather and record data to help in answering questions.

Helping plants grow well

Revise
● Display the large outline of an entire plant used in week 4, lesson 3 and ask the children to identify parts as you point them out. Begin revising from the roots up; show the children the hyacinth you have been growing over water and look closely at how its root system has developed. Compare this with the bean seedlings planted in pebbles. Ask the children to tell you why roots are important and show them a photograph of the healthy busy lizzie plant. Encourage them to identify it and to recall what happened to make the second plant look different. Display the photograph taken of the busy lizzie that had not been watered for a few days and talk about what had happened. Establish that the children understand there was no water in the soil for the roots to absorb and so the plant began to dry out. Check that the children also recognise the role of the roots in holding plants in the ground; remind them of the trees and other plants they have looked at and talk about why they don't blow away in the wind.
● Next, show images of the trays of plants that were used for your investigation of light and dark. Ask the class to recall what happened to the tray they put in a cupboard for a few days and display the photograph taken when you took the tray out again and compared it with the one that had stayed in the light. Draw the children's attention to the yellow leaves and long, straggly stems of the plants that have been in the dark and establish that light is important for healthy plants.

Assess
● Reuse photocopiable page 138 'Plant parts' and ask the children to label the plant independently.
● Provide each child with a sheet of paper with printed images of the dry busy lizzie and tray of plants that was kept in the dark. Tell the children they are going to be 'plant doctors' and write by each picture what the plants need to make them better.
● Provide the children with a selection of torn-up coloured papers and a sheet of paper with two blank outlines of a flowering plant. Tell them to select colours to show the plant is healthy and stick these onto one of the outlines to make a collage. Then ask them to repeat this activity for the other plant, but this time selecting and gluing on colours to make it look unhealthy. Once they have completed the collage work, ask them to label the plants 'healthy' and 'unhealthy'.

Further practice
● Support children with initial-letter clues to help them label the plant parts; provide labels with instructions for the 'plant doctor' activity, such as 'water this plant' and 'put this plant in the light'; and provide 'healthy' and 'unhealthy' labels for the plant collage activity.
● Challenge children when they are naming the parts of the plant to write a sentence explaining why they are important. They could also add more detail to their 'plant doctor' advice and to the plant collage activity.

Name: _____   Date: _____

Botanical gardens

■ Add labels to the plants and colour them in.

I can name some plants in the botanical gardens.

How did you do?

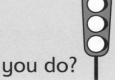

Who am I?

■ Match the names of the flowers the pictures.

lily

rose

busy lizzie

pansy

daffodil

tulip

I can name some garden flowers.

How did you do?

Name: _____ Date: _____

Bean diary

■ Record how your beans grow and change each week.

Day 1	After 1 week

_____ _____ _____	_____ _____ _____
After ____ weeks	**After ____ weeks**

_____ _____ _____	_____ _____ _____

PHOTOCOPIABLE

Plant parts

■ Label the parts of the plant.

| root | stem | leaf | flower |

I can name parts of a flowering plant.

How did you do?

PHOTOCOPIABLE

SCHOLASTIC
www.scholastic.co.uk

Horse chestnut tree story

■ Match the leaves, flowers and conkers to the right horse chestnut tree. Show how the leaves change at different times of year.

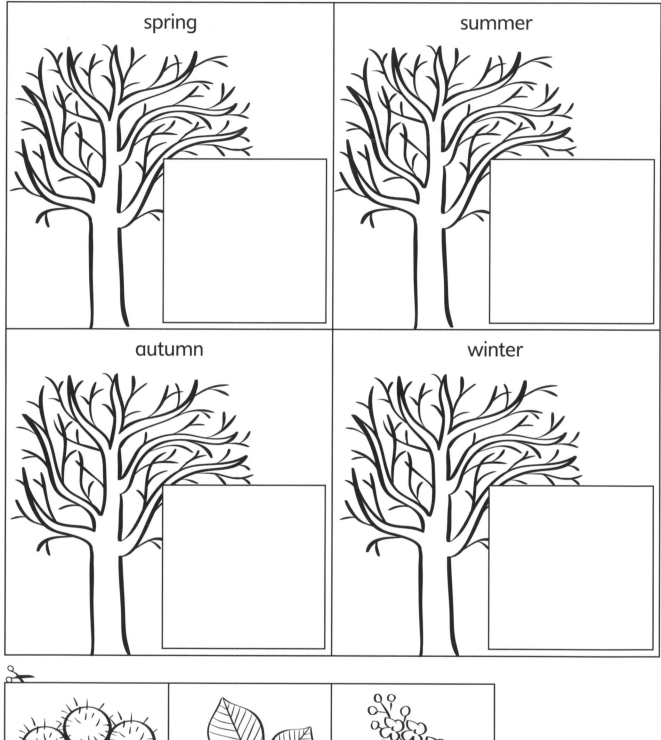

spring

summer

autumn

winter

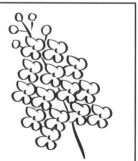

Evergreen trees

■ Look carefully at these trees. Which one has berries?
Which one has cones? Draw these on the right trees. Write in the
name of each tree.

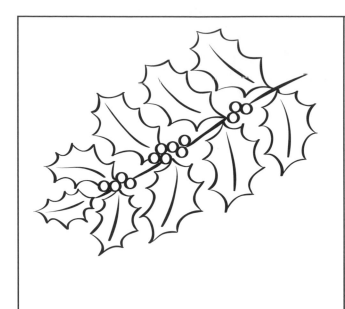
_____

_____

_____

_____

holly   Scots pine   spruce   privet

I can describe some evergreen trees.

How did you do?

PHOTOCOPIABLE

SCHOLASTIC
www.scholastic.co.uk

Where do plants live?

■ Link these plants to the part of the world they came from.

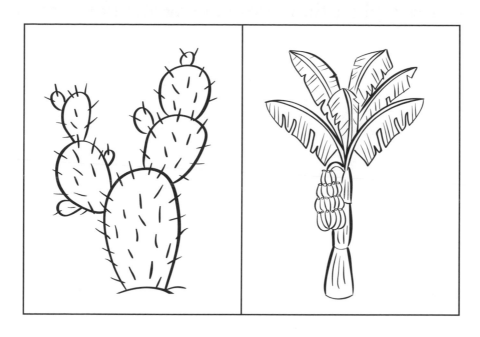

(our park)   (rainforest)

(desert)   (warm, dry country)

I can say where some plants live.

How did you do?

Name: _____   Date: _____

How does your garden grow?

■ Match these garden plants to their names.

■ Can you name a plant that gardeners would not want in their gardens?

lily

rose

busy lizzie

pansy

daffodil

tulip

I can name some plants that grow in gardens.

How did you do?

PHOTOCOPIABLE

SCHOLASTIC
www.scholastic.co.uk

Seasons: spring and summer

Expected prior learning

- Observations about some changes in weather and day length.
- Names of some common plants and animals.
- How seasonal change can affect plants and animals.

Overview of progression

After completing this chapter the children should know about:

- weather associated with spring and summer
- some changes in day length
- how plants, animals and humans are affected by seasonal changes associated with spring and summer.

Creative context

- This topic provides many opportunities for children to make observational drawings and use images to present their findings.
- Children will be required to deploy their design and technology skills when making model birds' nests and sunflowers.
- The natural environment lends itself to various forms of creative writing, song, music and dance.

Background knowledge

Farm animals

Farm animals are bred for many purposes: eggs and meat from chickens; milk and beef from cows; wool and lamb from sheep; and pork from pigs. Chicks are traditionally associated with spring. They hatch after an incubation period of around 21 days. Lambs are also associated with spring. Ewes usually give birth to one or two lambs, often in a small pen away from the main flock, where they stay until the lambs have bonded with their mothers. Sheep are generally sheared in the summer months to prevent them from overheating.

Wild animals and plants

By the summer solstice, daylight in the UK increases to over 16 hours a day (from around 8 hours in the depths of winter). For many animals, this increase provides opportunities for courtship, reproduction and raising their young. Plants also take advantage of the increase in day length to photosynthesise and grow prolifically. Flowering plants exploit the abundance of insect pollinators at this time of year.

Speaking scientifically

In this chapter, the children will have opportunities to work scientifically and observe changes across spring and summer, observe and describe the weather at this time of year, and observe the apparent movement of the Sun and how daylight varies. A simple scientific vocabulary will enable the children to comment on their observations and could include: temperature, daylight, arable, pastoral, cereal, harvest, cattle, sheep, poultry, adult, offspring, life cycle, breeding, incubating, hatching, dawn, shadow, sunscreen, photosynthesis, air pressure, anemometer, water vapour and spectrum.

Preparation

Ensure that your class understands that it is never safe to look directly at the Sun and remind them of this when you are undertaking any of the activities relating to day length or sunny weather.

You will need to provide: cameras; video and images of spring and summer scenes, including plants and animals; weather measuring equipment; clipboards; gardening gloves; sunhats, sunglasses, sunscreen; travel brochures

On the CD-ROM you will find: photocopiable pages 'Spring and summer weather', 'The early bird catches the worm'; interactive activities 'Animals', 'Life cycles', 'Wind', 'Rainbow colours', 'Changing seasons'; media resources 'Bird nests', 'Dawn chorus'

Chapter at a glance

Week	Lesson	Curriculum objectives	Lesson objectives	Main activity	Working scientifically
1	1	• To observe changes across the four seasons.	• To look for evidence of spring. • To identify some common farm animals. • To find out what work needs to be done on a farm at different times of year.	Visiting a farm to find out what happens in spring/summer.Gathering information on lambing, egg hatching, returning cattle to fields after winter, crop planting, and so on.	• Asking simple questions. • Identifying and classifying. • Observing closely. • Making comparisons. • Gathering and recording data to help in answering questions.
	2	• To observe changes across the four seasons (spring/ summer).	• To learn the names of animals and their young. • To match adult animals to their offspring.	Recapping animals observed on farm visit. Matching pictures of animals to their young.	• Identifying and classifying. • Observing closely. • Making comparisons.
	3	• To observe changes across the four seasons (spring/ summer).	• To investigate life cycles. • To review the life cycle of a frog. • To order the life cycles of a butterfly and a chicken.	Recapping on frog life cycle covered previously. Looking at images of stages of chicken's life cycle and ordering them correctly.	• Identifying and classifying. • Observing closely. • Making comparisons.
2	1	• To observe changes across the four seasons (spring/ summer).	• To observe similarities and differences between some common birds' nests. • To identify materials that could be used to build a birds' nest. • To build their own 'birds' nest'.	Looking at images of birds gathering material for nests and comparing with finished articles. Talking about why good nests are necessary. Making model nests.	• Asking simple questions. • Identifying and classifying. • Observing closely. • Making comparisons. • Gathering and recording data to help in answering questions.
	2	• To observe how day length varies. • To observe changes across the four seasons (spring/ summer).	• To understand that there are more hours of daylight in spring and summer. • To discover that birds sing at dawn. • To understand the position of the Sun in the sky at sunrise.	Listening to dawn chorus recording and discussing why birds sing loudly. Comparing with birds in the evening. Making pictures of sunrise.	• Asking simple questions. • Observing closely. • Making comparisons. • Gathering and recording data to help in answering questions.
	3	• To observe and describe weather associated with the seasons and how day length varies.	• To compare different weather conditions. • To identify activities suitable for a warm summer's day.	Using images identify what you can do in the sunshine.	• Observing closely. • Making comparisons. • Gathering and recording data to help in answering questions.
3	1	• To observe how day length varies.	• To suggest and investigate the shadiest spots in the playground. • To observe and record shadows throughout the day. • To explain why the shadows have changed during the day.	Finding a shady spot for Teddy in the playground by observing what happens to shadows throughout the day.	• Asking simple questions. • Identifying and classifying. • Observing closely. • Making comparisons. • Gathering and recording data to help in answering questions.
	2	• To observe how day length varies.	• To understand that too much sunlight can be harmful. • To identify ways of protecting yourself from too much sunlight.	Using images to identify hazards connected to exposure to strong sunshine. Producing a poster.	• Gathering and recording data to help in answering questions.
	3	• To observe how day length varies.	• To explore how some plants move to follow the Sun during the course of a day. • To revise the apparent movement of the Sun across the sky during the day.	Watching time-lapse footage of heliotropic plants and making paper-plate models. Turning model flowers to face the Sun as it appears to move.	• Observing closely. • Making comparisons.

Chapter at a glance

Week	Lesson	Curriculum objectives	Lesson objectives	Main activity	Working scientifically
4	1	• To describe weather associated with the seasons.	• To suggest ways of investigating wind direction. • To investigate the effect of bubble size. • To investigate how to make the biggest bubble.	Recapping wind speed/direction readings. Investigating a variety of bubble makers.	• Asking simple questions. • Identifying and classifying. • Observing closely. • Making comparisons. • Gathering and recording data to help in answering questions.
	2	• To describe weather associated with the seasons.	• To observe different cloud formations. • To record cloud cover over the course of a week. • To match cloud formations to the weather they bring.	Displaying images of clouds and talking about the weather they bring. Comparing amounts of cloud cover and keeping a record of cloud observations.	• Identifying and classifying. • Observing closely. • Making comparisons. • Gathering and recording data to help in answering questions.
	3	• To describe weather associated with the seasons.	• To investigate rainbows. • To discover the colours of the rainbow and their order.	Singing songs about rainbows. Ordering colours of the rainbows correctly. Making rainbow pictures.	• Observing closely. • Making comparisons.
5	1	• To observe how day length varies.	• To recall the work on shadows from the autumn term. • To conduct a new investigation of shadow length and position. • To compare shadow length between autumn/winter and spring/summer.	Recapping shadow size observations taken in autumn. Repeating investigation to chart shadow length changes. Comparing string lengths used to take earlier measurements.	• Asking simple questions. • Identifying and classifying. • Observing closely. • Making comparisons and deciding how to sort and group. • Gathering and recording data to help in answering questions.
	2	• To observe changes across the four seasons (spring/summer).	• To make some predictions about temperature. • To suggest seasonal activities and clothing. • To make daily temperature recordings.	Reminding children of the weather measurements taken earlier in the year. Taking temperature readings over a week.	• Asking simple questions. • Observing closely. • Making comparisons. • Gathering and recording data to help in answering questions.
	3	• To observe how day length varies.	• To observe and describe seasonal changes to hours of daylight. • To make observational drawings of 'bedtime' in winter and summer.	Reading letter from Teddy: he's having difficulty sleeping because, it's no longer dark when he goes to bed. Responding to letter and explaining what has happened.	• Asking simple questions. • Observing closely. • Making comparisons.
6	1	• To observe changes across the four seasons.	• To identify and record signs of early summer. • To identify changes to a tree across all four seasons.	Revisiting park to look for further signs of change. Looking at photos from previous visits and predicting how the park will have changed.	• Asking simple questions. • Identifying and classifying. • Observing closely. • Making comparisons. • Gathering and recording data to help in answering questions.
	2	• To observe changes across the four seasons.	• To observe a tree closely for seasonal changes. • To record their tree investigations.	Revisiting the tree observed previously to look for further signs of seasonal change. Predicting how a tree will change again.	• Asking simple questions. • Observing closely. • Making comparisons. • Gathering and recording data to help in answering questions.
	3	• To observe changes across the four seasons.	• To revise the months of the year and the seasons to which they belong. • To sort evidence according to season. • To explain their sorting.	Recaping on the seasons mobile made in the autumn term. Reviewing learning over the year on seasons.	• Asking simple questions. • Identifying and classifying. • Making comparisons.
Assess and review					

Objectives
● To look for evidence of spring.
● To identify some common farm animals.
● To find out what work needs to be done on a farm at different times of year.

Resources
Seasons mobile from autumn 1, week 1, lesson 2; children's work and photographs from previous autumn/winter/spring seasons topics; photographs of animals on a farm; photographs of the farm children will be visiting; images of common farm animals; clipboards and paper; cameras; photocopiable page 168 'A farm in spring'; photographs of wildlife, trees, wild plants, garden plants

Speaking scientifically
arable, cereals, harvest, cattle, sheep, poultry, adult, offspring

Lesson 1: Farm visit

Previous knowledge
During the Early Years Foundation Stage, children will have had opportunities to develop their understanding of similarities and differences between living things. They should have found out about different features of their immediate environment compared to others. They will also have made observations on how animals and plants occur or change. In addition to this, they should have completed the Year 1 seasons topics on autumn/winter and winter/spring, where they began to observe seasonal changes, weather associated with different seasons and how day length varies over the year.

Introduction
Look at the seasons mobile and talk about which months have passed since you set it up in the autumn. Check that the children are able to name and order the seasons and that they are aware that spring has started and that summer will follow. Remind the class of all the work they did previously on seasons and display some of this, along with photographs from any off-site visits they made to observe changes in the environment. Make a list of what they found out about changes in autumn, winter and early spring and challenge them to suggest questions about how the seasons are changing and what will happen next. Display some photographs of animals on a farm and tell the children that farms are very busy places at this time of year. Ask the children to identify the animals and describe what they know about farms. Explain that they will be going on a visit to one and will find out more about these animals and why they are important.

Whole-class work
1. Plan a visit to a local farm. There are a number of farms throughout the UK that have developed an educational role and can provide a quality learning experience for your children. Many education authorities have links with these and can provide information about who to contact and how to arrange a visit. Whenever you make an off-site educational visit, you will need to prepare by carrying out a thorough risk assessment and obtaining permission from parents and carers. Consider details such as transport, food, clothing, medical requirements (including any allergies) and an appropriate level of adult support.

2. Show the children some photographs of where they will be going and ask what they might expect to see there and what they would like to find out. Make a list of their questions and ideas. Explain that they will be able to see how the farmer looks after the animals and grows crops to feed them and us. Farms are busy places with big animals and lots of machinery, so establish some ground rules for staying safe, such as dressing appropriately, wearing robust footwear and staying with the group and accompanying adults. Hygiene is also very important so ensure the children are aware that they will need to keep their hands clean.

Group work
3. Consult with the farmer about how best to organise your class for the visit. He or she may suggest dividing the class into small adult-led groups and directing them to different locations around the farm, or recommend that the children stay together in one large group for the visit.

4. When outside: tell the children to look carefully at the animals, trees and plants, as well as on the ground, to find evidence of spring. Tell them to ask lots of questions to find out as much as they can about how the farmer works with the animals and crops. They should also make drawings and take photographs of what they see. Challenge them to find out what jobs there are on the farm at different times of the year and why the weather is so important to farmers.

Checkpoint
● What are the months of the year?
● What are the names of the seasons?
● Which season has just ended?
● Which season is just beginning?
● What happens in spring?
● How do trees change?
● How do animals change?
● What will change between now and autumn?

5. There may be opportunities to visit some of the sheds to watch cows being milked or to feed chickens. Encourage the children to make close observations and ask questions about life on the farm.

6. At various points during the visit, if appropriate, bring the whole class back together and talk about what they have found. Compare each group's observations about life on a farm in spring and send the children out to new locations to repeat their investigations.

Whole-class work

7. Back in class, remind the children of their visit to the farm and invite them to recall what they saw. Make a list of the information they have found out about farm animals and growing plants for food at this time of year, and display the photographs and any other evidence they collected.

Independent work

8. Provide children with photocopiable page 168 'A farm in spring' and ask them to label the animals and draw in some more signs of spring. They should shade it using appropriate colours.

Introducing the new area of study

Sing 'Old MacDonald Had a Farm' and other songs about animals or spring and talk about the lyrics. Display the weather charts the children used in the two previous terms and explain that they will be finding out more about weather in spring and summer, as well as ways in which the Sun affects us at this time of year. Show them pictures of garden birds and other local wildlife, farm animals, trees and wild and garden plants and explain that they will be finding out about how busy animals and plants are in the spring and summer.

Differentiation
● Support children with the photocopiable sheet by giving first-letter clues or labels to glue onto their farm scene.
● Challenge children to label their farm scene and write some information about life on a farm.

Science in the wider world

Terrain, soil type, rainfall, temperature and proximity to a market can all affect the type of farming possible in a particular region. Cattle are generally reared on extensive grasslands in milder parts of the UK, while sheep are often farmed on cooler upland hills and moors. Crops require fertile soil in flat areas.

Review

Children could be assessed on the observations they have made about life on a farm and signs of spring. They could also be assessed on their completion of the photocopiable sheet and inclusion of relevant detail such as colour, labels and sentences about their observations.

Objectives
- To learn the names of animals and their young.
- To match adult animals to their offspring.

Resources
Photographs from the farm visit; images of frog, tadpole, lamb, sheep, cow, calf, horse, foal, butterfly, caterpillar; name labels for images of animals; photocopiable page 169 'Parents and babies'; interactive activity 'Animals' on the CD-ROM

Speaking scientifically
sheep, lamb, cow, calf, chicken, chick, horse, foal, frog, tadpole, butterfly, caterpillar, adult, offspring

Lesson 2: Baby animals

Introduction
Remind your class of their farm visit and talk about what the children found out. Sing 'Old MacDonald' again and make a list of all the animals you observed on your visit. Talk about what you saw these animals do, how they were looked after and whether they had any babies with them. Work through the interactive activity 'Animals' on the CD-ROM together, matching parent and baby animals. Talk about the animals' role on a farm. Young children may find it upsetting to learn that the animals they have been patting or feeding end up as food, so it may be better to stick to products such as wool from sheep, milk from cows and goats, and eggs from chickens. Ask the children if baby animals have the same names as the adults.

Whole-class work
1. Show the children the images of young farm animals, one at a time, and ask them to identify them. Clarify with them that while they are a baby sheep, cow and horse, each has a special name. Display a name label by each picture and practise saying the names together.

2. Check that the children recognise the connection between the parents and offspring by playing a game. Tell them that they are to guess which animal you are thinking of, but they can only ask questions which have a yes or no answer. Once they have guessed the animal, challenge them to say the parent or baby that goes with it.

3. Display pictures of both the parent and baby animal for each species. Ask the children to look at these closely and describe any differences they notice. Draw their attention to the fact that the parents and offspring are very similar, but the adults are much bigger.

4. Display the images of a frog and butterfly. Explain that these are both parents, but that they look very different from their offspring. Encourage the children to describe the differences and reveal images of a tadpole and caterpillar. Ask the children to say which one goes with which adult.

5. Tell the children that they are going to match up parents and babies and put the correct names by each one. Show them an enlarged version of photocopiable page 169 'Parents and babies' and explain how to fill it in. Draw lines to join the correct parents and babies.

Independent work
6. Provide children with the photocopiable sheet or the interactive activity 'Animals' on the CD-ROM and ask them to match the young animals to the appropriate adults.

> ### Differentiation
> - Support children with name labels for them to glue into the empty boxes on the photocopiable sheet.
> - Challenge children to say which animal groups the examples belong to.

Science in the wider world
There are around 1.8 million dairy cows in the UK, producing over 13 billion litres of milk each year – around 7000 litres per cow. Around 29 million laying hens in the UK produce over 9 billion eggs per annum. There are more than 60 different breeds of sheep in Britain, producing around 60,000 tonnes of wool each year.

Review
Children could be assessed on their observations about the animals they saw on the farm and how they linked young animals to their parents on the photocopiable sheet or in the interactive activity.

Objectives
● To investigate life cycles.
● To review the life cycle of a frog.
● To order the life cycles of a butterfly and a chicken.

Resources
Chicken incubator kit or images of chickens and eggs; images of frogspawn, tadpoles, froglets, frogs; images of butterfly life cycle; images of chicken life cycle; interactive activity 'Life cycles' on the CD-ROM

Speaking scientifically
life cycle, adult frog, frogspawn, tadpole, froglet, gills, tail, leg, adult chicken, egg, chick, egg tooth

Lesson 3: Chicken or egg?

Introduction

Some educational suppliers can provide incubator tanks, eggs and heaters to schools so that children can observe chicks hatching out in their classroom. Alternatively, you could display some images of an adult chicken and an egg. Ask the children the age-old question: *Which came first, the chicken or the egg?* Invite the children to make suggestions, before explaining that it isn't easy to agree on an answer. Tell the children that by the end of the lesson, they will see why there is no straightforward solution.

Whole-class work

1. Remind the children about the jumbled images of stages in a frog's life cycle that they looked at during the autumn term (as part of the session on amphibian structure in autumn 2, week 5, lesson 3). Display these out of order and encourage the children to tell you the correct order. Lay the images out in a line as the children direct you and when you have got to the adult frog stage, ask the children what happens next. Encourage them to recognise that it is the adult frogs that lay the frogspawn, from which the tadpoles emerge to grow into new adult frogs. Gradually slide the pieces around to form a circle. Remind the children that this arrangement is called a 'life cycle' because it carries on with new adults laying eggs and young frogs growing from tadpoles every year.

2. Ask the children to help you make a life-cycle picture for a butterfly. Display jumbled images of eggs, caterpillars, chrysalides and butterflies and talk about each stage, sliding the images into a circle at the children's direction.

Paired work

3. Provide pairs of children with images of stages from a chicken's life and ask them to work together to put these into a circle to show the chicken's life cycle. Tell them to glue these onto card and label each stage: 'adult chicken', 'egg', 'chick with egg tooth' and 'young chicken'.

Whole-class work

4. Compare pairs' ideas and ask the children if they are any closer to answering the question: *Which came first, the chicken or the egg?* Encourage them to explain that this is impossible to answer because they are both part of the chicken's life cycle and one couldn't happen without the other. Work together through the interactive activity 'Life cycles' on the CD-ROM.

Science in the wider world

Female chickens (hens) lay eggs which contain a yolk that will provide the developing chick with food until it is ready to hatch out, usually after 21 days. The yolk floats in the egg white, which protects it and provides liquid for the chick. When ready to hatch, the chick uses an egg tooth to peck holes in the shell, but this will fall off after a few days, as the chick no longer needs it. Chickens reach full maturity when they are around 20 weeks old when, as pullets, they can start to lay eggs. They can live for about 10 years.

Review

Children could be assessed on how accurately they can describe the life cycles of frogs and butterflies as well as ordering the life cycle of a chicken.

● To observe similarities and differences between some common birds' nests.
● To identify materials that could be used to build a birds' nest.
● To build their own 'birds' nest'.

Resources
Images or video of garden birds gathering nesting materials; media resource 'Bird nests' on the CD-ROM; disposable gloves and bags for collecting natural materials in; a selection of 'nesting materials' – pipe cleaners, wool, tissue paper, cotton wool; recording of cuckoo song

Speaking scientifically
nesting, courtship, breeding, brooding, incubating, hatching

Lesson 1: Feathering nests

Introduction
Show the class some images or video footage of garden birds gathering material for building nests. Encourage the children to suggest why the birds are gathering these things. Explain that the prime time for garden birds to lay eggs and raise their young – sometimes in three or four broods – is between March and August. For many species, this process starts with building a nest in early spring, as daylight, temperature and food supplies increase.

Whole-class work
1. Display the media resource 'Bird nests' on the CD-ROM. Blackbirds' nests are generally the most common and are neatly constructed from grass and twigs, while magpies' nests are much larger, with small branches and bigger twigs criss-crossed into an untidy inverted dome shape. Talk about any similarities and differences in the choice of materials and design.

2. Ask the children to list other materials they notice that have been used for each nest, such as leaves and feathers, and explain that many birds smear mud around the inside of their construction. Encourage the children to say why.

3. Tell the children that they are going on a 'nesting safari' in the school grounds or local parkland. They will look on the ground for suitable materials, as well as watching out for birds and signs of nesting activity in trees or hedges. Ensure that the children realise they should only collect fallen materials while wearing gloves, that they should not pick anything that is still growing and that they should place their selection in a collecting bag. Explain that they will have more chance of seeing garden birds if they work quietly and do not make any sudden movements. Take photographs of any birds or nests that you come across.

4. Back in class, look at the materials. Talk about how birds weave these into a bowl shape secure enough to support their eggs.

5. If you have collected a large amount of natural materials, you may decide that the class could use them to make nests with, but be aware that these will not be clean and take suitable precautions to ensure the children can work safely. Alternatively, show them the craft materials, and demonstrate how these could be woven into a secure shape.

Paired work
6. Provide pairs of children with a selection of materials. Challenge them to make a nest strong enough to hold some marbles.

7. Display the finished nests alongside examples of natural nesting materials you found and images of garden birds and real nests.

Whole-class work
8. Play the children a recording of a cuckoo song. Ask if they can name the bird. Explain that the song is often taken as a sign that spring has started. cuckoos are notorious for leaving their eggs with other birds to hatch and feed.

Science in the wider world
Blackbirds can take around two weeks to build their nests, before laying between three and five eggs, which are then incubated for about 14 days. Magpies can take several weeks to complete their nests and then lay between five and eight eggs, which are incubated for about three weeks.

Review
Children could be assessed on their observations about nest building and the model nests they make.

Objectives
- To understand that there are more hours of daylight in spring and summer.
- To discover that birds sing at dawn.
- To understand the position of the Sun in the sky at sunrise.

Resources
Media resource 'Dawn chorus' on the CD-ROM; examples of sunrise–sunset timelines and models made by children earlier in the year; images of sunrise; video of birds returning to roosts in the evening; paints and paper; black paper; scissors

Speaking scientifically
dawn, sunrise, sunset, horizon, territory

Lesson 2: Dawn to dusk

Introduction
Play the class a recording of the 'Dawn chorus' on the CD-ROM and ask the children to suggest what sort of animals are making the sounds and what time of day they think this is happening. Explain that they are listening to birds singing in the early morning and that when large numbers of them all sing together at the same time it is called the 'dawn chorus'. It is particularly noticeable during the spring and summer months when birds are breeding. Remind the children of the timeline and model work they have done previously on sunrise and sunset and check that they recognise that 'dawn' is another word for sunrise.

Whole-class work
1. Display an image of sunrise and point out the position of the Sun – just coming into view above the horizon. Explain that the early light of dawn wakes the birds up and they begin singing to let other birds know that they are there, either to attract a mate or guard their territory. The first birds to start singing are the ones with big eyes, such as blackbirds, because there is still not much light. Later stirrers are the ones with smaller eyes, as it becomes light enough for them to feed on insects or peck at seeds; but the early birds are the worm catchers!

2. Remind the children of the 'What's the time Mr Wolf?' game they played during their last topic on seasons, which started at 'sunrise' and ended when the wolf gave chase at 'sunset'. Compare playing this in the summer and winter and talk about when there is more daylight. (The wolf called sunrise much earlier and sunset much later in the summer game than in the winter one.)

3. Look at footage of birds returning to their trees to roost in the evening and explain that there is also a chorus at dusk, though generally this is considered to be quieter than the morning one.

Independent work
4. Tell the children to choose suitable colours and to paint a sunrise scene. While these are drying, ask the children to out cut tree shapes from black paper to glue onto their work.

Group work
5. Display the finished sunrise pictures and listen to the dawn chorus again.

Science in the wider world
Birds have a specialised voice box called a 'syrinx'. It is thought that the dawn chorus lets neighbouring birds know that the singer is still there, and by singing loudly, possible mates are alerted: a strong bird that is good at foraging will have more energy for singing. There is also a chorus at dusk and while this is generally quieter, some species such as tree sparrows and blue tits appear to sing more at this time of day. An International Dawn Chorus Day is held in early May each year.

Review
Children could be assessed on their observations about sunrise and sunset at different times of the year and on their sunrise pictures showing the Sun low in the sky.

Objectives
• To compare different weather conditions.
• To identify activities suitable for a warm summer's day.

Resources
Photograph of winter scene showing people dressed warmly and photograph of summer scene showing people lightly dressed; images of different types of weather – snow, rain, wind, sunshine; photocopiable page 170 'What can you do when the Sun is warm?'

Speaking scientifically
sunrise, dawn, sunset, dusk, higher, lower, sunlight, shortest, longest

Lesson 3: What can you do in the sunshine?

Introduction

Display a photograph of the 'winter wonderland' visit you made earlier in the year or a general wintery scene of people dressed warmly for ice and snow. Ask the children to recall what it was like in the winter and make a list of their observations. Next, show them an image portraying a warm summer's day, with people dressed accordingly and taking advantage of the sunshine. Make comparisons between the two seasons and ask the children to identify similarities and differences. Encourage them to say which they prefer and why. Teach the children a verse of 'The Sun Has Got His Hat On'.

Whole-class work

1. Play a game to reinforce the children's understanding about different types of weather. Show them a succession of images portraying a variety of weather scenes on the interactive whiteboard. Explain that when they see rain, they should form an umbrella with their hands above their heads. If they see ice or snow, they should shiver and give themselves a hug, and if it looks very windy, they should all lean in the same direction. When they spot the Sun, they should shade their eyes and sing a verse of 'The Sun Has Got His Hat On'. Start off changing the images slowly, but gradually speed up and challenge the children to perform the corresponding action each time.

2. Display some additional images of warm sunny days and invite the children to say what they like to do in this sort of weather. Encourage them to explain why their example is a good activity to do on a warm sunny day and what would happen if they tried to do it during any other sort of weather.

3. Show the class an enlarged photocopiable page 170 'What can you do when the Sun is warm?' and point out the descriptions at the bottom. Read out one or two as examples and ask the children to choose whether these are warm sunshine activities or not. Ask them to circle the ones that are.

Independent work

4. Ask the children to complete the photocopiable sheet by writing description labels by each activity.

> **Differentiation**
> • Support children by providing labels which describe each activity for them to glue by each picture.
> • Challenge children to write sentences to suggest other activities they can do in warm sunshine, or explain why attending a firework display in the early evening, or building a snowman, cannot be done.

Science in the wider world

May is often the month in the UK with the highest number of hours of sunshine, nearly 200, although temperatures are generally higher in July. The month with the lowest average amount of sunshine is December. The sunniest parts of the UK are on the south coast of England, enjoying around 1750 hours of sunshine per year. Eastbourne, in East Sussex, currently holds the record for the most sunshine in a month, with over 383 hours in July 1911.

Review

Children could be assessed on their comparisons between different types of weather and their recognition of activities that are best done on a warm, sunny day.

■SCHOLASTIC

Objectives
- To suggest and investigate the shadiest spots in the playground.
- To observe and record shadows throughout the day.
- To explain why the shadows have changed during the day.

Resources
Letter from Teddy; work and photographs relating to shadow investigations from autumn 1, week 2, lesson 1; camera; chalk; photocopiable page 171 'Letter to Teddy'

Speaking scientifically
sun, shadow, sunlight, direction, length

Lesson 1: Finding shade for Teddy

Introduction
Set the scene for this lesson by telling the children that a cuddly toy, Teddy, has written to your class asking for help. Read them a letter from Teddy, which explains that he is making a visit to your school soon. He has heard that the playground is a great place to play and wants to find out for himself. He is planning to spend a whole day outside, watching all the activities, such as playtimes and outdoor PE lessons, but he is a little worried as, with his furry coat, he gets hot very easily. He would like to stay in a shady spot all day. Can your class recommend where he should sit? Once you have finished reading the letter, ask the children to make some initial observations about parts of the school grounds that are very sunny or shady.

Whole-class work
1. Remind the class of the work they did earlier in the year on shadows. Display the photographs and work relating to the investigation they carried out. Encourage the children to recall what they found out about their shadows, pointing out the changes in size and direction.

2. Ask your class to suggest how they might find out which are the shadiest spots in the playground and make a list of their ideas. Go on an initial walk around the area to identify the parts in Sun and those in shade. Take some photographs and make a note of the time.

3. Point out that some sections of the playground that are in shade in the morning could be in full Sun by the afternoon, and vice versa, so observing different parts of the area throughout the day would give them a better idea of how to advise Teddy. Select three or four different locations around the grounds to observe more closely.

4. Choose a sunny day when the forecast is for settled weather and begin by checking on shade and Sun early in the school day. Ask the children to record their observations by drawing outlines of shaded areas with chalk and taking photographs. Repeat this process throughout the day.

5. When you have collected all your data, display the photographs and encourage the children to talk about their observations. Focus on parts of the playground that started off either in Sun or in shade, but as the day goes on try to identify the area that is in the shade the longest. Perhaps the children will have to advise Teddy to move to a different location in the afternoon?

6. Challenge the children to explain why the shadows changed.

Independent work
7. Ask the children to use photocopiable page 171 'Letter to Teddy' to write to Teddy explaining what they found out and to draw a picture to show him the best place to sit in the playground.

> **Differentiation**
> - Support children by reducing the amount of writing they are required to do in the letter.
> - Challenge children to add more detail to their letter and explain why shadows move.

Science in the wider world
The Sumerians are thought to have been the first people to use shadows to tell the time and the ancient Egyptians are believed to have first devised a way of dividing the day into parts and using a tall pillar to calculate times of the day.

Review
Children could be assessed on their observations about how the shadows changed and the advice they give to Teddy in their letter.

Objectives
● To understand that too much sunlight can be harmful.
● To identify ways of protecting yourself from too much sunlight.

Resources
Sunhats, sunglasses, sunscreen; yellow paper or card cut into large Sun shapes for posters; old travel brochures or magazines; images of being safe in the Sun for the interactive whiteboard; scissors; glue

Speaking scientifically
sunshine, strong, sunburn, shade, sunscreen, SPF, UVA

Lesson 2: Care in the Sun

Introduction
Remind the class about the letter from Teddy in the previous lesson, requesting a shady spot in the playground. Ask the children if they can remember the reason he gave – he gets too hot in his fur coat in the Sun. Ask whether they can suggest any other reasons why shade is important. Encourage them to think about what they wear when there is strong sunshine and list their ideas, prompting further with examples: sunhats, sunglasses, sunscreen, and so on.

Whole-class work
1. Explain to the children that, although being out in the sunshine can be enjoyable, getting sunburnt is not. Sunburn is painful and damages the skin, so it is very important to take care in the sunshine.

2. Review the items you showed the class at the beginning of the lesson and talk about why each one is important. A sunhat protects the wearer's head from the Sun, a wide brim keeping the face in shade. Some children's hats have a flap that hangs over the back of the neck, protecting that too. Sunglasses reduce glare and can offer some protection to the eyes, while regularly applying sunscreen and wearing a t-shirt prevents exposure of delicate skin to the Sun. Show the children a bottle of sunscreen and explain that a number bigger than 15 is best.

3. The Australian 'Slip! Slop! Slap!' message resonates well with children around the world. The Cancer Council campaign featured Sid the Seagull, who recommended that people slip on a shirt, slop on sunscreen and slap on a hat when out in the Sun. Practise actions for each rule with your class to help them remember these three activities for reducing the risk of sunburn.

4. Explain that it is a good idea to stay out of the Sun between 11am and 3pm and remind the children about where the Sun is in the sky at this time. The higher the Sun, the stronger the damaging rays. The children should also be aware that they need to top up regularly on sunscreen, especially if they have been swimming.

5. Provide the children with old holiday brochures and magazines and tell them to find some good examples of people taking care in the Sun. Look at their selections, compare them with some images displayed on the interactive whiteboard and recap the rules.

Independent work
6. Ask each child to make a poster. Tell them to choose pictures from the magazines and brochures and cut and stick these onto their yellow card background. Encourage them to think of a simple message to add to their poster to advise people to take care in the Sun.

Science in the wider world
It is estimated that children spend around 90 minutes outside during the school day. While skin cancer among children is rare, sunburn during childhood can increase the risk of developing this in later life. As babies and young children have more delicate skin than adults, exposure to sunshine is more likely to result in sunburn.

Review
Children could be assessed on their choice of pictures portraying care in the Sun and the message they put on their posters.

Objectives

● To explore how some plants move to follow the Sun during the course of a day.
● To revise the apparent movement of the Sun across the sky during the day.

Resources

Time-lapse video footage of heliotropes; images of sunflowers; paper plates; yellow paper cut into petal shapes; dried lentils or small craft beads; glue

Speaking scientifically

plant, heliotrope, sunlight, photosynthesis, flower, leaf, stem, root, seed, soil

Lesson 3: Follow the Sun

Introduction

If using foodstuffs for the model-making activity, check for allergies among the children in your class first.

Remind the children about the work they did on plants in the previous term and ask them to recall what plants need to grow well. Emphasise the importance of sunlight and recap what happened to the plants that were left in a dark cupboard for a few days. Explain that most plants need light to grow properly and that some plants have found a way of getting as much light as possible by ensuring their flowers and leaves always face the Sun. As the children have found out, the Sun seems to move across the sky during the day and the flowers and leaves of some plants gently move to follow it. This happens too slowly for us to see, but you could show your class some time-lapse video footage of heliotropes, such as arctic poppies, moving over the course of a day.

Whole-class work

1. Encourage the children to recall why many plants produce flowers – to attract insects to drink nectar and collect pollen. Ask the children what they think might happen if a flower is facing the Sun all day and guide them to suggest that it will warm up. Explain that some plants are able to turn their flower heads to follow the Sun as its position in the sky changes.

2. Display an image of a sunflower field and ask the children if they can name these flowers. A chemical inside the stem causes newly opened sunflowers to tilt towards the Sun (once these have been pollinated the movement stops).

3. Show the class how to make sunflower models by attaching yellow petal shapes to the edge of a paper plate and either drawing in seeds or gluing on lentils or small craft beads.

4. Once the children have made their sunflowers, use these to play a game along the lines of 'Simon says'. The children stand in a group with their sunflower models above their heads facing you. Every time you say *The sunflower says, 'turn'* and point in a particular direction, the children shuffle round to face that way. If you just say *Turn*, the children should stand still and anyone who continues to move is out.

Science in the wider world

Heliotropism – or solar tracking – is a growth movement in plants that is prompted by sunlight. The snow buttercup and arctic poppy are both heliotrope plants but despite its French name (Tournesol), mature sunflowers no longer track the Sun. A sunflower is actually made up of many tiny flowers. The plants are cultivated for their seeds, which can be eaten or crushed to produce oil.

Review

Children could be assessed on their observations about how the Sun appears to move over the course of the day and the effect this has on plants.

Objectives
- To suggest ways of investigating wind direction.
- To investigate the effect of bubble size.
- To investigate how to make the biggest bubble.

Resources
Wind measurers from autumn 1, week 3, lesson 3, or images of them; images of the effects of wind – chimney smoke, flags, trees leaning, and so on; video footage of children playing with bubble makers and blowing bubbles; bubble makers; bubble solution; a camera; sheets of paper for recording; interactive activity 'Wind' on the CD-ROM

Speaking scientifically
wind, wind sock, air pressure, anemometer; Beaufort scale: calm, light air, light breeze, gentle breeze, moderate breeze, fresh breeze, strong breeze, near gale, gale, strong gale, storm, violent storm, hurricane

Lesson 1: Bubble fun

Introduction
Remind the children of the wind measurers they made earlier in the year and show them images or examples of their work. Talk about how they used these and what they found out about the direction of the wind. Display the images showing the effects of wind and ask them to compare these. Encourage them to describe what the wind is moving in each picture and how hard it must be blowing. Reuse the interactive activity 'Wind' on the CD-ROM to remind them about the speed of the wind – from a light breeze to a gale.

Whole-class work
1. Show the class some video footage of children playing with bubble makers and blowing bubbles. Ask how they could use these in the playground to find out which direction the wind is blowing in. Encourage the children to suggest other investigations, such as whether big bubbles go further than small ones, or higher bubbles go quicker than lower ones. Make a list of questions you could investigate in the playground.

2. There are a number of commercially produced bubble-making kits that your class could try out, or have a go at making your own bubble solution and ask the children to make wands by attaching pipe cleaners to pieces of dowelling and bending the pipe cleaners into rings.

3. Begin by standing the children in a line and asking them to blow bubbles in unison and watch the direction they float away in. Ask them to say which direction the wind is blowing from and how they can tell this from the bubbles.

4. Encourage the children to think of a way of making their bubble races fair: by starting from the same height and changing the size of the bubble wands; or using the same size of wands, blowing at the same time and altering the height they start from?

5. Set the children a challenge to see who can blow the biggest bubble, make a bubble go the furthest, or pop the most bubbles. Take photographs.

6. Back in the classroom, look at the photographs you took of the children's investigations and ask them to describe what they did and what they found out. Encourage them to describe what might happen to the bubbles on a more or a less windy day.

Independent work
7. Provide children with sheets of paper and ask them to record what they did with sentences and drawings.

> ### Differentiation
> - Support children by providing them with thumbnail photographs and a wordbank of appropriate words, such as 'big bubbles', 'small bubbles', 'high', 'low', 'far', 'near'.
> - Challenge children to write sentences describing what they did and making comparisons between different bubbles.

Science in the wider world
Bubble solution can be made by mixing water, washing-up liquid and glycerine together. Glycerine/glycerol is generally sold in chemists in the UK as a soothing remedy for dry skin or coughs, but check that none of the children are allergic to it before bringing it into the classroom. You may also prefer to use a natural washing-up liquid product. Mix the ingredients in a shallow container so that the solution is easily accessible.

Review
Children could be assessed on their observations about wind strength and direction they made during the bubble investigations and comparisons they made about bubble size, distance and so on.

Objectives
- To observe different cloud formations.
- To record cloud cover over the course of a week.
- To match cloud formations to the weather they bring.

Resources
Examples of children's weather report videos from autumn 1, week 3, lesson 1; weather forecast symbols; images of different cloud formations; images of a foggy day and boiling kettle, steamy bathroom; cloud observation chart (see whole-class work)

Speaking scientifically
water vapour, cumulus, stratus, cirrus, nimbus, altocumulus, altostratus, nimbostratus

Lesson 2: Looking at clouds

Introduction
Remind the children of the weather observation work they carried out earlier in the year and show them some of the weather report videos they made. Display examples of weather forecast symbols used to describe different types of weather and recap what these mean. Draw the children's attention to the one for cloudy weather and talk about what sort of weather we might expect when we see this symbol. Point out that sometimes the Sun peeps out from behind the cloud symbol or there are drops of rain or snow falling from it. It can be fun to imagine shapes and faces when you look up at the clouds; invite the children to describe any unusual ones they have noticed and show them some images of different clouds, ranging from high, fair-weather cirrus 'mackerel skies' to thunderstorm cumulonimbus.

Whole-class work
1. Ask the class if they know what clouds are made of. Show some images of a foggy day, boiling kettle and steamy bathroom and encourage the children to recognise that these are linked with water. Explain that clouds are made up of tiny drops of water and, when they get too heavy, the drops fall as rain or snow.

2. Display the cloud formation images and ask the children to suggest what sort of weather the clouds might bring. Point out high, wispy (cirrus) clouds in a blue sky and compare these with thick, low grey (nimbostratus) rain clouds. Encourage children to notice differences in thickness and colour.

3. Tell the children that they are going to keep a record of cloud cover over the course of a week. Display a cloud observation chart: a large sheet showing days of the week with space for drawings of clouds and observations such as 'it's raining' or 'high wispy clouds'. Recall the other weather measurements the children took earlier in the year and explain that this time they will record the amount of cloud cover at the same time every day.

Science in the wider world
Clouds are composed of a large collection of tiny droplets of water or ice crystals which are small and light enough to float in the air. Cirrus clouds are very high and thin and can be blown into long streamers by high winds. Alto clouds form lower in the sky. Puffs of altocumulus clouds might be the first sign of bad weather approaching, while grey altostratus clouds usually cover the entire sky and appear ahead of major rain clouds. Stratus clouds are low, grey and fog-like, and generally cover the entire sky. They may produce a light drizzle, while darker nimbostratus clouds bring continuous rain or snow. Cumulus clouds are usually associated with fine weather. However, in certain atmospheric conditions they can grow upwards into towering cumulus and develop into cumulonimbus clouds, containing huge amounts of water vapour. These are thunderstorm clouds.

Review
Children could be assessed on their observations about various types of cloud and simple comparisons they make about their colour, size and altitude.

Objectives
• To investigate rainbows.
• To discover the colours of the rainbow and their order.

Resources
Images of rainbows; red, orange, yellow, green, blue, indigo, violet papers; photocopiable page 172 'Rainbows'; interactive activity 'Rainbow colours' on the CD-ROM

Speaking scientifically
prism, spectrum, refracted, red, orange, yellow, green, blue, indigo, violet

Lesson 3: Rainbows

Introduction
Display an image of a rainbow and ask the children to say what it is and when they might see one. Explain that rainbows appear in the sky whenever the Sun shines onto drops of rain. The children may also have noticed mini-rainbows inside bubbles, or on compact discs when they are held up to the light. Rainbows happen when the light shines onto shiny surfaces, like raindrops and CDs, in a certain way. Teach the class a song about rainbows – it may not necessarily list the colours in the order they actually appear!

Whole-class work
1. Ask the children to recall the colours mentioned in the song and display paper samples of each one on the board. Compare the colours they have listed with a picture of a real rainbow and challenge the children to spot the differences. Move your paper samples so that the colours appear in the correct order: red, orange, yellow, green, blue, indigo, violet. Explain that the colours of the rainbow always appear in this order, with red at the top and violet at the bottom.

Independent work
2. Provide each child with photocopiable page 172 'Rainbows' (or use the interactive activity 'Rainbow colours' on the CD-ROM) and tell them to list the colours of the rainbow in the right order and to colour in the picture of the Sun, rainbow and rain cloud.

Whole-class work
3. Display some more images and ask the children to describe occasions when they have seen rainbows.

4. Tell the children a story about a rainbow. Noah knows the great flood has ended when he looks out of the Ark and sees a rainbow in the sky; and in Irish folklore, the end of the rainbow is where a leprechaun is believed to keep his pot of gold. Leprechauns are reputed to have the magical power to grant three wishes – but a human has to catch one first!

Differentiation
• Support children by providing colour name labels for them to cut and stick in order.
• Challenge children to write sentences about what sort of weather rainbows happen in.

Science in the wider world
Although sunlight looks white, it is actually made up of seven different colours, known as the spectrum. These always occur in the same order: red, orange, yellow, green, blue, indigo, violet. When white light is refracted (bent) through a prism, all the colours of the spectrum become visible. Prisms are generally a type of glass lens, but other materials can behave like prisms when light shines through them at a certain angle, including the shiny metal side of a CD, bubbles and water. The Sun makes rainbows when white sunlight passes through raindrops because the raindrops act like tiny prisms.

Review
Children could be assessed on their observations about rainbows, the order they list the colours in and how they complete the picture on the photocopiable sheet.

Objectives

- To recall the work on shadows from the autumn term.
- To conduct a new investigation of shadow length and position.
- To compare shadow length between autumn/winter and spring/summer.

Resources

Lengths of string and photographs from shadow observations in autumn 1, week 2, lesson 1; sunrise–sunset timelines from autumn 1, week 2, lesson 2; coloured string; chalk; a camera

Speaking scientifically

sun, shadows, sunlight, direction, length, solstice

Lesson 1: Summer shadows

Introduction

Remind the class of the shadow size observations they made in the autumn term. Display the photographs you took to record how the children's shadows changed in size and direction over the course of the day, along with the pieces of string you used to measure the length of some children's shadows. Encourage the class to recall what they did and what had happened to their shadows on that occasion. Check that they can make simple links between shadow formation and the position of the Sun in the sky, such as in the early morning, at midday and in the afternoon. Show the class some of the sunrise–sunset timelines they made in the autumn term and talk about the amount of daylight there was in the autumn and winter. Ask the children to suggest what they might find if they took some more shadow measurements now that it is almost summer.

Whole-class work

1. As before, choose a sunny day with a settled forecast before embarking on this activity. Explain that the class is going to carry out another shadow investigation, but this time they will use different-coloured string to make some new measurements.

2. At an early point in the school day, take the children into the playground to make their first observations. Begin by playing a quick game, so that the children can check that their shadows still move with them whether they run or turn on the spot.

3. Return to the same area in the playground that you used in the autumn and mark out another line with chalk. Remind the children that they will need to put their toes on this line and stand still while their partner draws around the shape of their shadow on the ground. They will then swap over so that everyone has a shadow chalked on the ground. As before, ensure that there is enough space for every child's shadow and that they all write their names at the base of their outlines.

4. Take photographs of the children and their shadows and use a piece of coloured string laid from head to toe of some of the shadows to take length measurements.

5. Repeat the chalking, photographing and measuring activities over the course of the school day.

6. When all the measurements have been collected, lay out the pieces of string and talk about the times of the day when the shadows were longest and shortest. Compare these with the photographs you have taken.

7. Select string lengths from children who have not had a major growth spurt over the winter and lay these alongside the original pieces of string from the autumn term, taking care to match the times of day. Encourage the children to make comparisons between the new and old lengths of string. The new shadow lengths should be shorter because the Sun will now be higher in the sky.

Science in the wider world

As the Earth moves towards the summer solstice – the point in its orbit at which the Earth's axis leans most towards the Sun – shadows become shorter. This is because the Sun appears higher in the sky.

Review

Children could be assessed on the observations and comparisons they make about shadow size.

● To make some predictions about temperature.
● To suggest seasonal activities and clothing.
● To make daily temperature recordings.

Resources
A large thermometer with a comparative scale showing 'cold', 'colder', 'warm' and 'warmer'; examples of children's work from earlier investigations on weather and temperature; a large temperature recording chart; photocopiable page 173 'Sunny ideas'

Speaking scientifically
temperature, thermometer, warmer, colder

Lesson 2: Sizzling summer?

Introduction

Remind the children about any temperature measurements they made earlier in the year. During the autumn term, they may have had an opportunity to take regular temperature readings as part of their work on weather recordings, which also included rainfall, wind speed and wind-direction. In the winter, they may have taken further temperature measurements, as well as investigating how long an 'icy hand' took to melt, or how warm 'huddling penguin' models kept a hot water bottle. Display some examples of the children's work from these previous lessons and check they are still able to explain that temperature is a measure of how warm or cold it is. Show them the thermometers they used to take temperature readings and recap on how these work.

Whole-class work

1. Talk about what the outside temperature was like earlier in the year and ask the children to suggest what might be similar or different in the middle of spring. Encourage them to say whether they think the weather will be warmer, colder or just the same as in the autumn, winter and early spring. Encourage them to compare clothing or activities appropriate to different seasons and weather, and make a list of their ideas.

2. Remind the class about how to check for temperature changes over a period of time. Take the large thermometer out to the playground and place it in the same area as previously. Once it has been in place for a few minutes, take your first reading.

3. Back in the classroom, add the information on temperature to a large chart. Explain that the children will carry on measuring the temperature and recording it on a daily basis for the next week and then try to say which days were the warmest and coolest.

4. Ask the children to suggest activities that are more enjoyable when there is a period of warm, dry weather and make a list of their ideas.

Independent work

5. Provide each child with photocopiable page 173 'Sunny ideas' and ask them to list or draw pictures of activities that are more enjoyable in warm, sunny weather, at the ends of the Sun's rays.

> **Differentiation**
> ● Support children by limiting the number of rays you ask them to list ideas by, or tell them to draw pictures of their ideas.
> ● Challenge children to make a fuller list of ideas and add explanations to some of the activities they suggest.

Science in the wider world

In April and May, average maximum daily temperatures in the UK are in the region of 12–15°C. The warmest months are generally July and August, with an average of just over 19°C. Faversham in Kent registered the highest daily maximum temperature currently on record, with 38.5°C on 10 August 2003.

Review

Children could be assessed on their observations on temperatures in late spring and the activities they associated with warm weather on the photocopiable sheet.

Objectives
● To observe and describe seasonal changes to hours of daylight.
● To make observational drawings of 'bedtime' in winter and summer.

Resources
Letter from Teddy; Robert Louis Stevenson's poem 'Bed in Summer'; examples of sunrise–sunset timelines children made in autumn 1, week 2, lesson 2; sheets of paper divided into two equal sections; a story with a bedtime theme

Speaking scientifically
sunrise, sunset, dawn, dusk, solstice, winter, summer, light, dark

Lesson 3: Why can't Teddy sleep?

Introduction
Tell the class that you have received another letter from Teddy. He is very grateful to the children for all their hard work in finding him a nice shady spot in the playground earlier in the term, but he's got another problem now, which he hopes your class will be able to help him with. Explain that Teddy says a very strange thing has started to occur at bedtime: even though he is still going to bed at the same time every evening, it is no longer dark outside. He can't understand what is happening. He is sure it used to be dark back in the winter, when he went to bed. Teddy hopes the children can help explain what is going on because he is feeling very puzzled.

Whole-class work
1. Ask the children if they have made similar observations to Teddy and encourage them to describe what has changed about their own bedtimes; perhaps it seems noisier, with older children in the neighbourhood still playing outside, or birds singing before they roost for the night. List the children's ideas.

2. Read the poem 'Bed in Summer' by Robert Louis Stevenson and talk about the differences the poet notices between his bedtimes in winter and summer. Add the poet's complaints and observations to your class list.

3. Ask the children if they can explain what has happened to the darkness they used to have at bedtime. Prompt them to make links to previous work they have done on variations in day length by displaying some of the sunrise–sunset timelines they made, or recalling the 'What's the time Mr Wolf?' games they played earlier in the year. Encourage them to recall that the Sun rises earlier and sets later in the summer than in the winter.

Independent work
4. Provide children with a sheet of paper divided into two boxes. In the top half, ask them to draw a winter bedtime scene, and in the bottom half a summer one. Ensure they include a window and tell them to label each of their drawings with the appropriate season and as 'light' or 'dark'.

Whole-class work
5. Ask the children to talk about what makes them feel sleepy at bedtime. Explain that having a story read out loud can help and that maybe they could suggest one for Teddy. Choose a story with a bedtime theme to read to the class.

Differentiation
● Support children with labels to glue onto their pictures.
● Challenge children to write sentences to say what happens to sunrise and sunset at different times of the year.

Science in the wider world
Sunset will gradually happen later each day, up until the summer solstice around 21 June. Light evenings can make it difficult for young children to fall asleep at their usual bedtime, but it is important they get around 11 hours sleep a night. A lack of sleep can lead to hyperactivity and irritability.

Review
Children could be assessed on their observations about the length of daylight in spring and summer compared to autumn and winter and the detail they present in their summer and winter bedtime scenes.

Objectives
● To identify and record signs of early summer.
● To identify changes to a tree across all four seasons.

Resources
Photographs and children's work from visits to park in autumn 1, week 1, lesson 1 and spring 1, week 6, lesson 1; cameras; paper; clipboards and pencils; disposable or gardening gloves; collecting bags; laminated photocopiable page 36 'Tree identification chart'; photocopiable page 174 'Trees in all seasons'

Speaking scientifically
season, autumn, winter, spring, summer, temperature, deciduous, evergreen, dormancy, growth, leaf, bud, blossom, flower, fruit

Lesson 1: Seasonal change

Introduction
Remind the children about the visits they have already made to a local park. Show photographs and display work from these visits and recap on their observations about signs of autumn, winter and early spring. They will have witnessed the leaves of deciduous trees changing colour and falling-, prior to the trees entering a period of winter dormancy. They will have observed the first buds and leaves beginning to reappear with other signs of spring, such as catkins, crocuses and daffodils. Ask the children to suggest how the park might look now. List their ideas and any questions they may have. Explain that they are going back to the same areas to see if summer has started.

Whole-class work
1. As before, prior to this lesson, you will need to prepare for an off-site educational visit by carrying out a thorough risk assessment and obtaining permission from parents and carers. Consider details such as transport, food, clothing, medical requirements (including any allergies) and an appropriate level of adult support. Once again, establish some ground rules for staying safe and remind the children to use gloves to collect natural objects that have fallen (they must not be picked) and tell an adult if they come across rubbish or dog mess.

2. Begin your visit in the same place as last time and encourage the children to notice further changes, for example, lilac or horse chestnut blooms, flowering shrubs and plants such as bluebells. They should also make a note of any weeds, such as daisies and dandelions, that they come across. Remind them to listen and watch out for birds flying between the trees, possibly with nesting material or food in their beaks for young chicks, also for squirrels and insects.

3. Divide the class into small adult-led groups and direct them to different locations in the park. Tell the children to use photocopiable page 36 'Tree identification chart' to name as many trees as they can and to collect any evidence of late spring/early summer, such as fallen blossom and downy feathers, using gloves and their special collection bags. Ask them to make drawings and to take photographs of any signs of change.

4. At the end of the visit, collect the whole class together again and review all their findings. Collate their drawings, photographs and other evidence of summer for a classroom display.

Independent work
5. Provide children with photocopiable page 174 'Trees in all seasons' and ask them to complete it with appropriate detail.

Differentiation
● Support children by providing seasonal clues for the photocopiable sheet, such as images of fallen leaves, frost on bare branches, flowering bulbs or trees in full leaf, and asking them to glue the appropriate one in each box.
● Challenge children to add further details such as evergreen trees, birds with nesting materials, flowering plants, and so on.

Science in the wider world
Spring bulbs fade and herbaceous borders grow in leaps and bounds as summer approaches. Grassy areas will once again require a mowing regime and weeds will be re-establishing themselves in areas left unchecked. Many woodland areas in the UK are carpeted in bluebells during the month of May.

Review
Children could be assessed on the observations they make about how the environment is affected by seasonal change and on their completion of the photocopiable sheet.

Objectives
● To observe a tree closely for seasonal changes.
● To record their tree investigations.

Resources
Photographs of 'adopted' tree from autumn 1, week 6, lesson 2 and spring 1, week 6, lesson 2; completed examples of photocopiable page 'Our tree' from the CD-ROM and photocopiable page 107 'Our tree in spring'; paper; a length of string or measuring tape; magnifiers; a camera; photocopiable page 175 'Our tree in summer'

Speaking scientifically
change, grow, branch, trunk, leaf, flower, fruit, spring, summer, autumn, winter

Lesson 2: Summer tree

Introduction
Remind your class of the observations they have made over the year of their 'adopted' tree in the school grounds or local area. Display photographs you took in the autumn and spring terms and recap what the tree is called, its location and how it has changed so far. Show the children some of the photocopiable sheets they completed on their adopted tree previously and ask if they think anything will have changed since their last observations. Encourage them to explain their ideas. List all the changes they have noticed since the initial photographs were taken.

Whole-class work
1. Take the class out into the school grounds to make some more observations of their adopted tree. As before, begin by looking at it from a distance and talking about what the children notice, before going up to it.

2. Tell them now to look carefully and use the magnifiers to make close-up inspections. Encourage them to look at how the leaves are growing and what colour these are. Ask the children to check for variations in the colour of the trunk and branches, and to try to recall whether this is the same as last time.

3. Look around to see if any of the roots are visible and talk about anything else the children notice under the tree. Ask them to check whether any plants, such as grasses or weeds, are starting to grow around the bottom of the tree.

4. Tell the children to take another measurement around the trunk with a length of string or a measuring tape and to take further photographs and bark rubbings of their tree.

5. Back in class, collate all their findings and straighten out the length of string that you used to measure the girth of the tree and compare it with the heights of the children, and to the lengths of string you used to take the trunk measurements in the autumn and spring terms.

6. Discuss how the tree has changed with the seasons so far, and ask the children to describe what they think the tree will look like when they return to school after the summer holidays.

Independent work
7. Give the children the 'Our tree in spring' work that they did in the previous term. Ask them to think about what has changed since then and to complete photocopiable page 175 'Our tree in summer', colouring the tree appropriately.

Differentiation
● Support children with the photocopiable sheet by providing labels and thumbnail photographs of the changing tree for them to paste on.
● Challenge children to add more detail and write further sentences about their tree observations.

Science in the wider world
Trees such as oak, ash and sycamore generally grow about 2cm in girth per year. In parkland, where conditions are more open, the growth rate may be nearer 2.5cm. It is possible to find the approximate age of a tree by measuring around the girth and dividing by 2. This method was devised by the dendrologist Alan Mitchell, who founded the Tree Register of the British Isles (TROBI), which holds records of more than 100,000 trees.

Review
Children could be assessed on their observations of changes to their tree and completion of the photocopiable sheet.

Objectives
● To revise the months of the year and the seasons to which they belong.
● To sort evidence according to season.
● To explain their sorting.

Resources
Seasons mobile from autumn 1, week 1, lesson 2; a selection of photographs and children's work from seasons topics; small hoops or circles drawn on sheets of paper; sheets of paper divided into 4 boxes; interactive activity 'Changing seasons' on the CD-ROM

Speaking scientifically
summer, autumn, winter, spring, season, lighter, darker, shorter, longer, day length

Lesson 3: Seasons mobile

Introduction

Display the seasons mobile that you made with the class early in the autumn term. Ask the children to explain what the yellow ball represents and why the hoop is divided into four differently coloured areas. Recap the Earth's annual journey around the Sun. Check that the children can relate this to the seasons. Practise saying the months of the year in order and then relating them to specific seasons. Point out the children's photographs. Talk about which birthdays are coming up. Play a game: explain that you are thinking of a child with a birthday in a particular season, which you name as an initial clue. The class then have to guess who – but you can only answer *yes* or *no* to their questions. Play a few rounds. Look together at the interactive activity 'Changing seasons' on the CD-ROM.

Whole-class work

1. Show the class some photographs taken during their work on seasons over the course of the year, along with examples of their photocopiable sheets, and drawings and models they have made. Encourage them to talk about how trees and plants change, how animals behave at different times of the year and how the weather and changing amounts of daylight affect all living things.

Group work

2. Provide groups of children with a selection of photographs and seasonal artefacts, and four sorting hoops. Tell the children to label the hoops with the names of the seasons and to sort the images and objects.

3. Ask each group to present a particular season to the rest of the class. Encourage other groups to compare their own sorting and share their ideas.

Independent work

4. Provide the children with a sheet of paper divided into four boxes. Tell them to write the names of the seasons at the top of the boxes and underneath to draw a picture to represent something they have found out, such as, whether it is light at bedtime or whether animals are hibernating.

5. The children could also complete the interactive activity 'Changing seasons' on the CD-ROM.

Differentiation
● Support children with ready-made labels and thumbnail photographs for each season to glue onto their sheet.
● Challenge children to write sentences making comparisons between the seasons.

Science in the wider world

Phenology is the study of recurring natural phenomena. It was originally developed in the 18th century by Robert Marsham. By noting significant dates for natural events, such as snowdrops blooming and the first sighting of swallows every year, he laid the foundations for an archive of signs of seasonal change. More recently, the Woodland Trust has been developing a phenological record for the UK called Nature's Calendar. Using observations from thousands of members of the public, a log is gradually being built up of how climate change is affecting wildlife.

Review

Children can be assessed on their observations about the changes associated with autumn, winter, spring and summer.

Objectives
- To make a recognisable representations of a deciduous tree in spring/summer and autumn.
- To attempt to label the main parts of their tree.
- To add appropriate evidence of wildlife to their tree, based on their observations.

Resources
For each child: a selection of coloured modelling clays; a board to work on; simple tools such as lolly sticks; labels – trunk, branches, bark, twigs, roots, leaves, buds, blossom, nests; two sheets of cardboard

Working scientifically
- To identify and classify.

Understanding seasonal changes (2)

Revise
- Use photographs and examples of the children's work, including the birds' nest models, made during this topic to recap the seasonal changes they have been finding out about. Remind the children of their visits to the park and the tree they have adopted in the school grounds. Challenge them to recall some of the names of deciduous trees they have observed, such as ash, horse chestnut, lime, oak and sycamore. Talk about what has been happening to these trees and make a list of the signs of late spring/early summer that they have spotted, including the production of buds, leaves and blossom. Also talk about ways in which animals change at this time of year and remind the children about birds singing loudly in the dawn chorus and gathering material to build nests.

Assess
- Provide each child with a selection of different coloured modelling clays, a board and some simple tools, such as lolly sticks. Tell them to begin by making a bare tree (just the trunk and branches) and to lay it carefully on one of their sheets of cardboard.
- Next, ask them to select some of the tree-part labels and gently attach these to their tree model.
- Tell the children to now use their clay to show how the tree looks in late spring/early summer, making buds, leaves and blossom to add to it. Remind them to think carefully about what they have seen recently on real trees.
- Ask them to add some evidence of animals living in their tree, such as a bird's nest or a squirrel climbing the trunk, and to label the sheet with the appropriate season.
- Check that the children have made a recognisable representation of a deciduous tree and have attempted to label the main parts of it. Also check that they have selected suitable colours for the leaves and flowers and have placed these, together with some wildlife, on their tree.
- When the children have completed their spring/summer tree model, ask them to draw how their tree will look in the next season on their second sheet of card. Suggest that they use different colours to show how the leaves will change and to label this piece of work with the appropriate season.
- Review each child's model, drawing and labelling to assess their knowledge and understanding of seasonal change associated with spring and summer. Check that they have drawn some leaves on the ground around their autumn tree drawing.

Further practice
- Support children by pre-labelling their sheets of card with 'summer' and 'autumn' and ask them to point out features on their model and drawing and talk about differences between them.
- Challenge children to further demonstrate their understanding of seasonal change by writing sentences about their tree model and drawing. Ask them to explain why birds are singing loudly and building nests at this time of year or why insects are busy visiting flowers.

Objectives
● To recap on shadow length and the position of the Sun in the sky.
● To choose the correct weather symbols to portray particular weather conditions.
● To correctly identify that there are more hours of daylight in the summer.
● To demonstrate their understanding of Sun safety.

Resources
Lengths of string and photographs from week 5, lesson 1 and autumn 1, week 2, lesson 1; the completed weather chart from this term; photocopiable page 'Spring and summer weather' from the CD-ROM; plain paper

Working scientifically
● To make comparisons.

Weather and day length

Revise

● Remind the children of their observations on shadows made earlier in this topic and in the autumn term. Show them the photographs you took to record how their shadows changed in size and direction over the course of a school day and the length of string showing each set of measurements. Point out the longest and shortest string lengths on each occasion and encourage the children to link these with the position of the Sun in the sky. Make comparisons between the string lengths in autumn and summer and talk about why the summer ones are shorter. Remind the children of the work they did for Teddy: finding him a shady place and making observations about why it is no longer dark at bedtime.

● Display the weather chart the class has completed and talk about how the temperature has been changing since earlier in the year. Recap other types of weather you have focused on this term, including cloud formation and rainbows, and talk about staying safe in the Sun. Point out the weather symbols that have been used to record the children's observations and check they can identify which ones signify temperature, rainfall, cloud cover and wind speed and direction. Challenge the children to tell you the colours of the rainbow in the order they occur and explain what the 'Slip! Slop! Slap!' message means.

Assess

● Give each child the photocopiable page 'Spring and summer weather' from the CD-ROM. Tell them to look carefully at the pictures and the weather symbols at the bottom of the page. For each image, they will need to think about how warm it looks, whether it is sunny or raining and how hard the wind might be blowing. They will then need to choose the correct weather symbols to match what is happening in the picture.

● Provide children with a plain sheet of paper and tell them to draw the view from their bedroom window at bedtime in summer. Check that they have sketched a daylight scene.

● Give the children further sheets of plain paper and ask them to make a poster to advise other children on how to stay safe in the Sun.

Further practice

● Support children by giving them weather symbol templates to cut and stick onto an enlarged photocopiable sheet. Talk to the children about bedtime in summer and what they notice about daylight at this time of year. Provide old holiday brochures or magazines for children to cut and paste appropriate images from.

● Challenge children to shade in the colours of the rainbow in the correct order on the photocopiable sheet. Ask them to write a sentence suggesting something that would help them get to sleep more easily in summer, such as thicker curtains. Encourage the children to add as much detail to their poster as they can, including wearing a t-shirt, hat, sunglasses and sunscreen; staying out of the Sun in the middle of the day; and topping up with sunscreen when they have been in the water.

- To name some farm animals and their offspring.
- To revise life cycles and independently complete a life cycle for a chicken.
- To revise the dawn chorus.

Animals in spring and summer

Revise

- Show the class the photographs taken during their farm visit at the beginning of this topic and talk about the animals they saw. Sing 'Old MacDonald Had a Farm', listing adult animals, and then ask the children to make up verses for young farm animals. Check that they are able to name lambs, calves, foals and chicks. Remind the class about the question you posed earlier in the term: *Which came first – the chicken or the egg?* Ask the children to explain why it is not a straightforward question to answer and display some of the life-cycle work they completed on frogs and chickens. Encourage them to explain why the pictures go round in a circle and talk about each stage of development for both the frog and the chicken. Play the class the recording of the dawn chorus and ask them to say what sort of animals are making these sounds, what time of day it is and why it may be quite loud. Remind the children that this is called the 'dawn chorus' and that spring is the time when birds start building nests ready to lay their eggs. They sing loudly to let other birds know they are in a particular area (so there is no room in it for others) and to impress potential mates.

Assess

- Provide children with a copy of photocopiable page 169 'Parents and babies'. Remind the children that they completed this earlier in the term, but that now you want to see how much they can remember, so this time you have covered up the name labels at the bottom of the sheet. Explain that you would like the children to name as many of the animals as they can without these clues, as well as matching the parents with their offspring.
- Provide children with a sheet of paper cut into the shape of an egg with arrows drawn around the edge at regular intervals. They will also need thumbnail images of stages from a chicken's life cycle. Explain that last time they worked with a partner to order the stages of the chicken's life cycle, but now they are going to do it on their own. Ask them to stick the pictures between the arrows around the edge of the egg in the order they think is correct and to write sentences in the middle of the egg to explain how chicks grow and change.
- Give each child the photocopiable page 'The early bird catches the worm' from the CD-ROM, containing a picture of a blackbird with an empty speech bubble emerging from its beak. Tell the children to imagine what message the blackbird might be giving in his song and to write this into the speech bubble.

Further practice

- Support children by providing them with name labels to glue onto the 'Parents and babies' photocopiable sheet. Provide a wordbank of labels to help with some simple sentence work on the chicken's life cycle and blackbird's song.
- Challenge children to list the names of any more baby animals they know – puppies, kittens, kids, and so on. Ask them to explain why chicks have an egg tooth and what happens to this once the chick has hatched. Encourage them to explain the saying 'the early bird catches the worm'.

Name: _____   Date: _____

A farm in spring

■ Label the animals you can see and show what the fields are like in spring.

(sheep)   (lambs)   (cows)   (chickens)   (chicks)

I can show what a farm is like in spring.

How did you do?

PHOTOCOPIABLE

■SCHOLASTIC
www.scholastic.co.uk

Parents and babies

■ Fill in the labels with the names of the baby animals and their parents.

_____   _____

_____   _____

_____   _____

_____  _____

_____  _____

frog	tadpole	lamb	sheep	cow
calf	horse	foal	butterfly	caterpillar

I can label baby animals and their parents.

How did you do?

PHOTOCOPIABLE

Name: _____   Date: _____

What can you do when the Sun is warm?

- Circle the activities you can do on a warm sunny day.
- Add labels to each activity you have circled.

(playing at the seaside)   (having a picnic)   (at a firework display)

(ice skating)   (at an adventure playground)

I can choose activities for a sunny day.

How did you do?

PHOTOCOPIABLE

■SCHOLASTIC
www.scholastic.co.uk

Letter to Teddy

■ Write a letter to tell Teddy where to sit in your playground.

Dear Teddy

I am writing to tell you that the best place to sit in our playground is

_____

_____

_____

_____

I can find the shadiest spot in the playground.

How did you do?

Rainbows

■ List the colours of the rainbow in the right order and colour in the picture.

The colours of the rainbow are

r _____   b _____

o _____   i _____

y _____   v _____

g _____

I can say the colours of the rainbow in the right order.

How did you do?

Name: _____   Date: _____

Sunny ideas

■ Which activities are more enjoyable when the weather is warm and sunny? Write your ideas in the Sun.

I can choose activities to do on a sunny day.

How did you do?

Trees in all seasons

■ Show how the tree would look in each season.

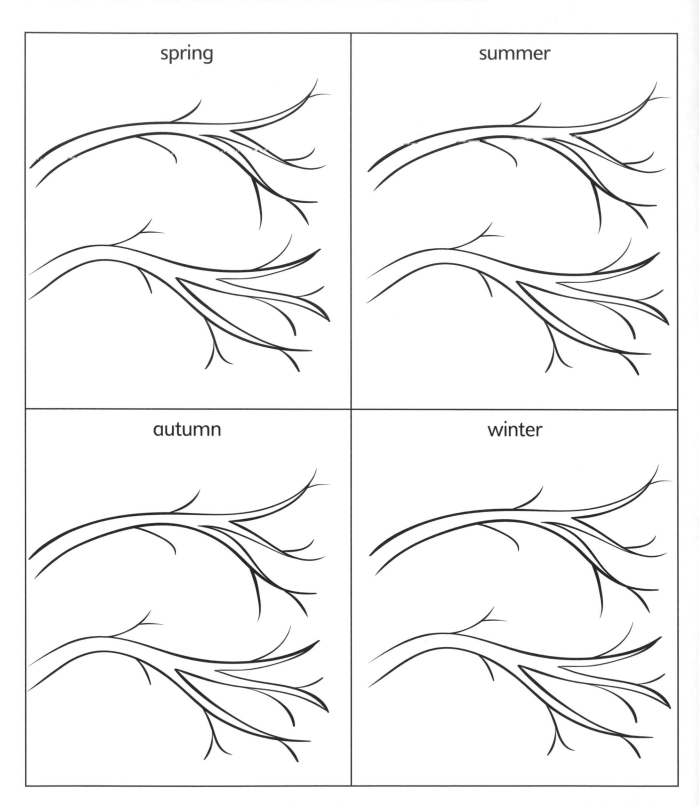

spring

summer

autumn

winter

I can show how a tree changes each season.

How did you do?

PHOTOCOPIABLE

Our tree in summer

■ Describe how your tree has changed. Colour the picture to show how the tree looks now.

This is our tree in _____

The tree measured _____ cm round.

We found _____

_____

_____.

I can show how our tree looks in summer.

How did you do?

Materials

Expected prior learning

● Making sense of the physical world through opportunities to explore, observe and find out about the environment.
● Know about some similarities and differences in relation to objects and materials.

Overview of progression.

● Names of everyday materials.
● Some properties of everyday materials.
● Comparing and grouping everyday materials.
● Changing the shape of solid objects made from some materials.
● Distinguishing between an object and the material it is made from.

Creative context

● This topic provides many opportunities for children to make observational drawings and use visual images to present their findings.
● Children will be required to deploy their design and technology skills when investigating changing the shape of play dough and working with wood.
● Everyday materials can inspire various forms of creative writing, song, and music.

Background knowledge

Make sure the children realise that the term 'material' does not just mean 'fabric'. Some materials have several useful properties. Wood is used for its strength and its insulating properties, and because it is relatively easy to cut and shape. Metal is strong, can be shaped and moulded and conducts electricity. 'Rough' and 'smooth' are often used as criteria for sorting, but these are usually properties of the objects rather than the material. A metal file is rough because it has been made to be so, not because metal is naturally rough. Natural rocks are rough, but a pebble has been worn until it is smooth.

Ensure magnets are always stored properly – complete with a keeper – to help them stay magnetic as long as possible. Store plastic-coated ceramic bar magnets in pairs in the box they were supplied in.

Speaking scientifically

Properties of everyday materials may include: soft, hard, light, heavy, waterproof, absorbent, shiny, dull, flexible and rigid. Iron and steel are the most common magnetic metals; others that the children are likely to come across at this stage – particularly aluminium – are not.

Preparation

Some initial research into likely sources of materials will help this topic run smoothly. Try to find out about possible manufacturing processes, such as chocolate production or car factories, that you could take your class to observe. Many museums offer hands-on activities for children to experience working with various materials.

You will need to provide: a range of everyday materials and objects made from different materials, including; fabrics, papers and card, wood, play dough, metals, plastic and rubber, as well as a magnet and a variety of magnetic and non-magnetic materials. The children will also need access to some simple tools, such as small hammers, nails, junior hacksaws and sandpaper which they can use under close supervision. Additionally, a selection of sandwich foods, rolling pints and save knives

On the CD-ROM you will find: photocopiable pages 'Properties of materials (2)', 'Play-dough recipe', 'Assessment – magnets'; interactive activities 'What is it made of?', 'Magnets', 'Bendy or stretchy?'

■SCHOLASTIC

Chapter at a glance

Week	Lesson	Curriculum objectives	Lesson objectives	Main activity	Working scientifically
1	1	• To distinguish between an object and the material from which it is made.	• To distinguish between an object and the material from which it is made. • To observe a manufacturing process.	Visiting a manufacturing plant – or museum of manufacturing – to observe materials being made into objects.	• Asking simple questions. • Observing closely. • Gathering and recording data to help in answering questions.
	2	• To distinguish between an object and the material from which it is made.	• To know what an assembly line is. • To create an assembly line to make a packed lunch.	Follow-up to visit to manufacturing plant: recapping on materials used and main stages of process. Creating a packed lunch production line.	• Observing closely. • Making comparisons.
	3	• To identify and name a variety of everyday materials.	• To identify and name a variety of everyday materials. • To observe materials closely. • To describe some of the properties of various different materials.	Looking at images and samples of different materials and matching with labels.	• Asking simple questions. • Identifying and classifying. • Observing closely. • Making comparisons.
2	1	• To identify and name a variety of everyday materials.	• To identify and name a variety of everyday materials. • To think about the properties of materials.	Walking around school and identifying materials in use. Talking about their properties.	• Asking simple questions. • Identifying and classifying. • Observing closely. • Making comparisons. • Gathering and recording data to help in answering questions.
	2	• To identify and name a variety of everyday materials.	• To identify and name a variety of everyday materials. • To think about why an object is made of a particular material. • To correctly identify the materials objects are made of.	Sorting collections of objects into sets according to the material. Playing 'material dominoes' game and completing 'It could be made from...' photocopiable sheet.	• Asking simple questions. • Identifying and classifying. • Observing closely. • Making comparisons.
	3	• To identify and name a variety of everyday materials.	• To identify the materials used to make objects. • To explain why each of the different materials has been chosen. • To identify materials that would be inappropriate for certain objects.	Looking at objects that are made of two or three different materials and identifying the properties that have made them suitable. Completing 'What is it made of?' photocopiable sheet.	• Asking simple questions. • Identifying and classifying. • Observing closely. • Making comparisons.
3	1	• To describe the simple physical properties of a variety of everyday materials.	• To know that some materials can be changed in shape by forces. • To identify pushes and pulls when using play dough and clay.	Investigating ways of changing the shape of dough and clay and using appropriate forces vocabulary.	• Asking simple questions. • Identifying and classifying. • Observing closely. • Making comparisons.
	2	• To describe the simple physical properties of a variety of everyday materials.	• To identify different pull and push forces. • To observe the use of forces to change the shape of a block of wood.	Investigating ways of changing the shape of wood and using appropriate forces vocabulary.	• Asking simple questions. • Observing closely. • Making comparisons.
	3	• To describe the simple physical properties of a variety of everyday materials.	• To identify materials. • To describe the texture of different materials.	Using a feely bag to identify materials. Sorting materials.	• Asking simple questions. • Identifying and classifying. • Observing closely. • Making comparisons.

Chapter at a glance

Week	Lesson	Curriculum objectives	Lesson objectives	Main activity	Working scientifically
4	1	• To describe the simple physical properties of a variety of everyday materials.	• To explore the properties of magnets. • To test objects to see if they are magnetic. • To sort objects according to whether they are magnetic or not. • To compare magnetic items.	Investigating a variety of materials and identifying the ones that are magnetic. Completing 'Magnets' photocopiable sheet.	• Asking simple questions. • Identifying and classifying. • Observing closely. • Making comparisons. • Gathering and recording data to help in answering questions.
	2	• To compare and group together a variety of everyday materials on the basis of their simple physical properties.	• To identify that only metals are magnetic. • To investigate whether all metals are magnetic. • To sort magnetic and non-magnetic materials.	Recapping on previous investigation; making predictions about variety of other metals. Sorting metals. Making fridge magnets.	• Asking simple questions. • Identifying and classifying. • Observing closely. • Making comparisons.
	3	• To describe the simple physical properties of a variety of everyday materials.	• To distinguish between shiny and dull materials. • To make observations about shiny materials. • To sort materials into shiny and dull groups.	Selecting materials for Cinderella's coach and dress. Selecting examples of shiny/dull papers to stick onto outlines of Cinderella before/after and the coach.	• Asking simple questions. • Identifying and classifying. • Observing closely. • Making comparisons.
5	1	• To describe the simple physical properties of a variety of everyday materials.	• To conduct a test to find out which materials are most waterproof. • To recognise conditions needed for a fair test. • To report back their findings and sort materials accordingly.	Testing a range of materials by pouring water over them. Sorting materials into waterproof/not waterproof groups.	• Asking simple questions. • Identifying and classifying. • Observing closely. • Making comparisons. • Gathering and recording data to help in answering questions.
	2	• To compare and group together a variety of everyday materials on the basis of their simple physical properties.	• To identify hard and soft materials. • To suggest why objects are made from soft materials. • To suggest why items of playground equipment are made from hard materials.	Looking at images of bedrooms and playgrounds and asking children to identify hard and soft objects in each. Talking about why there are more soft materials in the bedroom.	• Asking simple questions. • Identifying and classifying. • Observing closely. • Making comparisons.
	3	• To describe the simple physical properties of a variety of everyday materials.	• To identify materials as either rigid or flexible. • To conduct an investigation into changing the shape of objects. • To identify whether a material is bendy or stretchy and sort accordingly.	Investigating a variety of materials such as socks, elastic bands, pipe cleaners, stretchy fabrics, and so on. Identifying which ones are bendy or rigid. Comparing the bendy materials and identifying stretchy ones.	• Asking simple questions. • Identifying and classifying. • Observing closely. • Making comparisons.
6	1	• To describe the simple physical properties of a variety of everyday materials.	• To carry out an investigation into absorbency. • To establish a fair test. • To make predictions. • To identify the most absorbent material. • To compare results.	Investigating materials to mop up a spill. Using different papers/fabrics of the same size and squeezing out water collected when used to mop same sized puddle.	• Asking simple questions. • Identifying and classifying. • Observing closely. • Making comparisons. • Gathering and recording data to help in answering questions.
	2	• To compare and group together a variety of everyday materials on the basis of their simple physical properties.	• To compare the strength of different materials. • To find out which is the best material for a bookshelf.	Discussing materials in the classroom. Testing different materials to see if they can support books.	• Asking simple questions. • Observing closely. • Making comparisons. • Identifying and classifying. • Gathering and recording data to help in answering questions.
	3	• To compare and group together a variety of everyday materials on the basis of their simple physical properties.	• To carry out an investigation into blackout material for curtains. • To decide which combination of properties would make the best curtains.	Deciding what properties curtains need: keeping light out and warmth in; light and flexible enough to pull and bend into folds; attractive to look at. Investigating a variety of materials.	• Asking simple questions. • Identifying and classifying. • Observing closely. • Making comparisons. • Gathering and recording data to help in answering questions.
Assess and review					

■SCHOLASTIC

Objectives
● To distinguish between an object and the material from which it is made.
● To observe a manufacturing process.

Resources
Clipboards; paper and pencils; cameras; information leaflets; large sheets of paper

Speaking scientifically
manufacture, factory, raw material, product, packaging, machine

Lesson 1: Factory visit

Previous knowledge
During the Early Years Foundation Stage, children will have begun to make sense of the physical world through opportunities to explore, observe and find out about the environment. They will also have developed some understanding of similarities and differences in relation to objects and materials.

Introduction
Plan a visit to a local manufacturing plant or hands-on museum so that the children have the opportunity to compare raw materials with finished products or watch materials being transformed. There are a number of manufacturers throughout the UK that have developed an educational role and can provide a quality learning experience for your children. Search online for information on your local area and any historical links with a particular industry, such as car manufacturing, pencils, hats, chocolate, and so on. You may be able to arrange a visit to the actual factory or find a local museum which covers a particular production process with hands-on simulations, videos and artefacts.

Whenever you make an off-site educational visit, you will need to prepare by carrying out a thorough risk assessment and obtaining permission from parents and carers. Consider details such as transport, food, clothing, medical requirements (including any allergies) and an appropriate level of adult support.

Spend some time in class familiarising the children with the names and simple properties of the materials they are likely to come across on their visit. Encourage them to think about tools and processes, such as heating and cooling, that might be involved in changing these into finished products.

Show the children some photographs of where they will be going and ask what they might expect to see there and what they would like to find out. Make a list of their questions and ideas. Explain that, depending on the nature of your planned visit, they may be able to watch how materials are changed and made into objects, or find a variety of objects that have been made from similar or different materials. Factories are busy places with lots of machinery, while museums can be open plan over several floors, so establish some ground rules for staying safe, such as staying with their group and accompanying adults.

Mass-produced goods have to leave the factory in perfect condition. This may involve a packaging process that involves other materials such as card, paper and plastic. Prior to your visit, display images and examples of foodstuffs and school equipment inside its original packaging and ask the class to identify the materials that have been used. Make a list of these and tell the children to watch out for ways in which goods are packaged ready to leave the processing plant during their visit.

Whole-class/Group work
1. Consult with the museum or manufacturing plant's educational liaison officer about how best to organise your class for the visit. He or she may suggest dividing the children into small adult-led groups and direct them to different locations around the building, or recommend that the class stays together in one large group for the visit.

2. Take photographs where possible throughout the visit, and collect samples of any information leaflets or publicity material that you can use in your follow-up work back in school. Provide the children with clipboards and tell them to make drawings of what they see.

3. At various points during the visit, if appropriate, bring the whole class back together and talk about what they have found out. Compare each group's observations about different stages of the process in transforming the original material into a finished product.

Checkpoint
● What materials do we know?
● What are objects made of?
● How are materials shaped with tools?
● How are materials changed?

4. Back in class after the visit, display all the information you have collected, including photographs, leaflets and the children's drawings, and recap on the stages and processes you found out about. Encourage the children to describe and compare the raw materials and finished objects they observed.

Paired work

5. Provide pairs of children with large sheets of paper and tell them to collate thumbnail photographs with their drawings and images or information cut from the leaflets to tell the story of the manufacturing process relating to their visit.

Introducing the new area of study

Show your class a selection of objects made from a variety of materials and play an 'I spy' game to identify them. Introduce the children to materials and their properties through stories such as the 'Three Little Pigs' and songs like 'There's a Hole in my Bucket'. Invite your site manager to talk to your class about some of the tools he or she uses to fix door handles, wall boards and plumbing leaks, and so on around the school.

> **Differentiation**
> ● Support children during the follow-up activities by providing a structured template with boxes and headings for stages of production, or for raw materials and finished products, which requires them to glue images and labels to record their observations.
> ● Challenge children to label the stages of production and write some sentences giving more information about their visit.

Science in the wider world

Cocoa trees grow in the humid, warm conditions of the world's tropical regions. They produce large pods full of beans, which have to be extracted, dried and have the shells removed to expose the nibs – the raw ingredient of chocolate. The nibs are ground into a liquid cocoa paste, which is then processed to create cocoa butter and powder. These are then blended together with other products such as sugar and milk to produce chocolate.

Car manufacturing begins with flat metal sheets that are shaped into panels, which are then pressed, bent and pierced. The panels are welded together to form the car body to which doors, bonnets and so on are added. Powerful chemicals prepare the metal bodywork for painting before the engine, suspension and steering components, together with smaller interior parts, are installed and fitted together to complete the car.

Review

Children could be assessed on the observations they make about the materials and objects they handle, or the manufacturing process they watch. They could also be assessed on drawings and writing connected to their visit on turning materials into useful objects.

Objectives
● To know what an assembly line is.
● To create an assembly line to make a packed lunch.

Resources
Photographs, leaflets and children's work from visit; images of production lines in action; sandwich ingredients, cartons of drink and pieces of fruit; child-safe knives for spreading and sandwich cutting; packaging and labels

Speaking scientifically
manufacturing, raw material, finished product, production line, changing. assembly line

Lesson 2: Assembly line

Introduction
Prior to this lesson, contact parents and carers to explain that the class is finding out about how goods are produced in factories, and that you are planning a packed-lunch assembly line day. Outline how you intend to organise this, clarify what additional food – if any – the children will require on the day of this activity and check whether any of them have allergies that could be triggered by foodstuffs before you introduce these into your classroom environment. Aim to select fillings that reflect the children's cultural and/or religious heritage. You may wish to invite some additional adults to help supervise your production line.

Display the photographs, leaflets and work done by the children following your visit to find out about a manufacturing process. Talk about how products are often put together one piece at a time because it is quicker than just one person doing everything. If products can be made quickly, they generally cost less money. Show the class some images of people working on production lines, including the preparation of foodstuffs and older car assembly lines where many workers were involved. Compare these with some more recent images of car plants where some of the humans have been replaced by robots.

Whole-class work
1. Explain to the class that you are going to set up an assembly line to produce a packed lunch for all of you. Ask the children to suggest different stages and make a list that should include putting spread onto slices of bread, laying out a filling, sandwiching the slices together, cutting into smaller portions and wrapping. The sandwich will then need to be presented attractively alongside a drink and a piece of fruit.

2. Establish that good hygiene is essential when working with food and point out that the production line images you showed the class included people wearing hats, nets and clean coats. Ensure that the children take the necessary steps to work safely around food that you are all going to eat at the end! Their hands must be clean, and the surfaces they work on must also be clean.

Group work
3. Decide how best to arrange your class. You could either have a different, specific task being undertaken by separate groups, or organise a mini-assembly line within each group. The aim is for the children to experience being responsible for one aspect of the packed lunch production and observing how the product is developed at each stage along the line.

4. Over lunch, review how the process worked. Ask the children to describe the order in which the sandwiches were put together and talk about any quality control issues there were.

Science in the wider world
Henry Ford is generally credited with developing assembly-line production methods. Rather than produce individually crafted expensive cars, Ford organised his workforce to perform repetitive tasks on parts of cars as they passed along an assembly line. This meant that complete cars could be produced quicker and more cheaply than in the past. The assembly line as a means of mass production has become common industrial practice across the world, although many tasks these days can be performed by robots rather than humans!

Review
Children could be assessed on their observations about the stages of the sandwich production to produce an edible packed lunch.

Objectives
● To identify and name a variety of everyday materials.
● To observe materials closely.
● To describe some of the properties of various different materials.

Resources
Samples of wood, glass, paper, metal, rock, plastics; labels with names of the materials; images of products made from glass; objects made from plastic such as, hard containers, bags, toys and clothing; images of a metal box, a canvas bag, a wooden toy and woolly jumper; interactive activity 'What is it made of?' on the CD-ROM

Speaking scientifically
stretchy, bendy, flexible, rigid, mould, hard, material, rough, smooth, strong, cold, warm, natural, made, manufactured

Lesson 3: Many materials

Introduction
Display some images of wood, glass, paper, metal, rock and plastics and ask the children to identify each one in turn. Explain that these are the materials from which many objects are made, often in large factories similar to the one the children visited. Show the images again, one at a time, and encourage the children to suggest which objects could be made from each material. Make a list of the materials along with the children's ideas.

Group work
1. Provide each group with a selection of materials and name labels (rather than asking children to work directly with glass, it may be advisable to use pictures of objects made from glass). Tell the children to match the materials and pictures to the name labels.

2. Check that the children have identified all the materials correctly and ask each group to choose a material to describe to the rest of the class. Add their descriptions to your list of materials and objects which could be made from them, to build up a list of properties such as hard, smooth, rough and strong.

Whole-class work
3. Together, work through the interactive activity 'What is it made of?' on the CD-ROM.

4. Discuss the fact that some materials can occur in different forms, especially manufactured materials. Talk about the variety of ways in which plastics are used and show the children examples, including hard containers, bags, toys and fleecy clothing.

5. Play the guessing game again, but this time the children have to try to find out which plastic item you are thinking of.

6. Explain that before plastic was invented, all the objects they have been looking at would have been made from a different material. Challenge them to suggest alternative materials for each item and then display some images of objects such as metal box, a canvas bag, a wooden toy and woolly jumper.

Science in the wider world
Most plastics are made from materials that are extracted from crude oil. Refineries process the oil to produce fuels, such as petrol and diesel, as well as a range of petrochemicals including plastic resins. These, in turn, are used to produce many different types of plastic. The plastic is often collected as small pellets, which can be melted and made into a wide range of objects. Moulds can be dipped into hot plastic, or the molten material may undergo extrusion or blow moulding depending on the specific properties required for a particular object. Fleece has many of the properties of wool. It is a synthetic polyester fabric that is lightweight, warm and suitable for outdoor use. Fleece is often made from recycled plastic bottles that have been crushed into small chips, and then melted down. The liquid plastic is forced through small holes to produce threads, which are then used to make the fabric.

Review
Children could be assessed on their identification of the materials looked at in this lesson and descriptions they give of specific properties.

Objectives
- To identify and name a variety of everyday materials.
- To think about the properties of materials.

Resources
Images of wood, metal and plastic from previous lesson; photocopiable page 201 'Materials at School (1)'; photocopiable page 202 'Materials in School (2)'; a camera

Speaking scientifically
metal, glass, plastic, brick, clay, wood, wax, paper, stone, concrete, tarmac

Lesson 1: Materials walkabout

Introduction
Recap on the materials, such as wood, metal and plastics, which the children looked at in the previous lesson and display images of these on the interactive whiteboard. Ask them to give examples of objects that are made out of these materials and describe what these look or feel like. Explain that the class is going on a 'materials walkabout' around school, to look for the materials from which things are made and also, to look for examples of different things that are made from the same material.

Whole-class work
1. Before leaving the classroom, name one or two objects they are likely to see outside (such as railings, benches and litter bins) and discuss the materials these are made of. Draw children's attention to some of the properties of these materials and talk about why they have been used in the manufacture of particular objects.

2. Walk around the school, first inside and then outside. Help the children to focus on various objects and the materials from which they are made. Encourage them to link the properties of materials with the objects and to compare and contrast some materials. For example, railings, lamp posts and chair legs are all made out of metal for strength, but chair seats would be less comfortable if they were also made of metal. A metal door would be strong, but might be too heavy to open and close.

3. Talk about materials, such as concrete, that have been made from a mixture of other materials. Ask the children how many examples of the same material they can find being used to make different objects.

4. Encourage the children to report back to the class on their observations. Talk about materials that were found both inside and out and the properties that made them suitable for each location. Challenge the children to explain why both doors and pencils are made out of wood; or whether tarmac would be a sensible flooring for the classroom.

Independent work
5. Give each child a copy of photocopiable page 201 'Materials in School (1)' and ask them to cut out the labels and stick them in the appropriate boxes. Children can then complete photocopiable page 202 'Materials in School (2)'.

Differentiation
- Support children by providing them with copies of the 'Materials at School' photocopiable sheets that depict fewer and less complex objects.
- Challenge children to answer questions such as: *Were any materials only indoors or outdoors, and why might this be? Was any one material found more often than the others?*

Science in the wider world
Plastics are now widely used in buildings, replacing traditional materials: roof tiles, pipes, window frames, doors and even paint are now often plastic. For this reason there may be confusion about the materials used to build a house. An old cottage may still have wooden window frames, a thatched roof and metal pipes, but a modern dwelling is likely to have a high plastic content. The surface finish of some materials may also be confusing for example, metals may be plastic coated and high gloss paint may hide wood or metal. Some materials such as concrete and tarmac are aggregates or composites. Concrete is often made to look like natural stone, as in paving slabs.

Review
Children could be assessed on their completion of the photocopiable sheets and naming of familiar materials correctly.

Objectives
● To identify and name a variety of everyday materials.
● To think about why an object is made of a particular material.
● To correctly identify the materials objects are made of.

Resources
A collection of similar objects made from different materials (such as toy cars made from wood, metal and plastic; cups made from paper, plastic and pottery; spoons made from metal, plastic and wood); photocopiable page 203 'It could be made of...'; images of other objects made from the same materials as those in the collection

Speaking scientifically
material, wood, plastic, metal, paper, clay, strong, pliable, shaped, joined

Lesson 2: It could be made of...

Introduction

Show the class the collection of objects and tell the children to name them and talk about what they are used for. Ask them to say what the objects have in common, as well as ways in which they are different from each other. Encourage the children to recognise there is more than one of the same object, but that they are made out of different materials. Sort the collection into sets according to the object: all the cups, all the spoons, and so on. When the collection has been sorted, look at each set and ask the children to name the material of which each object has been made. Explain that the pottery objects have been made from clay.

Whole-class work

1. Now ask the children to suggest how to re-sort the objects according to the material of which they have been made. Talk about why different materials might be used to make each object. For example, plastic cutlery is useful at parties because it is safe and saves lots of washing up; but it is not really strong enough for everyday use, so metal is better. Wooden bowls look nice and are good for keeping fruit in; but they would burn if put in the oven, so are not suitable for cooking.

2. Invite a child to choose an object and challenge the rest of the class to guess which one it is by asking questions that can only be responded to with 'yes' or 'no'. Allow several children to have a turn selecting an object to encourage the class to make close observations and think about all the materials used.

Group work

3. Split the children into groups of three to play 'material dominoes'. One child chooses an object from the collection and places it on the table. The next child chooses a different object that is made from the same material. The third child chooses a similar object made from a different material and they go on alternating, for example, wooden fork, wooden bowl, metal bowl, metal spoon, plastic spoon then plastic cup.

Independent work

4. Provide each child with a copy of photocopiable page 203 'It could be made of...'. Tell them to write the names of the materials of which the object could be made in the space opposite each picture.

Differentiation
● Support children by giving them a version of the photocopiable sheet with fewer words for them to choose from.
● Challenge children to think of further examples of objects made of metal, wood and plastic.

Science in the wider world

Many materials have more than one useful property and are suitable for a range of purposes. For example, metal can be shaped (when heated) into bowls, cups or jewellery; but it is also strong and so can be used to make furniture, ships or bridges. Both of these properties make it ideal for making tools to work with other materials. Wood is warm to the touch, is strong, can be shaped and joined, and is pleasing to look at, so it is ideal for use in building and furniture making.

Review

Children could be assessed on their contribution to the dominoes game and on their completion of the photocopiable sheet.

Objectives

- To identify the materials used to make objects.
- To explain why each of the different materials has been chosen.
- To identify materials that would be inappropriate for certain objects.

Resources

A collection of objects made up of two or three (fairly evident) materials, such as a shoe, a trainer, a wellington boot, a pencil, a pencil case, an umbrella, a chair, scissors (with plastic handles), a plastic sharpener, a torch; photocopiable page 204 'What is it made of?'

Speaking scientifically

manufactured, plastic, wood, stone, leather, paper, strong, waterproof, bendy, pliable, flexible, rigid

Lesson 3: What is it made of?

Introduction

Recap on some familiar materials and ask the children to describe what these look and feel like. Choose a familiar object that has been made of one material and invite the children to suggest why that particular material has been used for that particular object. Next, introduce an object that is made of two or three materials and ask the children to identify each one. Encourage them to say why the different materials have been chosen. Invite the children to handle and explore several simple objects that are made of more than one material and then identify and discuss the ones that have been used. Talk about what the objects are used for and how the materials relate to these uses. For example, the outside of a wellington boot is made of plastic and plastic is waterproof, while the insole is generally cotton, which is warm and makes the boot comfortable to wear.

Group work

1. Provide each group of children with the photocopiable page 204 'What is it made of?' and examples of each object listed on the sheet. Tell them to look closely at each object and talk about the materials they are made of. When they are sure they have found all of the materials used, they should record these by ticking the appropriate boxes.

2. Next, tell each group to think about materials that could NOT be used for each particular object and why. For example, a paper shoe would get very soggy in the rain and fall to pieces and would not wear well even if you could keep it dry. This activity could be purely oral, or children could draw pictures of the wrong material and write sentences to explain why something could not be used.

Differentiation

- Support children with a photocopiable sheet that contains fewer objects and materials for the children to match together.
- Challenge children to look at more objects, identify the materials used and write sentences to describe some of the properties that make them suitable for the job.

Science in the wider world

Many objects are made of more than one material because no single material is the most suitable for every aspect or function of the object. The materials of which composite objects are made are chosen largely for their properties, but also for their price, availability and appeal. For example, wood makes a pencil strong and more comfortable to hold. The lead alone would break easily, be messy to use and be difficult to hold. (The 'lead' in a pencil is actually graphite.) Scissors need metal blades to cut efficiently, but may have plastic handles for more comfortable and secure handling. It is not always easy to identify the individual materials that go to make up an object in particular plastics can be made to mimic a wide range of other materials.

Review

Children could be assessed on their identification of materials in objects that are made of more than one material and on their explanation as to why these have been chosen.

Objectives
● To know that some materials can be changed in shape by forces.
● To identify pushes and pulls when using play dough and clay.

Resources
Clay or play-dough (see photocopiable page 'Play-dough recipe' on the CD-ROM); rolling pins; cutters; safe knives; clay

Speaking scientifically
squeeze, squash, push, pull, roll, press, tear

Lesson 1: Changing shape

Introduction

Remind the children of their visit to a manufacturing plant and their sandwich assembly line work and talk about some of the actions that were necessary to change the raw material into a finished product. Focus on actions that caused the materials to change shape and explain that pushes and pulls can change the shape of things. Show the class some of the play dough you have made and ask them to suggest as many ways as they can think of to change its shape. Encourage them to use appropriate vocabulary such as, 'roll', 'push', 'press', 'squash', 'pinch', 'pull', 'stretch' and 'cut'. Discuss the fact that we are using force every time we change the shape of the play dough. As you demonstrate changing the shape, ask the children to say whether this is a push or a pull.

Whole-class work

1. Provide each child with a ball of play dough. Tell them to reshape their dough in as many ways as they can: into pancakes, sausages, worms, and so on. Ask them to cut the play dough with safe knives and cutters, make pancakes with rolling pins and press their fingers into it to make patterns. Encourage them to say whether they are using a push or a pull force as they shape their play dough and then tell them to roll their play dough back into the ball they started with.

Independent work

2. Tell each child to roll out some clay to make a tile and then to push smaller pieces of clay into the tile to make a pattern. Remind them not to make the base tile too thin or they will end up with something that is full of holes! Talk about the fact that they are changing the shape of both the actual tile and the little pieces of clay they are pushing into it. If possible, the patterned tiles could be glazed or fired.

> **Differentiation**
> ● Support children to relate what they are doing to the idea of using a force to change the shape of an object.
> ● Challenge children to describe forces they have observed in other contexts, such as using playground equipment and moving around school.

Science in the wider world

At this stage, children should simply be taught that they are using a force to change the shape of things. Most forces are basically a push or a pull. Children will be familiar with the fact that they can change the shape of a material or object by such actions as banging, pressing, squashing and rolling (which are all types of push). They will also know that stretching and tearing (which are types of pull) will cause materials to change their shape. They need to be made aware that the above are all types of force, and that the use of force is necessary to cause a change in shape. Aim to use the correct vocabulary with the children and provide definitions. For example, *Use a little more force to flatten your play dough – push it harder.*

Review

Children could be assessed on the forces they are able to identify that can be used to change the shape of a material.

Objectives

● To identify different push and pull forces.
● To observe the use of forces to change the shape of a block of wood.

Resources

Small light hammers; junior hacksaws; blocks of wood (balsa is ideal); nails; sandpaper; a workbench and vice; coloured wools; ribbons and threads

Speaking scientifically

hammer, saw, cut, smooth

Lesson 2: Working with wood

Introduction

Display the clay tiles the children made in the previous lesson and talk about how they were made. Encourage the children to describe the forces they used to shape the clay tiles and make a list. Remind them that all their ways of changing the shape of the play dough and clay were either pushes or pulls. Ask them to suggest other activities where forces are used to change the shape of objects, such as squeezing the sponge out in the bath, or cutting up their dinner. Show the children a ball of soft clay and ask them to compare this to clay that has been baked, or allowed to dry out. Talk about the properties of damp clay and those of clay that has been changed through drying or firing. Show the class some blocks of wood and ask them to suggest ways in which these could be changed. Display the tools and talk about how these could be used safely.

Whole-class work

1. Provide groups of children with a selection of wooden blocks, and some sandpaper. Tell them to use the sandpaper to smooth around the edges of a block of wood and talk about how they have changed the appearance and feel of the wood. Encourage them to recognise that sanding is a pushing force.

Group work

2. Arrange for groups of children to have the opportunity to use junior hacksaws on and hammer nails into pieces of wood. Check your school policies for guidance on using this sort of equipment in your classroom and providing appropriate levels of supervision. Demonstrate to the children how to use the tools safely, for instance, placing a block of wood in a vice before sawing it in half.

3. Once all the children have hammered in some nails, they can decorate their blocks by winding coloured wool, ribbon or thread around and between the nails.

4. Recap on the vocabulary the children have learned and practised. Ask them to list all the forces they used to create their wood decoration and relate the hammering, sawing and sandpapering of the wood to pushes or pulls.

Science in the wider world

Wood is the oldest and most commonly used engineering material in the world. Light in weight, it is easily shipped and handled and worked into various shapes. Wood can be fastened with nails, staples, screws or glue and its surface smoothed and then treated with either paint or preservative. When working with children, aim to use balsa or other soft woods such as pine, which will be easier to hammer nails into. Nails with large heads are easier to hit, but ensure that they are about two thirds of the depth of the piece of wood in length, so that there is no danger of the points coming through the bottom of it. Beware of bags of offcuts of wood, which are often too hard, thick and splintery to use safely.

Review

Children could be assessed on their observations about the use of forces to change the shape of a piece of wood.

- To identify materials.
- To describe the texture of different materials.

Resources
Images of a range of materials; a collection of materials that feel different, such as – wooden/plastic blocks, synthetic sponge, a section from a drinks bottle, a piece of carrier bag, metal, fabric, glass (paperweight), cork, wax; feely bags – enough for each group of four children; a variety of materials

Speaking scientifically
rough, smooth, slippery, hard, soft, ridged, bumpy, bendy, stretchy, flexible, rigid, cold, warm

Lesson 3: What's in the bag?

Introduction

When preparing for this lesson, check that there are no objects with sharp edges on which the children could hurt themselves. As a general rule of hygiene, ensure that the children wash their hands before and after playing the feely bag game.

Display some images of a range of materials (try to find pieces or lumps of raw materials rather than manufactured objects to show the class) and invite the children to describe how these might feel. Make a list of their ideas and then ask them to feel some materials around them, such as the carpet they are sitting on, their clothes, whiteboards, whiteboard erasers, and so on. Talk about the materials these objects are made from and encourage the children to think of words to describe them and add these to your list, introducing any new words you think might be relevant.

Whole-class work

1. Show the children your selection of 'feely' materials. Pass these around and ask them to think of words to describe how each one feels.

2. Put one of the objects into the bag, without the children seeing, and invite a child to try to describe it using just their sense of touch. Encourage them to use any words they can think of, but help them to focus on the words from the class list. Ask the children to guess what material is in the bag and then reveal it to them.

3. Next, put two materials in the bag. Name one of the materials and ask a child to find that one in the bag.

Group work

4. Explain that each group is going to carry on with the feely bag game. One child should describe what he or she can feel, while the other children in the group try to guess which material it is. Encourage the children to use the vocabulary from the class list you made earlier in the lesson.

5. Working in groups of four, tell the children to make 'feely' pictures. Using a large sheet of paper, they should 'take a pencil for a walk' to create a random pattern, and then fill in each area with a different collage material. Encourage the children to describe the materials they are using in terms of what they feel like. Alternatively, you could stick several large sheets of paper together and have six to eight children at a time making a class feely picture (to cover a display board).

Science in the wider world

It is important to be clear about the differences between the intrinsic properties of materials and their attributes (properties that can be given to them in the manufacturing process). For example, all plastics are waterproof and have a relatively low melting point. These are properties of the material. However, plastics can be made rigid or flexible, transparent, translucent or opaque. These are attributes of the manufactured products. Wood is strong, it floats and insulates – these are properties. However, it can be made rough or smooth, flat or curved, it can be dyed or polished – these are attributes.

Review

Children could be assessed on their identification of a variety of everyday materials and descriptions of different textures.

Objectives
- To explore the properties of magnets.
- To test objects to see if they are magnetic.
- To sort objects according to whether they are magnetic or not.
- To compare magnetic items.

Resources
Good magnets of different shapes and sizes, including ring magnets on a stick; a collection of materials such as – small pieces of wood, plastic, synthetic sponge, a section from a drinks bottle, a piece of carrier bag, metal (paper clip, a nut, a washer) – plain metal discs are useful for this activity, fabric, paper, cork, wax, string; PE hoops/set rings for sorting; photocopiable page 205 'Magnets'

Speaking scientifically
magnet, magnetic, attracts, attraction, repels, repulsion, pick up, stick to, metal, non-metal

Lesson 1: Magnets

Introduction
Show the class a range of magnets and ask the children if they know what these are. Invite them to say what they already know; perhaps they have a collection of fridge magnets at home, or have noticed magnetic catches on cupboard doors. Tell the children that you can use the ring magnets to do a trick. Show them how these stack one on top of the other on the stick to begin with. Then pick up all but the bottom one and turn them over. Now when you put them back on the stick, these magnets will float above the bottom one. You can carry on creating more floating magnets by turning each ring in turn. Ask the children if they are able to give a scientific explanation and guide them as necessary to talk about the properties of magnets and use the terms 'repel' and 'attract'.

Whole-class work
1. Tell the children that some of the magnets in the collection are stronger than others. Demonstrate that a stronger magnet will pick up more or heavier objects than a weaker one. Talk about the importance of keeping magnets well away from televisions, computers, phones and watches because of the damage they can do.

2. Go through the names of the materials in the collection and ask the children to predict which of these materials will be attracted to a magnet. Encourage them to explain their ideas and make a 'yes' or 'no' list on the board.

3. Test out two of the materials – one magnetic and one non-magnetic – and allocate these to two PE hoops.

Paired work
4. Provide pairs of children with a collection of materials and sorting hoops and ask them to use a magnet to check these and place them in the right hoop.

5. When all the materials have been sorted, share each pair's findings and compare with the class's earlier predictions. On the interactive whiteboard, make two hoops and write in the names of the materials the children have sorted into their magnetic and non-magnetic groups.

Independent work
6. Provide each child with photocopiable page 205 'Magnets' and ask them to record the materials in the correct hoop. Encourage them to recognise that all the magnetic materials are metals.

Differentiation
- Support children by providing them with images and small samples of materials that can be cut and pasted appropriately or with a wordbank of labels.
- Challenge children to make observations about magnetic materials and to write sentences about these.

Science in the wider world
Bar magnets are available from most educational suppliers. Old audio speakers (often available from car boot sales) can be a source of really strong magnets that would otherwise be expensive to buy. Magnets should always be stored properly in order to help them remain magnetic for as long as possible. Store ceramic bar magnets in pairs in the box they were supplied in. Store other magnets complete with a keeper. Magnets will lose their strength if dropped continually, though plastic-coated ceramic magnets (which have iron particles baked into the clay) are a little more resilient.

Review
Children could be assessed on their observations about magnetic and non-magnetic materials and their completion of the photocopiable sheet.

Objectives
• To identify that only metals are magnetic.
• To investigate whether all metals are magnetic.
• To sort magnetic and non-magnetic materials.

Resources
Interactive activity 'Magnets' on the CD-ROM; magnets, a collection of coins; a set of discs of different metals (named if possible); PE hoops/set rings for sorting; magnetic tape; card; scissors, adhesive; felt-tipped pens

Speaking scientifically
magnet, magnetic, iron, cobalt, nickel, steel, attracts, attraction, repels, repulsion, pick up, stick to, metal, non-metal

Lesson 2: Non-magnetic metals

Introduction

Recap on what the children found out about magnetic materials in the previous lesson. Use the interactive activity 'Magnets' on the CD-ROM to remind them of how they grouped materials into those that were attracted to a magnet and those that were not. Ask the children to explain what the materials in the 'magnetic' group all have in common. Show the class the photocopiable sheets they filled in to record their observations and invite some children to check these results again by demonstrating to the rest of the class whether a particular material is attracted to a magnet or not. Once you have established that all the children recognise that only metals are magnetic, show them a strip of magnetic tape and an aluminium soft drinks can. Ask them if they think the can will be attracted to the magnet and then demonstrate that it is not.

Whole-class work

1. Display the set of coins and metal discs. Explain that the coins are different colours because they are made from different metals. Each disc is also made of a different sort of metal, such as brass, zinc, copper and aluminium.

2. Ask the children to suggest how they could find out which of the metals are magnetic and encourage them to consider a similar sorting activity to the previous lesson: testing out each metal with a magnet and putting it in the appropriate PE hoop or set ring.

Group work

3. Provide groups of children with magnets and a selection of coins and metal discs and tell them to sort into magnetic and non-magnetic sets.

4. Ask each group to report back their findings to the class and check that everyone agrees. List the magnetic metals on the board and link these with some of the objects, such as paper clips and bottle tops, which were attracted to the magnet.

Paired work

5. Give each child a piece of card, scissors and felt-tipped pens. Explain that they are going to make a fridge magnet by decorating and shaping the card and then attaching it to a piece of magnetic tape. Ask the children to explain why their magnet will attach itself to the fridge and encourage them to use words such as 'attracted' and 'magnetic' in their explanations.

Science in the wider world

Iron, cobalt and nickel are magnetic metals. As steel is composed mostly of iron, it is also magnetic, while metals such as aluminium, copper and gold are not. Before using sterling coins for the class investigation described, check whether the ones in your collection are magnetic. Pennies and 2p coins made before 1992 were made mostly of non-magnetic copper, but more recently minted ones are generally made of copper-plated steel which is magnetic. Newer 5p and 10p coins are also magnetic; since 2012, the Royal Mint has been issuing nickel-plated steel ones into circulation. Twenty pence coins are made from an alloy called cupro-nickel, which is mainly copper and is therefore not magnetic.

Review

Children could be assessed on their observations and sorting of magnetic and non-magnetic metals.

Objectives
- To distinguish between shiny and dull materials.
- To make observations about shiny materials.
- To sort materials into shiny and dull groups.

Resources
Images from the story of Cinderella; images of objects made from shiny or dull materials; tinsel, old CDs, paper towels, torches; shiny and dull materials such as – papers, tin foil, fabrics, plastics, play dough, and so on; PE hoops or set rings; template outlines of Cinderella in rags and dressed for the ball, or in the carriage; scissors and adhesive

Speaking scientifically
shiny, dull, reflecting, absorbing, heat, light ray, fluorescent

Lesson 3: Helping Cinderella go to the ball

Introduction
Show the class images from the tale of Cinderella, or watch some video extracts, and ask the children to tell the story in their own words. Encourage them to describe some of the differences between the Cinderella character at the beginning of the story and later, when she is ready for the ball. Make a list of their ideas and prompt them as appropriate to use words such as shiny and dull.

Whole-class work
1. Draw two large circles on the interactive whiteboard and display some images of objects that are made from a variety of materials. Encourage the children to identify the material that each object is made from and ask them to help you sort these into shiny or dull groups. Talk about their ideas and check that everyone agrees with where each example should go before dragging the image into a circle according to their instructions.

2. Hold up a piece of tinsel and a paper towel and challenge the children to describe these and explain how they know whether they are shiny and dull. Shine the torch onto each one in turn and encourage the children to make further observations. Draw their attention to the way in which the light is reflected from the surface of the tinsel.

3. Play an 'I spy' game, introducing the article to be guessed as 'I spy a shiny (or dull) object beginning with...' Model this game yourself and then give children the opportunity to have a turn.

Paired work
4. Provide pairs of children with a selection of the shiny and dull materials you have collected and two PE hoops or set rings. Explain that they are going to sort the materials into a group of shiny ones and another of dull ones.

5. Once the children have created their two sets of materials, provide them with an outline of Cinderella in rags and another of her dressed for the ball, or in the carriage that has been transformed from a pumpkin. Ask them to select materials from the appropriate set to glue onto these pictures to make a collage.

6. Once the children have finished their work, ask pairs to present these to the class and talk about their choice of materials. Make a classroom display of shiny and dull collages.

Differentiation
- Support children by providing them with a choice of template outlines and asking them to complete just one collage.
- Challenge children to think about how reflective materials can help with road safety when it is dark.

Science in the wider world
Whether a material is bright or dark depends on the amount of light that is absorbed or reflected by it. Matt black surfaces do not reflect much light because most of it is absorbed and turned into heat. Shiny surfaces, on the other hand, are poor absorbers of heat and so light rays are reflected away. Spacecraft are shiny to reflect away the Sun's heat. Light from car headlamps does not pick out dark clothing well at night, but is easily reflected if fluorescent materials are worn.

Review
Children could be assessed on their sorting of shiny and dull materials and their observations on these.

Lesson 1: Teddy's umbrella

Introduction

Read 'Happiness' by AA Milne. Ask the children to recall what John is wearing in the poem and make a list of his clothing on the board. Encourage them to suggest further items of waterproof clothing to add to this list and prompt them, if necessary, to include umbrellas. Remind the children of previous letters they have had from Teddy (asking for help with finding shade and why it is light at bedtime in earlier chapters on seasons) and explain that he has written to the class again. Read out a letter in which Teddy explains that he is fed up with getting wet when it rains and wants to buy a new umbrella. The problem is that there are so many to choose from in the shop and he doesn't know which will be the most waterproof. He hopes the children can give him some advice on the best material for an umbrella.

Whole-class work

1. Show the children a real umbrella and talk about how to use it effectively. Ask how they could find out if it was waterproof and guide them to consider pouring water over the top of it and seeing if whatever was underneath stayed dry.

2. Display a selection of materials and ask which one they think would be best for making an umbrella. Encourage them to give reasons for their choices. Draw their attention to the holes between the threads in a woven fabric and ask what they think might happen if they poured water over that.

3. Explain that they are going to test out each material by putting a piece of it over the top of a container and securing it in place with an elastic band. The children will then pour some water over the top of the material and see whether the small plastic teddy inside the container has got wet. Check that they recognise that if the teddy stays dry, the material must be waterproof.

4. Demonstrate what to do by attaching pieces of fabric over a couple of the containers, making one obviously bigger, or folded into several layers and pouring very different amounts of water over each. Encourage the children to recognise that doing their investigation like this would not be fair. Establish that each piece of material needs to be the same size and the same amount of water will have to be used each time.

Group work

5. Provide groups of children with the containers, teddies and a selection of materials (you may wish to prepare these so that they do not have the fiddly job of securing the covers in place with elastic bands). Tell them to stand the containers in a large tray and pour the same amount of water over each one.

6. Alternatively, the children could investigate one material at a time, or you could provide each group with a different cover to test.

Whole-class work

7. Ask the children to report back on their findings and assign the tested materials to groups of waterproof and not waterproof materials.

Science in the wider world

Umbrellas are thought to date back to ancient civilisations and were originally intended to be sunshades. The Chinese are credited with being the first to wax and lacquer paper parasols to provide protection from the rain. In the middle of the 19th century, an English inventor called Samuel Fox designed a steel-rimmed umbrella, which replaced earlier wood and whalebone models.

Review

Children could be assessed on their observations about waterproof materials and whether they can identify these at the end of their investigation.

Objectives

- To identify hard and soft materials.
- To suggest why objects are made from soft materials.
- To suggest why items of playground equipment are made from hard materials.

Resources

Images of soft play areas and traditional outdoor playgrounds; cuddly toys; pillow; duvet; a selection of hard and soft objects – foam; cotton wool, fabrics such as cotton, towelling, fleece and microfibers, metal discs, pebbles, wood, plastic; PE hoops or set rings; bedroom pictures from old magazines or a simply drawn template; collage materials

Speaking scientifically

soft, hard, impact, absorb, comfort, spongy, ductile, malleable, rigid, warm, cold

Lesson 2: Soft or hard?

Introduction

Show the class a pillow, duvet and cuddly toys you have collected together and talk about what these are used for. Ask the children to describe how each item feels and encourage them to include words such as soft, spongy, warm and cosy. Make a list of their ideas. Talk about some of the materials that have been used to make these items, including cotton/polyester, feathers, microfibers and foam. Display the images of a variety of play areas, such as a soft-play ball pool, a bouncy castle and traditional children's playground. Ask the children to say whether there are soft or hard materials in each picture; identify what these are and suggest why they have been used.

Whole-class work

1. Take the class for a walk around the playground and note the materials that have been used for large items of play equipment such as climbing frames and slides. Encourage the children to describe how these feel and talk about the properties of plastic, wood, and metal. Point out any absorbent surfaces around the play structures and compare these with other parts of the playground. Talk about why such surfaces are generally used around children's play equipment.

2. Back in class, show the children a large image of a child's bedroom. Ask them to list all the soft items they can see in the picture: curtains, bedding, pillows, toys, cushions and so on, and talk about why there are so many soft materials in a bedroom.

Group work

3. Provide groups of children with a selection of materials and hoops. Tell them to sort their materials into hard and soft sets. Explain that they will need to talk about each example and come to a decision as a group.

4. When they have completed the sorting element of this activity, ask each group in turn to select a material and explain why they placed it in a particular set. Encourage the children to describe what it feels like and invite the rest of the class to add their comments. Repeat for each group.

Independent work

5. Provide each child with a smaller version of the bedroom picture. Tell them to select suitable collage materials and to glue these onto all the soft objects they can see in the bedroom.

Science in the wider world

British Standards (BS) require that softer surfacing is used around children's play equipment to cushion the impact of accidental falls. A variety of materials, including rubber tiles, mats and grass may be suitable, depending on the height of the play structures. BS regulations also determine the depth to which these materials should be laid so that they can provide a sufficiently cushioning layer. More absorbing surfaces can lessen the severity of an injury, compared to harder surfaces such as tarmac and concrete.

Review

Children could be assessed on their observations about soft and hard materials and their uses; how they have grouped examples of these and their selection of materials for a bedroom collage.

Objectives
• To identify materials as either rigid or flexible.
• To conduct an investigation into changing the shape of objects.
• To identify whether a material is bendy or stretchy and sort accordingly.

Resources
Images of flexible and rigid materials – modelling clay, elastic bands, drinking straws, pipe cleaners; items made from stretchy fabrics – socks, beanie hat, lycra, and so on; photocopiable page 206 'Bendy and stretchy'; interactive activity 'Bendy or stretchy?' on the CD-ROM

Speaking scientifically
squashing, bending, twisting, stretching, flexible, pliable, rigid, elasticity, stiff

Lesson 3: Bend and stretch

Introduction
Display the clay tiles made in a previous lesson and ask the children to recap on how these were formed. Remind them that they used pushes and pulls to shape the clay and encourage the children to use appropriate vocabulary including, 'roll', 'press', 'squash', 'pinch', 'stretch' and 'cut' as they describe what they did. Prompt them to say how the clay felt as they worked with it and draw out properties such as bendy, squashy and soft. Ask them if they can suggest any other materials that can be changed easily into different shapes.

Whole-class work
1. Show the class images of a variety of materials on the interactive whiteboard, alongside two large empty circles. Explain that you are going to play a guessing game to sort out the materials into two sets, depending on whether they are bendy or not. Introduce the terms 'flexible' and 'rigid' to describe these properties.

2. Tell the children that you will start by thinking of an object that is easy to bend, but can only answer 'yes' or 'no' to their questions. Encourage them to ask ones that relate to physical properties of the materials displayed and as they guess each one, either bendy or stiff, drag it into the appropriate circle. Continue until all the materials have been allocated to the correct set.

Group work
3. Provide groups of children with a variety of objects made from stretchy or bendy materials. Tell them to investigate changing the shape of their collection and talk about the actions they have used to do this.

4. Ask each group to report back to the class about their observations and check whether any of the children have noticed that some of the objects stay in the new shape they have been pushed or pulled into, while others spring back to their original shape as soon as the children let go.

5. Tell the groups to sort their materials into hoops, making a group of objects that stay in a new shape and a group that return to their original shape.

Independent work
6. Provide children with a copy of photocopiable page 206 'Bendy and stretchy'. Tell them to look carefully at the images displayed around the circles and think about what happens to the shape when these are pushed or pulled. If they are items that stay in a new shape, the children should put them all together in one circle, while any they think will spring back into their old shape again, should go into the other circle. Children could also complete the interactive activity 'Bendy or stretchy?' on the CD-ROM.

Differentiation
• Support children by telling them to draw lines from each object to the correct circle, or provide images for them to cut and stick on appropriately.
• Challenge children to use words such as 'flexible' and 'elastic' to describe objects and write sentences about their observations.

Science in the wider world
The Mayans are thought to be the first people to have used sap from rubber trees to create an elastic material that could be wrapped around objects to bind them. An English inventor called Stephen Perry is credited with patenting the modern rubber band in 1845. They were originally made from natural rubber, they are now generally made of a synthetic material derived from oil.

Review
Children could be assessed on their observations about differences between bendy and stretchy materials and their completion of the photocopiable sheet activity.

Objectives
● To carry out an investigation into absorbency.
● To establish a fair test.
● To make predictions.
● To identify the most absorbent material.
● To compare results.

Resources
A selection of materials such as – newspaper, paper towel, towelling fabric, dishcloth; large plastic trays; small beakers; large plastic bowls; large measuring cylinders; a funnel; food colouring

Speaking scientifically
absorbent, soaking, mopping

Lesson 1: Mopping up spills

Introduction
Prior to this lesson, collect all the equipment and resources that you will need. Plan to test four different materials that have been cut into pieces all the same size. Have extra samples of differing sizes to show the children. Measure a small amount of water into enough beakers for each piece of material and have a corresponding number of large plastic bowls that the children will be able to squeeze their materials over. Attach a sample of material to each bowl to guide the children to wring out a particular material over its matching bowl.

Explain that Teddy has emailed another question for the class to answer. He spilled a drink of water on the floor recently and couldn't find anything to mop it up with. He wants to get something suitable when he goes shopping, but is not sure what will be the best material to buy. He hopes the children can find out for him.

Whole-class work
1. Remind the class of the umbrella investigation they carried out for Teddy. Encourage them to recall how they kept all the pieces of the materials they were testing the same size and poured the same amount of water over each one. Talk about why this was important and prompt the children as necessary to recognise that it will make this test fair if they do the same. Establish that each piece of material needs to be the same size and the same amount of water will have to be used each time.

2. Demonstrate what might happen if you didn't keep the size of the materials or the amount of water the same each time.

Group work
3. Give each group samples of all the materials they are going to test. Tell them to choose the one they think will mop up the most, and least, amount of water. Make a note of all their predictions by attaching the materials they select onto a display board underneath headings for best and worst mops.

4. Provide all the groups with a large plastic tray, pieces of each material cut to the same size and small pre-measured beakers of water. Tell the children to make a spill in their tray and then use one piece of material to mop up as much water as they can. When the material looks soaking wet, they should squeeze it out over the collection bowl for that material.

5. Collect all the bowls together and pour the contents of each one into a large measuring cylinder – one for each material. Add a drop of food colouring to make the water level more visible.

6. Line up the measuring cylinders to form a simple bar chart and ask the children to say which was the best, and which the worst, material for mopping up spills and how they can tell. Take a photograph of your results and compose a class email to send to Teddy, with the photo attached.

Science in the wider world
Natural sponges are primitive sea animals. Synthetic ones are generally made from celluloses which attract water molecules and store them in holes between the fibres. The water is forced back out of the holes as the sponge is squeezed. Terrycloth – made from either 100% cotton or a polyester mix – is woven on special looms which create loops of fabric. The longer these loops, the greater the surface area to absorb water; making this fabric ideal for bath towels.

Review
Children could be assessed on their observations on the absorbency of materials and on their understanding that the more water collected, the more absorbent the material.

Objectives
● To compare the strength of different materials.
● To find out which is the best material for a bookshelf.

Resources
Images/samples of a variety of materials to demonstrate a range of properties; photographs of children carrying out earlier investigations in this chapter; similar sized samples of wood, plastic, metal, fabric, wool, cardboard; selection of exercise books (to ensure identical size and weight each time); shelf supports (such as wooden or plastic blocks); lengths of string, rulers or tape measurers; a camera

Speaking scientifically
strong, hard, rigid, rough, smooth, soft, ridged, bumpy, bendy, stretchy, flexible

Lesson 2: Making a bookshelf

Introduction

Display images or samples of a variety of materials and invite the children to identify each one. Ask them to suggest a use for these materials and encourage them to explain their ideas. Remind the class about earlier investigations they may have carried out during this topic – such as finding a waterproof material for an umbrella – and display any photographs you have taken of the children working on these activities. Talk about what they did and what they found out about the materials they investigated. Hold up the lengths of wood, plastic, metal, fabric, wool, cardboard and a set of exercise books. Ask the children to say which material would make the best bookshelf. Encourage them to consider properties such as hardness, rigidity and strength.

Whole-class work

1. Look around the classroom – or take the class on a tour of the school – and point out a variety of bookshelves. Talk about the number of books each one is holding and whether the shelves are rigid or bending under the weight. Ask the children to identify which material the bookshelves are made from and encourage them to explain why they are made from this.

2. Display the materials you are going to investigate and encourage the children to suggest ways of finding out which one will make the best bookshelf.

Group work

3. Set up workstations with identical piles of books and shelf supports all the same length apart. Ensure that these are set up safely – where any falling books will not present a hazard to children. Ask some children to check the distance between the supports – either with lengths of string, rulers or tape measurers – and confirm that this is the same at all the workstations.

4. Provide the groups with lengths of shelving materials and ask them to find out if these will support their books by laying one at a time across the supports and placing the books on top.

5. Tell the children to group their materials according to whether they supported the books or not. Encourage them to use words such as 'hard', 'strong', 'rigid', 'bendy', 'flexible' or 'soft' to describe what happened when they tried out each one. Make a note of their comments.

6. Take photographs of the children's investigations and display these together with the materials tested and some transcripts of the children's observations.

Science in the wider world

Early books were written by hand and often stored in boxes or chests. However with the development of printing techniques, bookshelves evolved to display books spine side out. The British Library in London boasts over 625km of shelves!

Review

Children could be assessed on their observations about the strength of each material tested and on the suggestions they make as to how to carry out the investigation.

Objectives
● To carry out an investigation into blackout material for curtains.
● To decide which combination of properties would make the best curtains.

Resources
Pieces cut from a plastic bag, tin foil, newspaper, modelling clay; swatches of fabrics including net, cotton or polyester, lycra, and so on; torches

Speaking scientifically
thin, thick, flexible, daylight, sunset, darkness, shining

Lesson 3: Curtains!

Introduction
Remind the children of the letter the class received from Teddy during their previous work on seasons describing how it was hard to go to sleep now that it was no longer dark at bedtime. Re-read the letter and ask the children to explain why it is no longer dark when they go to bed. Establish that in summer, there is much more daylight than in winter and that at this time of year, it doesn't get dark until after bedtime. Ask the children if, now that they know so much about properties of materials, they think it might be possible to recommend some curtains for Teddy that would keep the light out and help him go to sleep at the right time.

Whole-class work
1. Talk about the types of curtain or blind the children have in their own bedrooms and whether these block out enough light at bedtime. Ask them what sort of properties they think effective curtains should have and make a list of their ideas. Prompt them as necessary to suggest keeping the light out, keeping heat in (in winter), hanging easily on a curtain rail and being light enough to pull open and shut easily.

2. Encourage the children to think about how they could find out which material would be the most suitable. Prompt them as necessary to suggest trying to fold each one into pleats, comparing how heavy the materials feel and shining a torch through it to see how much light is visible.

Group work
3. Provide groups of children with a selection of materials to test. Tell them to begin by folding each one into pleats and observing what happens when they let go. Ask them to put to one side any that cannot be bent, stay folded into their new shape or feel like they would tear if pulled too much. Check that each group is making similar observations and choices.

4. Tell the children to test their remaining materials by shining a torch on them and putting to one side any that they can see a lot of light through.

5. Out of the swatches they have left, ask the groups to think about whether any other properties are important, such as whether the colours and patterns are suitable for a child's bedroom, and choose the one they would recommend to Teddy.

6. Compare each group's findings, encouraging children to give explanations for their choice of curtains, and compose a class letter for Teddy explaining what they found out and attaching swatches of their recommended material.

Science in the wider world
The first curtains were thought to be animal hides hung across entrances. Originally, window curtains would have been a preserve of the affluent, but as the mass-production of textiles evolved from the mid-19th century onwards, household fabrics would become more readily available. As towns developed, lace curtains became a way of maintaining privacy between neighbours living in close proximity to each other.

Review
Children could be assessed on their observations about the properties of the materials used in this investigation and their ideas about what made some of these suitable for curtains.

Objectives
● To recap on all the properties of materials they have investigated.
● To match materials to their properties.
● To suggest why objects are made from certain materials.

Resources
Photocopiable page 207 'Properties of materials (1)', images and examples of a variety of materials; photocopiable page 'Properties of materials (2)' from the CD-ROM

Working scientifically
● To identify and classify.
● *To make comparisons.*

Properties of materials

Revise

● Remind the children of the work they have done during this topic to identify various properties of different materials. Display examples of their work relating to some of these properties, such as helping Cinderella go to the ball, choosing soft materials for a bedroom collage and sorting out bendy and stretchy materials. Ask them to recall as many properties as they can and add these as headings to a large table on the interactive whiteboard, prompting the children as necessary to ensure this includes: flexible, rigid, soft, hard, rough, smooth, shiny, dull. Next, display images of a variety of materials around the table and ask the children to name these. Taking one at a time, talk about some familiar properties and drag the image into the appropriate column in the table. Repeat until all the materials have been allocated, pausing where appropriate to talk about materials that share a number of properties. Make enough copies of these images to put into other boxes, or write the name of the material in the correct columns.

● Select one of the materials from the table and ask the children to suggest objects that are made of it. Talk about why a particular object is made of a certain material and make up sentences similar to those on the photocopiable page 'Properties of materials (2)' from the CD-ROM. Remind the children of the work they carried out shaping wood with tools and sandpaper and finding a waterproof umbrella material for Teddy. Model writing several sentences using the word 'because' to explain why an object is made out of a particular material.

● Refer back to the table and ensure that the children can name all the materials in each column before scrolling up the completed table so that it is no longer visible. Tell them that you are thinking of a material that is... (give a specific property) and challenge them to guess by asking questions to which you can only answer 'yes' or 'no'. Gradually, build up a list of all the materials from the previous table that can then be left on the board as an aide memoire, or printed out for individual children to use.

Assess

● Provide each child with a copy of photocopiable page 207 'Properties of materials (1)' and point out the column headings: flexible, rigid, soft, hard, rough, smooth, shiny, dull. Tell them to sort the list of materials from the board (or on their own copy) by allocating each one to the appropriate column. Remind them that they can use materials more than once.

● Give each child a copy of photocopiable page 'Properties of materials (2)' from the CD-ROM and ask them list examples of objects that are made out of particular materials and say why.

Further practice

● Support children by providing them with a material label wordbank that they can cut and stick onto their 'Properties of materials' sheets. Limit the number of materials you ask them to sort.

● Challenge children to add further examples of materials and write sentences to explain why some materials appear in more than one box.

Objectives
● To recap on elasticity.
● To recap on the forces needed to change the shape of a solid.
● To think about different pushes and pulls.

Resources
Play dough (see photocopiable page 'Play-dough recipe' on the CD-ROM); boards; pastry cutters and safe knives; large sheets of card divided into 8 boxes; a camera

Working scientifically
● To identify and classify.
● To make comparisons.

Changing shape

Revise

● Show the children images or examples of the work they did earlier in this topic on changing the shape of play dough and clay. Remind them that they used a variety of pushes and pulls and ask them to recall some of the specific actions they carried out to make different shapes, prompting as necessary to produce a list that includes: 'roll', 'push', 'press', 'squash', 'pinch', 'pull', 'stretch' and 'cut'. Write these actions clearly on the board. Talk about what happened once they changed the shape of their play dough, asking the children to recall whether it stayed in its new shape or sprung back to the old one when they let go. Establish that play dough does stay in its new shape, but that elastic materials such as rubber bands will not. Point out that the clay they used to make their patterned tiles, not only stayed in its new shape, but changed from being soft and squidgy to being hard and dry.

Assess

● Provide each child with a ball of play dough and a board to work on. Tell them to practise reshaping their dough in as many ways as they can and check that there are able to make pancakes, sausages and worms when asked. Encourage them to think about whether they are using a pushing or a pulling force as they shape their play dough. After they have practised for a few minutes, tell the children to roll their play dough back into a ball again and leave it on their board.

● Distribute a large sheet of card to each child and point out that these have been divided into eight boxes. Remind the children of the vocabulary list on the board that you made at the beginning of the lesson. Read through this again together.

● Tell the children that they can also use the pastry cutters or safe knives to help them shape their play dough and to think about which actions these may be particularly useful for.

● Ask them to choose one of the actions from the board and to copy the word carefully into one of the boxes on their sheet of card.

● Next, tell them to break off a piece of play dough and using the action they have just written down, work on their board to change the shape. Once the piece of play dough has been reshaped, ask them to carefully move it from their working board to the box on the sheet of card where they wrote down the appropriate action.

● Continue this process until the children have filled all their boxes.

● Take photographs of the children's work to form a permanent record of this assessment activity.

Further practice

● Support children by providing them with boxes that have already been labelled with appropriate headings – or limit the number of actions you ask them to carry out.

● Challenge children to write a set of simple instructions for making a particular shape, using the appropriate vocabulary. Pairs of children could then work together to try following each other's instructions.

• To revise magnetism.
• To carry out an investigation to show which magnet is the strongest.
• To sort metals according to whether they are magnetic or not.

Resources
Magnets; paper clips; blank paper; a collection of materials such as – small pieces of wood, plastic, synthetic sponge, section from a drinks bottle, piece of carrier bag, metal (a nut, a washer), plain metal discs, fabric, paper, cork, wax, string; photocopiable page 'Assessment – magnets' from the CD-ROM; drinking straw, nail, drawing pin, stamp, string, button, paper fastener, scissors; A3 version of the photocopiable page 205 'Magnets'; interactive activity 'Magnets' on the CD-ROM; metals wordbank or name labels

Working scientifically
• To identify and classify.
• *To make comparisons.*

Magnetic strength

Revise
• Remind the children about the work they carried out during their lessons on magnets. Show them the magnets they used for these activities and ask them to explain how they work; checking that the children can use the words 'attract' and 'magnetic' and describe how some of the magnets were stronger than others. Demonstrate how you can make a chain of paperclips dangle from a magnet. Show the class the materials they investigated previously along with examples of the 'Magnets' photocopiable sheets they filled in – sorting materials into magnetic and non-magnetic groups. Show them the materials that will appear on the photocopiable page 'Assessment – magnets' from the CD-ROM and encourage them to make predictions about these. Demonstrate what happens with each material. Re-do the interactive activity 'Magnets' on the CD-ROM to remind the children of how they can group materials according to whether they are attracted to a magnet or not. Establish that only the metal objects were magnetic and challenge the children to say if this was the case for all metals they tested. Focus on the collection of metal discs that were used previously and ask the children to say whether all of these are magnetic. Demonstrate using a magnet to show that some of them are not.

Assess
• Provide children with two magnets of differing strengths and some paperclips. Ask them to find out which magnet is the strongest by counting how many paperclips can be attached to each one. Observe how the children carry out this practical activity and tell them to record what they found out by drawing the magnets, with the appropriate number of paperclips attached, onto a blank sheet of paper.
• Provide each child with the photocopiable page 'Assessment – magnets' from the CD-ROM and ask them to complete the activities; colouring in magnetic objects and crossing out those that are not magnetic; then answering the questions at the bottom of the page.
• Following this, provide each child with an A3 version of photocopiable page 205 'Magnets', which they used in an earlier lesson. They will also need a magnet and a small collection of metal discs – including iron, steel, nickel and some non-magnetic metals such as copper and aluminium. Tell the children to test out each disc and place it in the correct hoop on their photocopiable sheet.
• Once the children have completed the practical sorting activity, ask them to use the wordbank or labels to record the names of the metals they have put in each group.

Further practice
• Support children by modifying the photocopiable sheet 'Assessment – magnets', so that it does not include the two questions at the bottom of the page. Limit the number of metals you ask them to test and take photographs of their photocopiable sheets to make a record of this sorting activity. If the discs they are using have the names of the metals embossed on them, the children could make rubbings of these using crayons and tracing paper and then cut around the shapes and attach these to their photocopiable sheet.
• Challenge children to explain what sorts of materials are magnetic and to name one or two examples of magnetic metals. Ask the children to write additional sentences about their observations regarding magnetic and non-magnetic metals.

Materials at School (1)

■ Cut out the labels and stick one in each box to show what the things are made of.

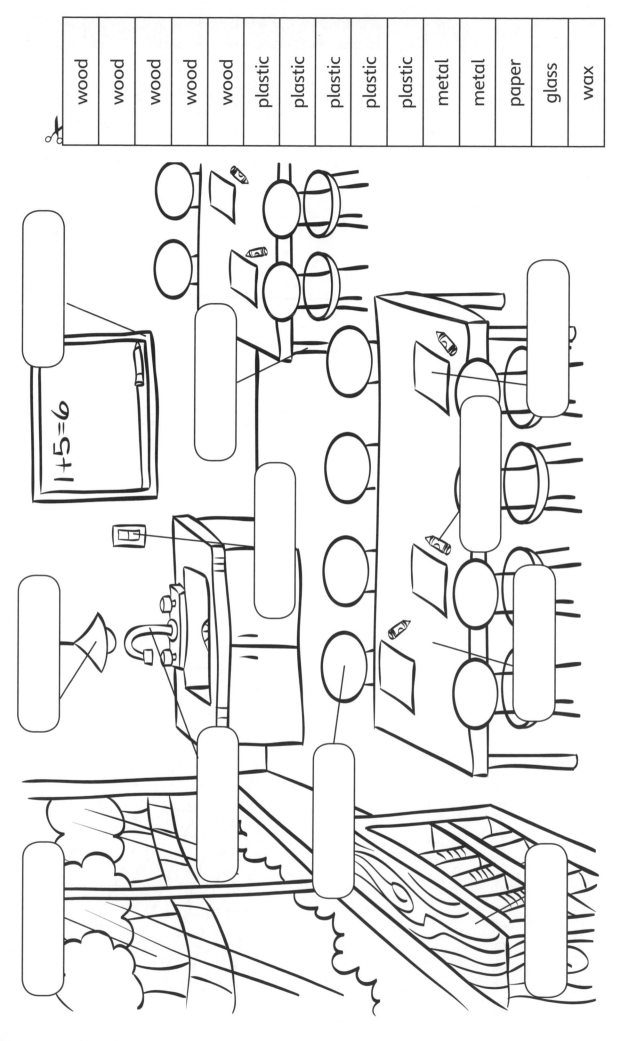

| wood | wood | wood | wood | wood | plastic | plastic | plastic | plastic | plastic | metal | metal | paper | glass | wax |

$1 + 5 = 6$

PHOTOCOPIABLE

Materials at School (2)

■ Cut out the labels and stick them in the correct places on the picture.

| glass |
| glass |
| metal |
| metal |
| metal |
| plastic |
| wood |
| wood |
| brick (clay) |
| brick (clay) |
| brick (clay) |
| brick (clay) |

It could be made of...

	A bowl could be made of:
	A bucket could be made of:
	A mug could be made of:
	A knife, fork and spoon could be made of:
	A toy car could be made of:

I can identify the materials that could be used to make an object.

How did you do?

Name: _____

Date: _____

What is it made of?

■ Put a tick against the materials that each object is made of.

	plastic	wood	metal	cotton	glass	graphite	leather	fabric

How did you do?

I can explain why different objects are made of different materials.

PHOTOCOPIABLE

SCHOLASTIC
www.scholastic.co.uk

Magnets

■ These things are attracted to a magnet:

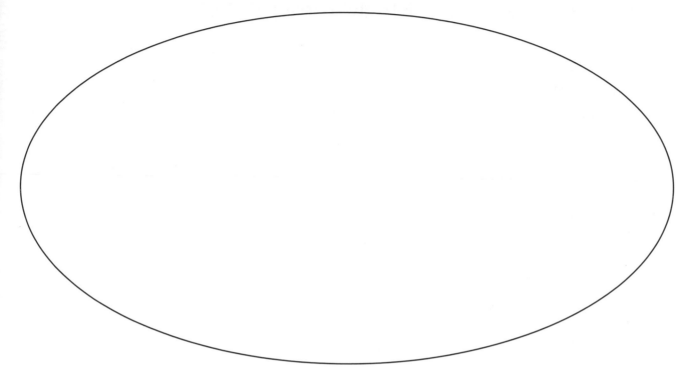

■ These things are not attracted to a magnet:

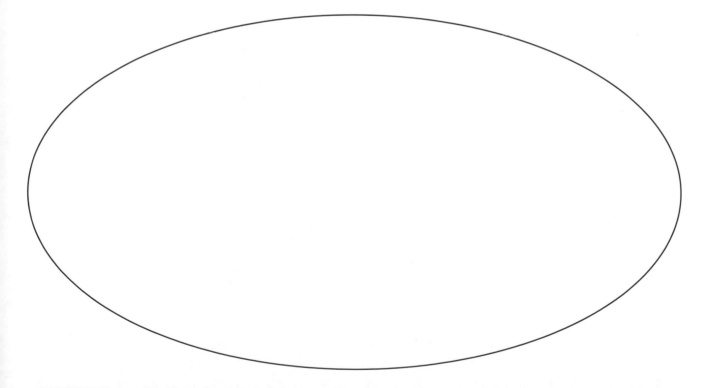

I can say which objects are attracted to a magnet.

How did you do?

Bendy and stretchy

■ Which items stay in a new shape and which spring back to their old one? Sort these objects into the correct circle.

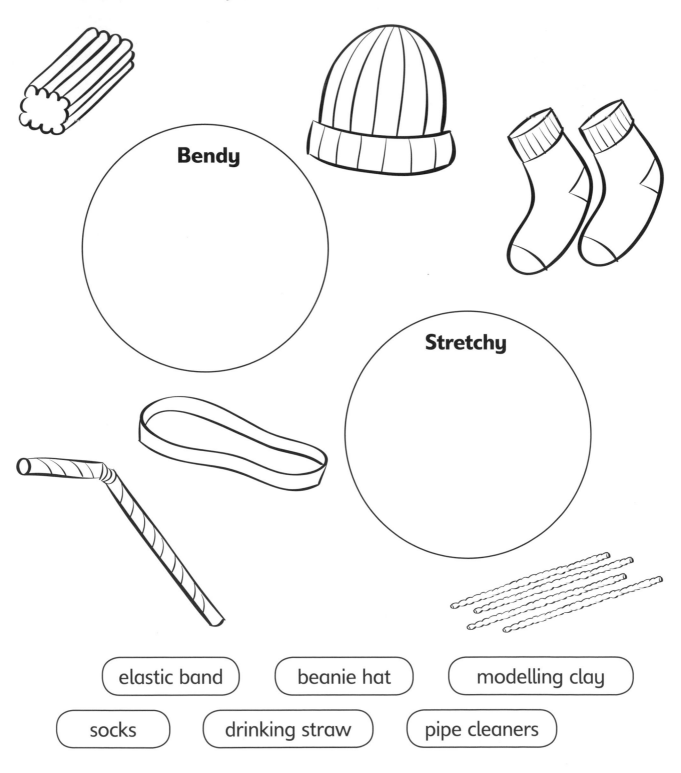

Bendy

Stretchy

(elastic band)   (beanie hat)   (modelling clay)

(socks)   (drinking straw)   (pipe cleaners)

I can say whether something is bendy or stretchy.

How did you do?

PHOTOCOPIABLE

■SCHOLASTIC
www.scholastic.co.uk

Name: _____   Date: _____

Properties of materials (1)

■ Give examples of materials that have these properties. Can you put any in more than one box?

flexible	rigid
soft	hard
rough	smooth
shiny	dull

I can describe the properties of different materials.

How did you do?

☐SCHOLASTIC

Also available in this series:

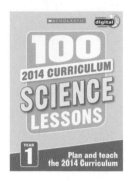

ISBN 978-1407-12765-1

ISBN 978-1407-12766-8

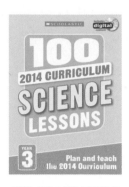

ISBN 978-1407-12767-5

ISBN 978-1407-12768-2

ISBN 978-1407-12769-9

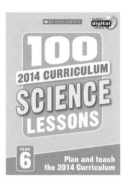

ISBN 978-1407-12770-5

English

Year 1   ISBN 978-1407-12759-0

Year 2   ISBN 978-1407-12760-6

Year 3   ISBN 978-1407-12761-3

Year 4   ISBN 978-1407-12762-0

Year 5   ISBN 978-1407-12763-7

Year 6   ISBN 978-1407-12764-4

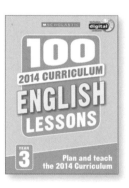

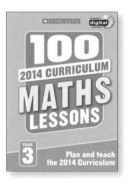

Maths

Year 1   ISBN 978-1407-12771-2

Year 2   ISBN 978-1407-12772-9

Year 3   ISBN 978-1407-12773-6

Year 4   ISBN 978-1407-12774-3

Year 5   ISBN 978-1407-12775-0

Year 6   ISBN 978-1407-12776-7

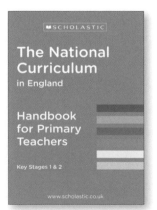

ISBN 978-1407-12862-7

To find out more, call: **0845 603 9091**
or visit **shop.scholastic.co.uk**